Several rounds popped overhead, and we cringed again. I dropped to the ground.

This couldn't be happening, I thought. It was worse than any nightmare I'd ever dreamed. In fifteen, maybe twenty minutes, we had been cut off and surrounded, lost two of our four platoons, half of our people, more than fifty men, and God knows what was happening to the rest of the battalion. They'd been strung out behind us when PAVN opened fire. They must be spread out, pinned down, and totally confused right now. And the firing hadn't let up at all. We were getting the shit kicked out of us!

Those dirty bastards, I thought, suddenly scrambling to the top of the anthill. It was sandy and dry but covered with plenty of grass and brush. I poked the barrel of my M-16 through it and looked out across the open field. Through the tangle of twigs and grass, I could see PAVN moving in the tree line, about two hundred meters away. Well within range. I saw one man, wearing a gray khaki shirt and a floppy hat, standing in the high grass near a thicket. I took a deep breath, steadied myself, lined him up in my sights, and slowly squeezed the trigger. My rifle bucked, and the little man dropped out of sight. I found another target, took aim, and fired. . . .

BAPTISM

A Vietnam Memoir

Larry Gwin

IVY BOOKS • NEW YORK

An Ivy Book
Published by The Ballantine Publishing Group
Copyright © 1999 by Larry Gwin

All rights reserved under International and Pan-American Copyright Conventions. Published in the United States by The Ballantine Publishing Group, a division of Random House, Inc., New York, and simultaneously in Canada by Random House of Canada Limited, Toronto.

Ivy Books and colophon are trademarks of Random House, Inc.

www.randomhouse.com/BB/

Library of Congress Catalog Card Number: 99-90659

ISBN 0-8041-1922-8

Manufactured in the United States of America

First Edition: November 1999

10 9 8 7 6 5 4 3 2 1

For my sons, Sam and Rob,

and

all the good men I served with in
Alpha Company, Second Battalion,
Seventh Cavalry Regiment,
First Cavalry Division (Airmobile)

Author's Note

I have reconstructed some of the dialogue in this book from memory and changed some of the names to protect families from further anguish. Other than that, everything in this book happened, and this is how I remember it.

A day came when I should have died, and after that nothing seemed very important. So I have stayed as I am, without regret, separated from the normal human condition.
—GUY SAJER, *The Forgotten Soldier*

Contents

Contents

Acknowledgments

I would like to thank the following people for their help with this book: Sanford Kaye, John Hallowell, Michael Curtis, and Lawrence Millman, writing teachers at Harvard Extension School, who helped me make the leap; Mike Alford, Bob Towles, David "Pat" Payne, and Jon Wallenius, 7th Cav veterans who shared their recollections, observations, writings, and expertise specifically for *Baptism*; Lt. Gen. Harold G. Moore and Joseph L. Galloway, coauthors of *We Were Soldiers Once . . . and Young,* for their friendship and support; Julie Moore, Christine Sydneysmith, Nancy Kelly Perelman, Gretchen Diller Harris, Jeanne O'Connell, Joanne M. Fletcher, Priscilla Mackie, Patience Mason, Allison Stokes, and Mary O'Neil for their love, encouragement, and technical expertise during the many years I worked on this book; Bill Iler, Charles B. "Cheeb" Everitt, Harry Houghton, J. D. Coleman, Bob Litle, Art Junot, Peter Maffitt, Don Cannava, Wayne Lougee, Len Ganz, Kenneth P. Sympson, Stewart O'Nan, Sam Hynes, Nat Tripp, Mel Gram, and Tim Millar, who either read one of the many drafts of the manuscript or encouraged me to complete it; Ethan Ellenberg, my agent; Owen Lock, my editor; and Dr. Michelle R. Ancharoff, at the VA Medical Center's PTSD Clinic, who helped me get past the pain.

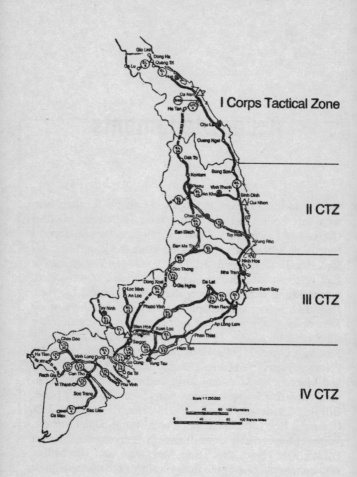

Republic of Vietnam

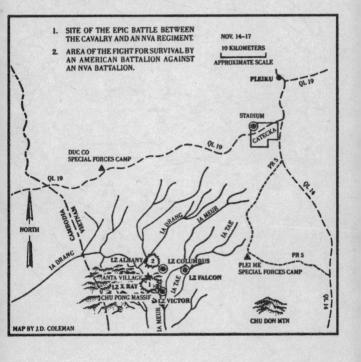

1. SITE OF THE EPIC BATTLE BETWEEN THE CAVALRY AND AN NVA REGIMENT.

2. AREA OF THE FIGHT FOR SURVIVAL BY AN AMERICAN BATTALION AGAINST AN NVA BATTALION.

NOV. 14–17

10 KILOMETERS
APPROXIMATE SCALE

PLEIKU

QL 19

STADIUM

CATECKA

DUC CO
SPECIAL FORCES CAMP

QL 19

PR 5

QL 19

QL 14

IA DRANG

IA MEUR

IA TAE

NORTH

IA DRANG

PR 5

LZ ALBANY

2

LZ COLUMBUS

PLEI ME
SPECIAL FORCES CAMP

ANTA VILLAGE

IA TAE

LZ FALCON

LZ X RAY

1

CHU PONG MASSIF

LZ VICTOR

IA MEUR

QL 14

CHU DON MTN

MAP BY J.D. COLEMAN

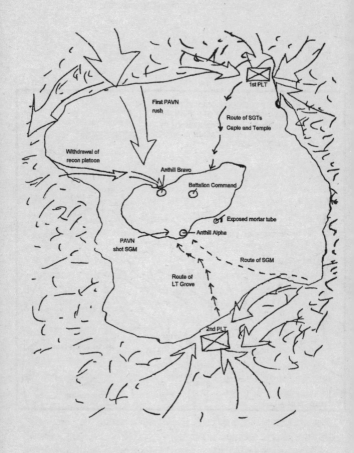

Last-ditch perimeter at LZ Albany

Introduction

A Taste of Fear

*Only the dead have seen the end
of war.*

—Plato

Alpha Company was point that day—a hundred gaunt exhausted men, trudging through the jungle with their sixty-pound loads. The rest of the battalion, roughly four hundred strong, was strung out behind us in one long, ragged column. We had five hundred meters to go before we reached our destination—a landing zone called Albany—where we could rest.

We continued forward, moving slowly, cautiously, silently— well dispersed but keeping visual contact—doing pretty well despite the heat, the humidity, our excruciatingly heavy loads, and having been awake for two days straight. As exhausted as we were, the prospect of a quick flight back to Pleiku kept us going.

We came to a very small stream. My map showed a tributary of the Ia Drang about four hundred meters east of the landing zone. If this was that stream, we were almost there.

We crossed it, filling our canteens as we did. About a hundred meters past the stream, the terrain changed dramatically, and the jungle seemed to engulf us. Tall trees, festooned with hanging vines and mosses, towered overhead, shutting out the sun. The thick, green jungle undergrowth was in our faces, and everything around us was obscured in a dim eerie light. The troops in front of me seemed to disappear as if they'd been swallowed by the earth.

Our progress slowed to a crawl. Captain Sugdinis, our

company commander, put out the word to tighten up the formation. We closed it up to maintain visual contact. We were still well dispersed, though, covering a hundred-meter front and moving noiselessly.

The battalion was called to a halt so the men behind us could fill their canteens. I couldn't help but wonder why the troops who hadn't seen any action the last two days, who hadn't been fighting off PAVN (North Vietnamese regulars) as we had, needed so much time to get their act together. Headquarters types. Cooks and clerks. Absolutely worthless.

We finally started up again, trudging slowly through the scrub. I was suddenly aware of how quiet it was and realized I hadn't heard our helicopters for a long time. Where the hell had they gone? The question came and went, though, because everything was getting confused and jumbled in my mind.

I had to concentrate. Had to keep Tom Costello (my radioman) in sight. He was in front of me now. I was having trouble staying alert. God knows how he was feeling.

Suddenly he stopped and raised his hand. I bumped into him anyway.

"What is it?" I whispered.

"Recon's just captured two PAVN," he said. "They walked right over them."

The Recon Platoon was with us on that trip. The captain had given them the point. His voice came over the radio, telling us to take another break. I went forward to have a look, to see what was going on. I could do that. I was the XO, the company's executive officer, the second in command.

Fifty yards ahead of where we'd stopped but hidden by the thick undergrowth, I came across the prisoners—two little men with their hands tied behind them, squatting wide-eyed on the ground. Sergeant Rodriguez, one of the captain's RTOs (radiotelephone operators), had the barrel of his rifle in their faces. They were well equipped, these little Viets—khaki uniforms, canvas harnesses and ammo pouches, potato-masher grenades, canvas sneakers—North Viet regulars, no doubt about it. The captain was inspecting one of their weapons, an SKS Chicom carbine with a folding bayonet. It was in mint condition. I was getting nervous. These guys were definitely PAVN, hard core all the way.

"Give them some water and treat them well," the captain said, handing the weapon to Rodriguez. "The colonel's on his way up here to interrogate them."

I studied the two little PAVN. So this was what they looked like up close—clean shaven, swarthy, high cheekbones, hair closely cropped on the sides, thin but not emaciated, and scared. More nervous than scared. One of them was shaking. Was it malaria, or fear?

"What are they doing here?" I asked the captain. We were three miles north of Xray, where we'd been fighting for two days.

"They're deserters, I think," he said. "There were some others, too, but they lit out when they saw us coming." He nodded in the direction we were headed.

Why had these PAVN just quit? It didn't make sense. Not after what we'd seen the last two days. Two days of heavy contact, and not a single PAVN had surrendered.

The battalion commander, Lieutenant Colonel McDade, arrived with his RTOs, his S-2 (intelligence officer), his S-3 (operations officer), and an interpreter, and they gathered round the prisoners. I didn't like the way they were clustered around them, especially at the head of the column, so I backed away from the group, back into the undergrowth to check our formation. From what I could see, we were still in pretty good shape, but I didn't like stopping again.

Don Cornett, Charlie Company's XO, came striding forward through the heavy undergrowth behind us. He saw me, smiled, and came over.

"What's happening?" he asked.

I told him as best I could. We had a cigarette and shot the breeze for a few minutes, then he went back to his people. I rejoined Costello and Denny Wilson (my other RTO), and we waited for the word to move. It came, eventually, and we resumed our trek to Albany.

We had gone less than a hundred meters when the direction of our march shifted slightly to the left, and our pace began to quicken. I felt a sudden sense of urgency, magnified perhaps, because I wasn't sure where Albany was. But then, in the distance, I saw a clearing, the first one we'd seen in three hours. Must be the LZ, I thought. Then Colonel MacDade suddenly strode by, followed by his entourage, heading toward the front of the column. He seemed to be in a rush.

Captain Sugdinis called me forward.

I found him kneeling on the edge of what appeared to be the LZ—a large, open, grass-covered field sloping gently to the left into a bog of some kind. A large clump of trees rose from the middle of the field about a hundred meters ahead of us. I was astonished to see the colonel and his crowd heading across the open field, toward the clump of trees.

The captain told me that he'd sent the Recon Platoon across the field to reconnoiter the far side, that he'd sent the 1st Platoon around to the right, and the 2d Platoon around to the left, to secure the LZ. I couldn't see any sign of them—the vegetation was too thick—but they were out there, circling the LZ. With that, the captain stood up and followed Mac-Dade's party into the open, and I, in turn, followed.

The field was fine for an LZ. The grass was waist high, the ground fairly flat. High trees surrounded it, but it could still take eight ships at a clip. We'd be out of there in no time.

When I reached the clump of trees, I noticed more open ground beyond it. The clump turned out to be a small grove in the open field, sort of an island, studded with saplings, clumps of thick undergrowth, and several six-foot-high anthills. We'd made it, I thought, collapsing into the grass. My whole body ached, my mouth was dry, my head hurt. But we'd made it.

Costello, Wilson, and the first sergeant plopped down beside me, and we watched as the rest of the company closed in behind us. Sergeant Braden's mortarmen staggered into the clump of trees behind us and dropped to the ground, exhausted. Captain Sugdinis and his two RTOs rested in the tall grass behind me. He had a handset to his ear, calmly waiting for our platoons to report. Several other troopers, probably headquarters types, straggled in behind us.

Brrrrrppp! Brrrrpppp! A couple of quick bursts of small-arms fire erupted from the jungle to our left, where the 1st Platoon had disappeared. It must be the PAVN stragglers I thought. I sat up, but couldn't see anything in the tree line across the field.

Brrrppppp! Another burst cracked overhead this time. I ducked back into the grass. Then an answering burst exploded from our left, across the open field, then another from the right, where we'd just been. Then, as if on cue, the entire jungle suddenly seemed to explode in an incredible crescendo of small-arms fire, as if everyone in the battalion had opened up around us with every weapon they had, and firecrackers started popping overhead.

I sprinted to a small tree on my left. The firing swelled around us. The air was alive with incoming rounds crackling overhead. People were shouting, but I couldn't hear a word because of the noise. And it kept getting worse. *Crack!* A quarter-size chunk of bark suddenly burst from the tree trunk in front of me, leaving a gash in the wood just inches from my face. Jesus, that was close! I had to get back to my radios, find out what was happening. I sprinted back to Costello and dove into the grass. Tom was lying facedown now, hugging the ground, his handset pressed to his ear. Wilson lay next to him, his eyes wide with fear. The captain was crouching against an anthill, just past us on the edge of our clump of trees, holding both handsets up to his ears, listening intently. I low-crawled to him behind the anthill.

The firing was raging around us.

"First Platoon's surrounded and taking fire!" the captain yelled at me through the din.

As the noise intensified, so did the confusion. From behind and to our left, in the middle of the clump of trees, I heard someone yelling, "Cease fire! Cease fire!" None of us was firing. None of us could tell what was going on.

The captain's face contorted. His eyes darted back and forth. The firing ebbed and then intensified again. Furiously.

"First Platoon's taking casualties," he yelled. "So is 2d."

The headquarters guys were still screaming "Cease fire! Cease fire!"

"Second Platoon's taking fire from Charlie Company," the captain said. "What's your position, Two-six?" he yelled into one handset. His brows knit in consternation. "Negative! Negative! Throw smoke. Affirmative!" he yelled into the other handset. "Negative, negative! My Two-six reports incoming fire from behind him! Roger. Wilco." Then, into the other handset, "Cease fire, all units! Cease fire!"

Despite the command, the shooting continued unabated, all around us, rolling back and forth in the jungle, swelling down the column, incoming rounds still crackling overhead.

I popped up and down again, quickly, but couldn't see anything. Bullets were exploding overhead like wildfire.

"First Platoon's surrounded," the captain said, looking at me in desperation. "Four-six, throw smoke for One-six. One-six, look for the smoke!"

"Roger," Sergeant Braden said. "Throwing smoke. Smoke is out."

The firing swelled again, all around us. It seemed to be rolling down the column, deeper into the jungle, where the rest of the battalion was.

"He says he can't see the smoke," I heard the captain yelling. "All his people are dead or wounded! They're being overrun!"

Whump! A loud, sickening *whump* erupted from the jungle to our right, down in the bog where the 2d Platoon had gone. Gordy Grove's men.

Mortars! PAVN had mortars registered on us, and they were dropping rounds on Grove's position. The first *whump* was followed by another, and another, and the ground shook with each concussion. The rounds kept crunching in, four, then five, then six, landing to our right, just below us, where the 2d Platoon was.

Joel was trying to raise Gordy on the radio, but nobody answered. "I've lost contact with 2d Platoon," the captain said to me, helplessly.

I'd never seen such anguish on his face. The fighting

picked up furiously to our front. Chaos, absolute chaos, from where we'd just been. Hundreds of small arms blasting away at each other, grenades exploding, men screaming or shouting hysterically. Worse than anything I'd ever seen, anything I could have imagined. The mortars suddenly stopped, but the firing continued furiously around us.

"I've lost the 1st Platoon," Joel said, his eyes wide with shock and disbelief. He glanced helplessly at the battalion CP behind us. "I've lost two platoons," he said, again. His jaw sagged. In the two months I'd known him, I'd never seen such anguish. I couldn't believe what was happening.

I jumped up and looked across the open field, back where we'd come from. Three GIs were coming across the field, Americans, coming right at us. I waved at them and yelled, "Over here!" One of them was a captain I didn't know, one was the battalion sergeant major, and the third guy was a young trooper with a bad stomach wound. He was holding in his guts!

Suddenly I saw movement in the trees beyond them. Men in uniforms, strange uniforms, mustard-colored shirts and floppy hats, running through the trees right behind them. PAVN! Jesus Christ, they were PAVN! Twenty, thirty, forty PAVN soldiers moving from left to right, running through the tall grass and trees on the far side of the field where we'd just been.

They were all around us now. We were cut off and surrounded. Cut off from the rest of the column. We'd have to fight our way out!

BOOK ONE

The ARVN

Chapter 1

Getting There

He was a soldier, he was marching to war, and the future looked bright.
—BERNARD CORNWELL,
Sharpe's Honor

Those of us who went had our reasons. As Jack Fuller wrote in *Fragments*, "It wasn't duty or honor or country or any lofty imperative. It had nothing to do with courage, moral or otherwise. It was simply who you were."

Well, almost. I went because my father had gone, and his father before him, and before that, my great-grandfather, who'd fought for the Confederacy. Had my dad been 4-F, or sold beef jerky to the War Department instead of volunteering for the army air corps in 1942, I might have felt otherwise. Who knows? What I'm trying to say is that I went because I thought it was the right thing to do, if I'd thought about it at all. About as much as the government had, I guess.

I "volunteered" for Vietnam in the fall of '62. I was a senior at Yale, in the Reserve Officers Training Corps (ROTC), and my understanding of the growing crisis in Southeast Asia had evolved from research for a political-science paper. I'd read that the U.S. military was advising the South Vietnamese and that the Communists were trying to wrest the country from its noble, dogged, democratic, pro-West leader, Ngo Dinh Diem. I'd heard my ROTC instructors expound on the domino theory. I'd leafed through *Life* magazine articles showing monkey-faced farmers in black pajamas and scarfaced blacks in the French Foreign Legion pitted against each other in a struggle over colonialism, too, but that was the extent of my expertise. I had thought about Vietnam, but not in global terms. I was intrigued by its potential for challenge, the unaddressed question of how I'd measure up in combat—a question that would not have concerned me, I'm sure, if I hadn't been aware of my father's proud service in the "Good War." We are, after all, who we are. So, I signed up.

ROTC policy required seniors to request duty stations and schools. I went for the gusto: First choice—10th Special Forces in Bad Tolz, Germany; second choice—82d Airborne Division at Fort Bragg, North Carolina; third choice (overseas assignment required)—Vietnam. Actually, I think the block said "Southeast Asia." Schooling was easy: First choice—Airborne School (jumping out of airplanes); second choice—Ranger School (long-range patrolling, commando raids, etc.). It was all very simple then, standing in the green-walled ROTC office, aiming my number-two pencil at the printed government form and checking the right boxes. What fascinates me in retrospect is the seeming inevitability of my ending up in Vietnam. Some whisper in my ear, some member of my brain trust, some director in my psyche, guided me, inevitably, to the choices I made. They all seemed subliminal. From the time I checked the box for Ranger School (which embodied all the physical challenges a young man could want), I was jogging on an ineluctable treadmill into the maws of combat. Little did I know what lay ahead.

Months later, when my orders came through, Bad Tolz was out. (I should have known.) Fort Bragg was in. The schooling came through as requested. I was on my way.

That I had a penchant, if not a morbid fascination, for things military is clear. The first recollection I have was the day my father came home from the war—Alaska, actually, where he'd spent two years manning airstrips on Attu and Kiska in the Aleutian Islands. I vaguely remember a parade in Washington on VJ Day, cars driving around honking their horns, people dancing in the streets, acting crazily, flags flying everywhere. Then there were the little lead toy soldiers that I'd arrange and rearrange in varied and sundry formations for endless hours in my room (and later, when I was older, outside, where I'd plink at them with my BB gun). Then there was "Victory at Sea" (which the family watched religiously on Saturday nights seated in front of our first television set), and the inevitable war games of youth, where friends and I, decked out in army surplus, would dash around the neighborhood, defending our shores against an unseen but clearly imagined enemy, reliving those poignant moments we couldn't possibly appreciate but had seen in black and white on our TV sets. Later, in college, I ended up as the battalion commander of our army ROTC detachment, a dubious distinction, at best, in times of peace. At any rate, let's say I had a calling, if not an obsession; prospects, if not talent.

I was reasonably intelligent, too—what you might call an A student, generally at the top of my class (until college, where I discovered that there were other things to do than studying—like boozing, sports, and wenching, albeit a relatively innocent form of it). My Yale roommates and I followed the simple dictum: "Never let your work interfere with your education." I played football, hockey, and lacrosse, too. All this biographical detail is in the way of introduction, not self-adulation. Perhaps I was destined to serve my country—certainly encouraged by John F. Kennedy's charismatic leadership. Signing up was just another step on the road. After all, we are who we are.

And all the Gwin men had gone. My great-great-grandfather, James Gwin, had joined Davy Crockett and his cronies as they traipsed through Tennessee on their way to fight Mexicans in Texas. James died at the Alamo, leaving a widow and two sons back on their hardscrabble farm. One of those sons, Sylvester, grew up to serve the Confederacy. He lost half of his jaw fighting for John Bell Hood at Franklin, but survived. His manservant, a full-blooded Choctaw, dragged him from the battlefield and cleaned his wound with maggots, and Sylvester went on to farm cotton and raise four sons. One of them, my grandfather Sam, signed on with the Mississippi Volunteers when the Spanish American War broke out. Though he never got close to the action, he bore the moniker "Cap'n" 'til he died. He raised my dad, whom I've mentioned.

* * *

Graduating from Yale in June of 1963, I commenced my apprenticeship with the 82d Airborne Division, the All American Division, and received the requisite training—three weeks of Jump School in August, ten weeks of the Infantry Officers' Basic Course at Fort Benning, and nine weeks of Ranger School, which I completed just before Christmas. Ranger School was the icing on the cake and gave me confidence in my credentials, confidence that I was as good as any of the best of the West Point graduates.

I took my job seriously, too. My generation had been raised under the shadow of the atomic bomb. During my junior year in college, I had watched the coverage of the Cuban missile crisis with more than thinly disguised interest and had applauded JFK's steadfast leadership. We, the United States of America, stood as the bastion of freedom, the watchdog of a tenuous peace. Arrayed against us at the time were the forces of evil, personified by the Soviet Union and the untold millions of the Red Horde, Red China, whose leaders had vowed openly to bury us. As an individual member of STRAC, the Strategic Army Corps, I was prepared to jump into the jaws of doom at a moment's notice. During almost every hour of my two years in the 82d Airborne Division, my instincts were honed for that seemingly inevitable eventuality. I served as a platoon leader in a rifle company, a battalion adjutant, and the commander of a raider platoon. I made more than forty jumps from a variety of aircraft, went on war games throughout the southern states and the Mojave Desert, and became increasingly aware of our growing military commitment in Vietnam. Many of my immediate superiors, whom I considered to be the finest officers in the army, were assigned there, and when I got my orders to proceed with several other first lieutenants to the MATA course (the Military Assistance and Training Advisory course), then to MACV (Military Advisory Command Vietnam) in Saigon, I was, believe it or not, quite thrilled. Saying farewell to friends in the 82d, we "chosen few" lieutenants signed out, drove four blocks up the street to Smoke Bomb Hill (where the Special Forces trained), and signed in to our six-week indoctrination in guerrilla warfare.

MATA was the prerequisite program for service in MACV.

The course consisted of morning lectures on counterinsurgency and afternoon lessons in the Vietnamese language. We had only one night exercise and a single parachute drop (to keep our Airborne status in case we opted to continue the tradition in Vietnam). After STRAC service, however, the MATA course seemed easy. Fun and games. What I was looking forward to was a two-month stint in Monterey, California, studying Vietnamese at the DLIWC—the Defense Language Institute, West Coast. Afterward, the treadmill would take us west, across the Pacific, to the jungle, and from there, who knew? I didn't think too much about it, though. MATA was too much fun.

Monterey was even more so, as our sole mission was to study Vietnamese at night and to speak it during the day. Too bad we never learned it. The rest of the time, we were busy cramming a life into the two months we had left in the good ole US of A. What else to do but fall in love? In my case it was the real thing (or so I believed with the absolute certainty of a twenty-three-year-old). Her name was Nicole, and she came from Montreal. When I departed for Vietnam, I was sure we would get married as soon as I came home.

Between trips to San Francisco, dinners on Fisherman's Wharf, walks through Cannery Row, camping at Lake Tahoe, and an unforgettable hike up Big Sur (eight miles on a steep trail with a sixty-pound rucksack), all with Nicki in tow, I studied hard at Monterey. I had two best buddies there, too: Gene Cargile, a six-foot-five-inch Georgia boy who had captained the West Point basketball team, and Burt McCord, a square-jawed tanker with a beautiful wife and two children (a son aged one and a daughter in utero). Burt and his wife Eddie had rented an apartment in the early '60s equivalent of a condominium complex on the Carmel coast. After Vietnamese classes, Gene, Burt, and I would adjourn there, run a few miles along the coast and back, savoring the sea air and the beautiful vistas and preparing our bodies for the rigors of our coming tour. After the run, we'd retire to the sauna and study Vietnamese. Burt would do push-ups, dozens and dozens of them, with his feet on the bench, while I sat there sweating in the hot, stifling air, barely able to breathe. Prepared for the next day's recitations, Gene and I would meet our girlfriends in Monterey, leaving Burt and Eddie with their son.

This idyllic two-month tour came to an end in July of '65.

Leaving wasn't easy, and saying good-bye to Nicki was one of the hardest things I'd ever done. We spent our last night at a friend's apartment in San Francisco, and he and his wife drove Nicki and me to the Oakland Army Terminal the next morning. After an unbearably painful parting, I donned my RAY-BAN glasses, turned away from my lady, and walked resolutely through the entrance gate and into the cold gray confines of the terminal. I looked back only once. Nicki was in the backseat of my friend's car. His wife was consoling her. Neither of them saw me looking back. I cast the scene from my mind and signed in.

Cargile, McCord, and I went carousing in San Francisco that night. No point in sitting around a bleak army barracks, waiting for our flight the next day, if we could go out and get hammered. We went to North Beach. I remember hitting a few of the local hot spots, Big Al's being the only one I recall distinctly. A gorgeous, full-breasted blonde in a see-through toreador jacket danced a crude flamenco on our table. How could you forget that? We were turned away from the Condor Club, where the inimitable Carol Doda was featured, because the place was jammed. We passed up Finochio's, a transvestite joint, and ended up in a local smut shop, where I purchased a nudie magazine that accompanied me throughout my tour. I bought it for the full-page spread of a luscious blonde lying spread-eagle naked on the wet sand of an unspecified beach, her breasts full, her skin tan, her womanhood exposed and enchanting. "Voluptua" I called her, and she represented, in a single photograph, everything we were fighting for.

On July 29, 1965, with Voluptua in my kit bag and what Ernest Hemingway would describe as a "mastodon hangover," I departed with forty-plus MACV advisers for the San Francisco Airport at 5:00 P.M. Arriving early, we congregated in the terminal's largest cocktail lounge and drank steadily and hard until our flight—a Pan American 707 Clipper bound for Saigon, via Hawaii, Guam, and Manila—was called for boarding.

As our "Champagne Flight" took off, Beethoven's Fifth Symphony was booming through the plane's plastic earphones. I sat back in my seat and shut my eyes. What a way to go to war!

We chased the dawn for hours, landing in Hawaii for a midnight nightcap, Guam for a pit stop, and Manila for a predawn swallow of San Miguel *cerveza*. Several hours later, I woke up in my seat with the sun streaming through the window and nothing but ocean below. The day of reckoning was at hand.

Vietnam's coastline appeared in the misty distance as the plane veered southward and the pilot announced our arrival. He also mentioned some "unspecified activity" below. I peered out the window and scanned the coastline, approaching fast on the right. Dark green mountains dropped precipitously to the sea. A single highway wended its way along the coastline like a copper-colored thread. Inland, the mountain range was swathed in a purplish mist, but the colors—the light blue sky, the purple-gray mountains, the dark green jungle, the shimmering silvery sea—boggled my mind. So did the bombing.

Forewarned by the pilot, I saw a silver glint in the sky above the coastline. A jet. Then another. The first dove toward the coast, pulled up sharply, and climbed to the west. In the jungle below, a tiny white puff of smoke blossomed into a cotton ball. The second jet dove, and another cotton ball materialized in the green below. My God, I thought, they're dropping bombs! Welcome to the war, Lieutenant.

If the pilot hadn't warned us that "for obvious reasons" our descent would be steep, he would have lost me with his landing. As it is, I'm nervous flying. My palms gush sweat whenever my plane takes off, turns sharply, or lands, and after two years of flying with a parachute on my back, I was actually scared to fly without one. Well, anyway, to escape Viet Cong sniper fire, we came close to the civilian equivalent of dive-bombing Tan Son Nhut, Saigon's international airport, and I left my stomach somewhere at fifteen thousand feet, I'm sure. What a way to land. I was beginning to understand why the civilian component of our flight's passenger list had thinned out to almost nothing back in Manila.

I looked out the window as we taxied toward the terminal. As far as the eye could see, the airfield teemed with activity. Small mountains of military hardware covered every available inch of the field's macadam surface. Jeeps and trucks and forklifts bustled through the maze. Shirtless American GIs struggled and sweated, pulled and tugged, lifted and lugged. An ant colony was unfolding before my eyes, and I was soon to be a part of it. Two camouflaged Phantom jets, their wings heavily laden with bombs, took off from an adjacent runway with a terrible roar, and I was reminded, once again, that there really was a war going on. I should have guessed from our approach into Tan Son Nhut who was winning it.

Anyone arriving in Vietnam for the first time has his own private recollection. Mine was of the heat. Stepping out of our air-conditioned aircraft into the blazing sunlight was like walking into an oven. The heat seemed to sear my lungs, I couldn't breathe, and by the time I negotiated the hundred yards from the plane to the MACV reception officer standing on the tarmac, my short-sleeve khaki shirt was soaked with sweat.

"Welcome to Vietnam, gentlemen," the MACV major said. We clustered around him like children. "You will now secure your baggage, board a bus, and proceed to MACV headquarters in downtown Saigon. There, you will be processed, briefed, and billeted. Do not—I say again do not—tip the porters in the baggage terminal more than twenty-five cents a bag, and spend as little time as possible in the terminal. It's been bombed twice in the last six weeks. Are there any questions?"

"Yes, sir," a voice drawled from the rear. We turned and looked at the speaker. "What time is it?" he asked.

Everyone burst out laughing.

Our bus was an army school bus, olive drab, with its windows protected by a one-inch wire mesh so Viet Cong couldn't toss a grenade inside. The half-hour drive to the MACV compound in Saigon was a kaleidoscope of culture shock. We left the airfield, where tanks and jeeps guarded the entrance, drove through the gate, and were treated with a fifteen-minute glimpse of the countryside. As the bus hurtled down the highway to the capital, we were entertained by a panoply of rice paddies, farmers wearing black pajamas and conical straw hats, water buffalo being herded by children, old women whisking along with poles on their shoulders (from which swung baskets filled with rice), buffalo carts loaded with produce for market, tin-roof shanties on mud-packed foundations, each with scrawny chickens pecking at the red earth and piglets rooting through the filth. The traffic on the highway consisted of ARVN jeeps and trucks, an occasional taxi, and one or two mopeds or motorcycles, all in a terrible rush.

We crossed a bridge and entered the city limits. For the first five blocks or so, all I could see were the high gray walls and empty sidewalks of the residential district. Behind the walls, French-style colonial buildings occasionally appeared, surrounded by palm trees and thick vegetation. I don't remember seeing any pedestrians until we hit the city proper.

Compared to Boston or New York, Saigon's streets were total bedlam. Absolute chaos. There were only two traffic lights in the city, and one of them was broken. The rule of the road was simple—the biggest vehicle had the right of way. Luckily, we were in a school bus. Pedicabs, little Renault taxis, civilian cars (Fords and Chevvies, mostly), jeeps, and trucks (deuce-and-a-halfs, three-quarter-ton trucks, even the huge cattle cars) clogged the streets, and everyone with a horn seemed to be blowing it. Jammed among the vehicles were pedestrians, cyclos, bicycles, and buffalo carts.

A block or two before we arrived at the MACV compound, somebody threw a bottle at our bus. It smashed against a window. Welcome to Saigon, GI.

The MACV headquarters compound was an imposing, multilevel stucco edifice with a red-tile roof. Several American military vehicles were parked next to it. The complex was surrounded by a high cement wall topped with broken glass and concertina wire. The entrance was guarded by American MPs in a huge, sandbagged bunker.

Safely inside the compound, we disembarked, and our MACV guide ushered us into an air-conditioned wing for orientation. Another batch of new guys was already there. I didn't know any of them, but Cargile and McCord recognized several West Point classmates, and we sipped coffee, smoked, and swapped jokes until the briefings began.

During the next few hours, we heard a series of lectures about the latest military and political developments in the country, the "do's and don'ts" of our mission, and the basics— where we would stay, how we would eat and pick up our gear, and when we would get our orders. Despite our jet lag and exhaustion, the lectures kept our attention.

We heard that the Viet Cong (VC, Victor Charlie, or Charlie) and units of the North Vietnamese Army (NVA or PAVN) were trying to cut the country in half up around the II Corps area. From all reports, they were succeeding. I had no idea I was going to end up in the middle of II Corps at the time, so my attention may have drifted, but I recall the lectures quite vividly. Around 4:30 in the afternoon, we picked up our field equipment, including our assigned weapons— M-2 carbines. (Under no circumstances were we to carry it, however, except in a duffel bag to our quarters, or load it until we left for the field.) With instructions like those, I should have known it was going to be a long year. I wasn't worried. A friend of mine back home had given me his army Colt .45 automatic as a talisman, and I carried it with me in my B-4 bag.

We survived the first day without mishap and boarded a bus to Cholon, the Chinese section of the capital, where we resided for the duration of our five-day stay in Saigon. I got off at a small *pensione* (whose name eludes me). Gene and Burt went on to the Commodore Hotel, one of the biggies, where we agreed to meet for dinner even though it had been car-bombed by the Communists the previous year.

I followed two army captains into the *pensione*. When I said *"Chao, ong"* (pronounced "chow, um" and meaning

"Hello, man") to the Vietnamese policeman leafing through a comic book at the entrance, he grinned and saluted. Ah, the power of language. When I tried to expand my newfound circle of Vietnamese intimates, however, I ran into a stone wall. My room was on the second floor. On the way, I passed a Vietnamese woman. I said *"Chao, co"* (Hello, unmarried woman), and she flashed me a smile. When I asked her how she was, she giggled. When I tried something clever, like "Where is the water?", I lost her, or she lost me, because whatever came out of her mouth was totally incomprehensible. Maybe she's Chinese, I thought, continuing upstairs.

My quarters consisted of a light green, stucco-walled room with a bed, bureau, and lamp. The window looked across an alley to a brick wall. There was a door in the corner. I knocked. No answer. I opened it. Another tiny room, with army gear and clothes strewn around it. I shut the door, stripped, set my alarm clock, and lay down for an hour's nap. There were four little lizards on the wall—an auspicious start. (Gecko lizards on the walls of your room were considered a luxury; they ate insects.) When the alarm went off, I dragged myself from the depths of a dreamless sleep, got up, dressed, ventured out on foot, and walked the five blocks to the Commodore. There, I rejoined my cronies.

The Commodore was a large hotel commandeered by MACV for transient officers or a BOQ. Its finest feature was the roof-top restaurant, an officers club with a good view of Saigon. You could drink at the bar, enjoy a cheap but decent supper in the restaurant, sip a nightcap under the stars, and watch the firefights erupt around the city. Nightly, I was told. Tracer rounds and flashes of mortar fire sparkled from the darkness around Tan Son Nhut, and eerie bumps and concussions—the rumble of distant artillery—often followed from farther west. We watched the show with thinly disguised interest, an apparent disdain bordering on bravado, and drank ourselves slowly silly. I slept badly that night.

The next day we suffered our first casualty. A navy lieutenant, a friend of Cargile's from Annapolis whom I'd met and liked, surprised us with a grand mal epileptic seizure during a

lecture on do's and don'ts. He was two rows in front of me
when I suddenly saw him stiffen. His body slid rigidly out of
his chair and onto the floor, and he started to writhe spasmodically. One of his friends tried frantically to get something
wedged between his teeth, but couldn't manage it. A few moments later, glassy-eyed and confused, he regained consciousness and found himself surrounded by a circle of concerned
faces. He was carried out of the room on a stretcher.

He returned the next day to say good-bye. "This must be
the shortest tour on record," he joked, but it was evident that
he was gravely disappointed. After four years at the Naval
Academy, latent epilepsy had cast his career into limbo.

We got our gamma globulin shots the next day, at the naval
hospital across town. Five cc's in each cheek for the big guys
like me. I spent the afternoon in bed, on my stomach, waiting
for the pain to go away. We'd received by that time the full
gamut of immunizations, shots for cholera, typhus, yellow
fever, and plague. Gamma globulin supposedly prevented
hepatitis and mononucleosis, so we needed it and didn't com-
plain. Too bad there wasn't something for malaria.

On the fourth day, we got our orders. Not until then did we
know where and with whom we would be spending the next
twelve months. We all had our druthers. Cargile wanted an
Airborne slot. I wanted to work with the Rangers. McCord
was a tanker, so he had armored duty in mind. None of us got
what we wanted. Par for the course. Gene landed a slot with
the Rangers. Burt got a mechanized outfit in the Iron Triangle. I was assigned to the 21st ARVN Division at Bac Lieu,
a province in the Mekong Delta.

"One of the best units in the country, sir," the assignments
sergeant said. "And it's quiet down there." I felt gypped.

We were leaving for the field the next morning, so the three
of us had a subdued farewell supper at the Commodore,
wished each other luck, and retired early for the night.

Chapter 2

Vi Thanh

*The hypocrisies in the whole
Vietnam situation were very nearly
asphyxiating.*
—WILLIAM F. BUCKLEY, JR.,
Tucker's Last Stand

Early the next morning, I met a lieutenant named Jones in
the IV Corps Liaison shack at Tan Son Nhut, and we hopped
a flight to Bac Lieu. Jones was a MATA course compatriot
who had been assigned to join a Ruff-Puff unit (Regional
Forces, Popular Forces, i.e., the local militia) in IV Corps,
and I was happy to have his company for the trip. We
were carrying all our gear—jungle pack, duffel bag, B-4
bag (a triple-compartment nylon suitcase), and carbine—
everything we'd need for the year, and we were nervous,
feeling green as grass, and wondering what the hell it was
like "down there."

We hopped a CV-2 Caribou, a two-engine army cargo
plane, and flew south. A member of the 21st ARVN Division
advisory team met us at the airstrip, drove us into Bac Lieu,
and escorted us immediately to the senior adviser's office in
the MACV compound there. Col. John Spellman commanded
a detachment of several hundred officers and men spread over
the southernmost provinces of the country. He was gracious
but busy. Advising us that he sent all his new lieutenants on a
familiarization tour of the division's AO (area of operations),
he immediately did. We would take off the next morning for
Ca Mau, then fly to Can Tho, and return to Bac Lieu. Afterward, Jones would join his unit in a strategic hamlet farther

south. I was to proceed to Vi Thanh—home of the 3d Battalion of the 31st Regiment of the 21st ARVN Division—situated on the Can Tho canal. None of this, of course, meant anything to us, but at least I knew I would end up with a regular army line outfit. Working with the Ruff-Puffs wasn't my idea of a job.

On August 7, 1965, we departed on our whirlwind tour. The culture shock I'd experienced in Saigon was doubled in the southernmost reaches of the country. The Mekong Delta was nothing but a seemingly endless expanse of rice paddies shimmering in the sun and crisscrossed by rivers, canals, and occasional roads. Flying over the paddies, I marveled at their crude symmetry, one after the other, side by side, like a never-ending patchwork of rain-soaked football fields, each with its own particular shade of brown. It was planting season, when newly sown rice shoots were just rooting, and all I could see below us were shimmering squares of brown, framed by thin paddy dikes, as far as the eye could see. The rivers that broke up the patchwork looked like thick, undulating snakes—bloated sidewinders—their banks thick with dark and foreboding vegetation.

Ca Mau was little more than an outpost on the northern edge of the U Minh Forest. The U Minh Forest, actually a mangrove swamp, was swarming with VC, so Ca Mau's MACV detachment was a tenuous presence, at best. The week before we visited, VC sappers had broken into the compound, shot up the place, and scared the hell out of everyone. The handful of lieutenants there regaled us with war stories, and that evening we went to the "Club" and got drunk.

The Club was an old French tennis sportif with a court I think I used. That night, the clubhouse was filled with a dozen or so members of the MACV team. I recall several tables, ceiling fans, lots of smoke, and a bar in the corner. Some of the local Viets were there, too. Girls. One was standing on a table surrounded by cheering GIs. They were betting on whether she wore underpants. She was laughing and smiling flirtatiously, ignoring the occasional look-see up her skirt—just a nice girl having some fun in a combat zone.

I drank my first *Bier La Rue*, or Tiger Beer, that night. Several, as a matter of fact. I learned later they were preserved with formaldehyde. Wow'd with war stories, flushed with excitement, and buzzing with booze, I went native. As the night wore on and the festivities increased in tempo, one of our hosts announced he had procured a woman for us. She appeared, smiling, a short, flat-faced, featureless one, the same who'd been twirling on the table. But she was all woman.

She came up to me, took my hand, and lead me into her room in back of the club. I figured "What the hell?" Why not? She seemed happy to have a new friend, and though I couldn't understand a word she said, she was more than able to express herself in the universal language, and we had a grand time for about twenty minutes. Oh, yes, she did say something I understood, now that I think of it. "Me no blow."

She seemed to enjoy our coupling, and I certainly did, and when we were finished and thoughts of Nicki flashed through my besotted brain, I rationalized my infidelity on the grounds that life here might be short, and Nicki was on the other side of the world. When my new friend and I left her room, she grinned happily, everyone cheered, and I felt like one of the boys. It all seemed very harmless at the time.

From Ca Mau we flew to Can Tho, which I can't remember at all thanks to the formaldehyde, and then returned to Bac Lieu. There I met Captain Moore, my new boss. Captain Moore was a fair-haired West Pointer, pleasant but emaciated from a recent bout with amebic dysentery (the particularly pernicious strain that hits you at both ends and renders you virtually worthless). He had flown to Bac Lieu to meet me and to introduce me to his counterpart, the *dai-uy* (translated captain and pronounced "die-wee"), CO of the 3d Battalion, 31st Regiment, 21st ARVN Division. The *dai-uy* was the first ARVN officer I met. He was actually a Cambodian, a Cham, one of the fiercer breeds. He'd been fighting Communists for twenty years, first with the French, then under Ngo Dinh Diem, and now with us. He was very short, very swarthy, and his teeth were full of gold. His dark eyes glinted when he grinned, and he seemed to grin every time I looked at him. I began to think it was a knee-jerk response. He was tough, though, and cruel I discovered, but whenever I looked at him, he grinned. Whenever I think of him, I see a cruel-eyed monkey of a man, grinning at me, and I remember the afternoon we toasted his "new wife."

Captain Moore had borrowed a jeep from headquarters, and, dressed in civilian clothes, we drove into town. The center of Bac Lieu was teeming with people—all Vietnamese. We parked the jeep, and started walking down the street through the crowd. That's when I had my first real taste of being a stranger in a foreign land.

"There he is," the captain said, smiling at an unending stream of Viets passing by. *"Bonjour."*

A tiny man in civilian clothes stopped and grinned at us. Captain Moore introduced me to him. The *dai-uy* and I shook hands. I said "Hello" in my best Vietnamese. The *dai-uy* grinned and nodded. He said something quickly to the captain, something I couldn't understand, not because I couldn't speak French but because I couldn't make out the *dai-uy*'s Cambodian version of French, and the captain laughed and the *dai-uy* grinned and nodded, and we adjourned to a nearby bistro for a drink.

Except for some young bar girls sitting around a table in back, the place was empty. We sat at the bar and drank a couple of *Ba-Mui-Ba*s (that's "33" in Vietnamese, the brand name of their most popular, and non-formaldehyde-preserved, beer), and I listened to the captain and the Cambodian make small talk about the war. Except for a smattering of French, I couldn't understand what they were saying. Whenever I tried out my Vietnamese, the *dai-uy*'s eyes would glaze over, his brows would knit, and he would look to Captain Moore for translation. Unfortunately, the captain couldn't speak Vietnamese, so we found ourselves at an impasse as far as a three-way conversation was concerned. Eventually, I gave up, sat back, kept my mouth shut, and listened to the veterans talking gibberish.

After a while, the *dai-uy* beckoned to the girls, and three got up to join us. We laughed nervously, and they giggled, and I stood up and bowed as cavalierly as I could. A sad-eyed girl of twenty, shy and very pretty with a pageboy haircut, sat with me and listened patiently to my groping efforts to speak her language. We all had several drinks, and then I heard the captain say, "Time to get back to work."

I looked at the *dai-uy*. He'd been having an uproarious time laughing and telling stories to the other girls at the bar, amusing them, I'm sure, with tales of derring-do. He saw me, flashed his grin, and grabbed the girl on his right. Then he reached up and squeezed her breast. I saw her wince. Captain Moore laughed and turned to me with his glass raised and proposed a toast "to the new wife." The *dai-uy* thought that was very funny, and squeezed the girl's breast even harder, glaring at me all the time with cruel, challenging eyes. The captain and I quaffed our beers and left. The *dai-uy* had some unfinished business.

"You did well back there," Captain Moore said, driving back. "I think the *dai-uy* liked you. That's important. If they like you, you'll be okay."

I wasn't sure what he meant by that, and I don't think I cared. All I could think about was the *dai-uy*'s cruel grin. So that was the face of our ally.

Captain Moore flew back to Vi Thanh that evening, and I followed the next day.

As soon as my Caribou rolled to a halt, the rear cargo door flew open. I saw a lone jeep careening toward us. It skidded to a halt. The driver, a black E-5 with a pencil-thin mustache, hopped out, introduced himself quickly, and began to offload cargo. By the time I had stowed my gear in his jeep, he was already ready to go. The Caribou revved its engines and rumbled back up the airstrip. By the time we'd reached the road, the plane was airborne. Landing and takeoff had taken only minutes.

"Welcome to Vi Thanh, sir," Sergeant Jeffries said. "Sorry 'bout the rush, but we don't want to spend much time on the ground."

We sped toward town, crossed a small bridge, turned left, and raced another hundred yards to the compound. As we entered through a barbed-wire gate, I saw several one-story, wood-frame buildings in a U-shaped configuration with a stucco, red-tile-roof building on the right and a large sandbagged bunker on the left.

"Welcome to Team 51," Sergeant Jeffries said, screeching to a halt in front of a tin-roof shack. Its screen door opened, and Captain Moore appeared.

"So you made it," he said. "Good. We're going out tomorrow. You can get your feet wet."

That evening, I met the members of the team. It was commanded by a major and consisted of Captain Moore's team (two sergeants and me), the artillery liaison officer (an army pilot), the air force liaison officer (an air force pilot), the regimental liaison team (another captain and his crew), and several senior NCOs who kept everything running smoothly while we were out in the field. Morale, I discovered, was high. Our team sergeants were seasoned regulars, both with time in country. Sergeant Hunter was a tall, blond, taciturn professional with a well-trimmed mustache. Sergeant Jones was equally quiet, but slightly shorter, dark haired, and sported a bushy mustache. Not knowing what kind of ninety-day wonder I might be, they were understandably reserved, but I liked them both immediately.

My quarters consisted of a bunk bed and a bureau in one of the open-air, wood-frame buildings that I shared with six others. The stucco building with the red-tile roof turned out to be the latrine, with showers and commodes. There were separate quarters for the enlisted men, a mess hall/rec center, and the headquarters shack. The compound was surrounded by a chain-link fence topped with barbed wire. Except for the sandbagged bunker, we were wide open to attack, but the place was clean and comfortable, so I settled in happily for my tour.

Chapter 3

Paddy Walk

The mechanical stupidity of infantry soldiering is the antithesis of intelligent thinking.
—SIEGFRIED SASSOON

Well before dawn the next morning, Sergeant Jones woke me with a gentle rap on the screen door. I heard his knock, mumbled thanks, and struggled to consciousness. It was pitch-black outside. The day of reckoning had come—my first operation. I got up, put on my shower togs, and padded to the latrine to clean up.

The mess sergeant scrambled eggs for us before we left. Well-fed and ready, we hopped in our jeep. Captain Moore drove with panache, roaring through Vi Thanh in the pitch-dark of the predawn hour, turning into the ARVN regimental compound and skidding to a halt near a rough-hewn shack with a tie rail in front of it, like a saloon in a western movie.

"Orient the lieutenant," the captain said. "I'll see what's up." He hopped out of the jeep and disappeared into the shack.

It was the ARVN battalion's headquarters building, and the compound, I learned later, consisted of thirty-six tin-roof, aluminum-sided structures with dirt floors. This was the home of the 3d Battalion's five hundred or so troops.

My eyes grew slowly accustomed to the dark. Ghostly shapes were moving quietly around the compound—ARVN troops, picking up their crew-served weapons for the upcoming operation. Despite repeated suggestions from Captain Moore, they kept the crew-served weaponry in the most

vulnerable, i.e., exposed, location in the compound. While
we waited in the jeep, the two sergeants pointed out the key
locations in the compound, described the routine, and com-
mented, not particularly favorably, on the ARVN. Though
their routine was much like any military organization's, their
competence didn't rank high in the minds of my teammates.

Captain Moore came back out of the shack and briefed us
on the regimental plan. We were going to head directly north
from the compound, walk five kilometers to the Snake River,
follow it east for five more kilometers, then head south along
a canal to the village of Cai Tac, where trucks would pick us
up and bring us back. Not only a fairly long paddy walk,
about fifteen kilometers, but also a classic example of a
search-and-destroy operation into VC territory.

"Larry," the captain said. "I want you and Sergeant Hunter
to walk with the lead company today."

I nodded.

"I hope you're in shape," he added.

"Me, too," I said, lighting another Camel.

The *dai-uy* came out of the headquarters shack, followed
by a tall *trung-uy* (first lieutenant) in a camouflage tiger suit.
He looked like Jack Palance, but his name was *Trung-uy* Tri,
and he was going to be my counterpart for the day. Captain
Moore introduced us, and we shook hands. The *trung-uy* sort
of grimaced at me, then turned and disappeared into the darkness. He, too, was a Cham, the captain said. We were blessed.

A whistle blew over the loudspeaker, and troops began to
swarm out of the buildings and congregate on the parade
ground for reveille. I watched them perform this time-honored
military ritual, forming up, standing stiffly and silently in formation as the commanders took the report. Somebody yapped
a shrill command, and the entire battalion, some four hundred
strong that day, came to a rigid attention. The sergeant major,
at least I assumed it was the sergeant major, reported to the
dai-uy and turned the battalion over to him. The *dai-uy*
yapped a short speech, but I couldn't understand a word of it.
Then a scratchy version of the Vietnamese national anthem
played over the loudspeaker while we stood at attention and

saluted the South Vietnamese flag unfurling from its pole over the headquarters shack. The *dai-uy* yapped another command, and the troops relaxed. They were ready for the operation and bristling with arms and ammunition. The sky began to lighten in the east.

So, this was it, I thought. Would we find VC?

Sergeant Hunter seemed relaxed, and I tried to relax, but I'd seen him glance nervously at Jones when the captain had mentioned the Snake River.

"We may run into something today," the captain said to me. "If we do, just keep an eye on Sergeant Hunter. He knows the drill."

Our RTOs (radiomen) arrived then, looking impish in their over-size tiger-stripe helmets. They carried PRC-10s, Korean War vintage radios, which we had used at Ranger School but which the army had junked years before. Not that they didn't work—they were fine for short-range communication—but they were difficult to calibrate and weren't renowned for their reliability.

Sergeant Jones introduced the two RTOs as *Ha Si* One and *Ha Si* Two. *Ha si* (pronounced "ha she") is Vietnamese for corporal. Jones had simply numbered them and let it go at that. The diminutive Viets stiffened and saluted smartly. I returned their salutes, smiled, and shook their hands. I learned later that the advisers' radiomen were usually decorated war heroes, longtime veterans whose service was rewarded by the honor of carrying our radios. They supposedly vied for the privilege, though my guess is that they did so because we never walked point during a mission.

The *Ha Si*s went about the tedious operation of calibrating their radios—tuning their sets to a common frequency. They accomplished this by tuning into transmissions from one specific set, the *dai-uy*'s, whose operator repeatedly counted from one to ten and back again until everyone was on his frequency. Every set was tuning into that transmission, and all around us I could hear the monotonous, continuous count of *"Mot, hai, ba, bon"* (one, two, three, four, etc.) echoing loud and clear around the compound. I asked Sergeant Hunter if the *dai-uy's* set was calibrated to the artillery's frequency. If it wasn't, we wouldn't be able to get artillery support if we needed it.

"No sweat, sir," he said. "The captain calls for all the heavy stuff." I didn't ask what we'd do if the captain was incapacitated, but I thought about it.

Some commotion in the compound's northeast corner indicated that we'd be moving out soon. *Trung-uy* Tri, looking very serious, was conferring with his troops. In the early light of dawn, he looked much meaner than Jack Palance. The *dai-uy* appeared with a retinue of bodyguards trailing along behind him, so I grabbed my M-2 carbine, nodded a quick farewell to Sergeant Jones, turned to Sergeant Hunter, and said "Let's go."

"Right, sir," he said.

"See you," I said to Captain Moore, trying to sound casual.

"Don't do anything I wouldn't do," he said, smiling. "Keep an eye on him, Sergeant," he added. Hunter grinned. I waved, started walking, and didn't look back.

At 0630, *Trung-uy* Tri's 1st Rifle Company clambered over the clay berm at the northeast corner of the compound and started across the rice paddies. Hunter and I watched the point platoon spread out and begin its long trek toward the far tree line, hazy in the distance, about a thousand meters away. I was relieved to see that the ARVN were staying on the paddy dikes and not jumping into the muck. They spread out expertly and began a fast zigzag course along the dikes heading generally north. The sun was blazing through the scattered clouds, turning the early morning mist to steam. I felt like I was standing in a steam bath.

Sergeant Hunter and I followed *Trung-uy* Tri across a retractable gangplank that spanned the moat surrounding the compound. Off we go, I thought, adjusting my harness and resting my carbine on my hip. I may have prayed a bit, too, but I don't think so.

Except for the stinking muck, the stifling heat, and the incredibly monstrous leeches, the first five miles weren't that bad. The paddies were very different on the ground from what they had looked like in the air. Each was blocked off by small dikes of packed mud, about a foot or so thick and a foot above the water. Some had weeds or grass growing on them. Apart from their agricultural importance, they served as dams, boundaries, and high-speed highways for our cross-country trek, and it didn't take long for me to master the secret of paddy humping. Concentration. If I didn't look where I was going, or watch where I put my feet, I'd slip off the dike and find myself mired in muck. And I mean muck. Under the water's shimmering surface was the stinkiest, slimiest, foulest-smelling goop I'd ever had the misfortune of wallowing in, and after one or two momentary lapses of concentration, resulting in a coat of stinky slime up to my knees, I quickly learned to watch my step. By the time we'd reached the first footbridge, I had almost gotten the hang of it.

The paddies were a weird and scary world. We were all alone out there—all four-plus hundred of us—and well within range of anyone with more than a peashooter, and all around us, the ARVN were trudging along, concentrating on keeping spread out and listening to their sergeants and officers telling them where to go, and it was up this dike and turn right or left onto the next one, and it was quiet, not because we were afraid anyone could hear us—that didn't matter because they could see us coming a thousand meters away—but because everyone was saving their energy, for the heat was close to unbearable and the humidity stifling, and nobody wanted to keel over and pass out. I felt totally naked and absolutely vulnerable out there during that first day's paddy walk, expecting almost every minute that some VC would open up on us with a machine gun from the far wood line and cut us to pieces. My sole comfort was Sergeant Hunter's stolid, steadfast presence. Not that he ever offered the slightest hint of encouragement, but he was there. Way behind us, well beyond earshot, I could see Captain Moore and Sergeant Jones, and the *dai-uy* surrounded by his coterie of bodyguards.

There were about four hundred of us out there—a full battalion. (ARVN battalions numbered about five hundred men, but they rarely exceeded four hundred in the field at any given time because of desertions, sickness, and wounds.) I took little comfort in the size of our force, however, because numbers don't mean much when you're exposed to automatic-weapons fire with absolutely no place to run. But that's what Uncle Sam was paying me for, so I concentrated on humping and watching where I stepped.

Eventually, we reached our first footbridge—across an irrigation ditch. As I've mentioned before, canals and irrigation ditches crisscrossed the paddies. This ditch ran about six feet wide. I couldn't tell how deep because the water was muddy. Light-coffee brown. Farmers crossed the waterways on crude footbridges set randomly along our route. Those wonders of primeval engineering consisted of little more than an occasional sapling or a couple of bamboo poles tied together in a sort of Rube Goldberg affair. That was all the Viets needed. Few of them weighed more than a hundred pounds. But for a two-hundred-pound, white Anglo-Saxon Protestant, those affairs left something to be desired.

The ARVN crossed the bridge without a mishap, though they bunched up terribly waiting for their turn. Suddenly it was mine. I've never been good at balancing acts and could never walk a tightrope, so when I stepped up to that springy little sapling footbridge, it seemed awfully thin.

"Will this thing hold?" I asked.

"I ain't broke one yet, sir," Hunter said.

That was no comfort. He couldn't have weighed more than one-eighty.

I glared at him. He looked a little odd. Then I realized why. For the first time since I'd met him, he was smiling.

I didn't think anything was so goddamn funny at the time, of course, but I had things to do, places to go, and people to see, and the Viets were patiently watching, so I started across. The sapling bridge couldn't have been more than three inches in diameter, and it yielded to my weight with the grace of a thin white birch, and there I was in the middle, teetering and tottering, showing my new brethren how well I could flail my arms, and suddenly, inexplicably, I was on the far bank, still dry. Without giving them time to laugh, as I did several times later that day, I turned and watched Sergeant Hunter negotiate the bridge without a thought.

I asked him later why the ARVN didn't spread out in one long line along the ditch and wade across it like the U.S. Army had been so carefully trained to do. He said the VC stuck punji stakes or similarly insidious booby traps just under the water's surface. And then he added that the Viets didn't like to get wet any more than we did. There was another reason, too, but he didn't mention it at the time.

On and on we trekked, farther and farther across the open paddies, until we stood well within small-arms range of that first distant tree line. About a hundred yards our side of it, *Trung-uy* Tri yelled something and raised his arms. The formation stopped. The point, or lead, platoon spread out. Tri yelled again, and the point platoon stepped into the rice paddy, the men sinking waist-deep into the water as they did, and began slogging toward the wood line. Everybody else waited to see what would happen. If the VC were there, they'd open up on the point platoon, killing the men in the water. That would give us time to react. Tensely, I watched the first wave wade through the muck. Beyond them, tall palm trees and the peaks of several thatch-roof huts jutted from the thick jungle growth. I couldn't see anyone in the tree line. The troops reached it without incident and disappeared into the heavy growth. Tri shouted again, and we resumed our march along the dikes into the village.

We'd made it. A thousand meters. My watch read 0730. At that rate, we were in for a long, long day.

That first wood line hid a hamlet, a group of thatched huts, a small island of humanity in a rice-paddy sea. I saw two old men in black pajamas, a girl in a light cotton shirt, and a handful of half-naked children near the entrance of a doorless, thatch-roof hut—what we called a hootch. They observed us impassively as we traipsed through their homestead, and I wondered fleetingly if some of them were VC. (Most likely they were.) We swept through the hamlet without stopping or paying any heed to its inhabitants, and continued into the next wide expanse of paddy. Looking across it, I saw a thin line of dark foliage on the far side, barely visible in the shimmering heat. We were halfway to the Snake.

"Be sure to drink plenty of water, sir," Hunter said. "And take your salt tablets. There's a well over there."

He was nodding across the paddy. Hearing that, I took a long swig from my canteen. The water was warm, but it tasted better than anything I'd had in a long time. "That's the only other paddy we have to cross," he said. "It's all hard ground after that."

I knew then that I'd make it.

The point platoon was deploying again. Tri stood alone in the shade of a palm tree, solemnly watching his people. He was doing pretty well, I thought. I'd let him do his job.

"We'll reach the river around eleven-thirty," Hunter said. "Then we'll break for lunch. That'll give Charlie time to fade into the bushes."

"Really?" I said, wondering if the rumors I'd heard were true. The Saigon commandos, American troops who stayed in the rear, were quick to bad-mouth the ARVN.

"I shit you not, sir." Hunter shook his head and spit. "And you should see what these guys eat. The *dai-uy*'s got himself a cook who fixes up five-course meals while him and his bodyguards sit around and shoot the breeze. Then they take a siesta. Yep. These guys operate in style. It drives the captain nuts."

"How often have you made this trip?" I asked.

"About eight or so times, one way or the other. Them ARVN, they don't mix things up much. The VC know we're coming, too. I guarantee you that. They probably knew it last week."

Christ, I thought, shaking my head. I hoped they weren't setting up an ambush.

I took another long drink and looked up. The lead platoon was two hundred yards into the paddy, three ragged lines of little men in painted helmets, zigzagging along the dikes. *Trung-uy* Tri's five-man command group stepped out of the shade and onto the paddy-dike highway. Tri moved like a cat, but he stood out in his tiger suit, an easy target for snipers.

"Let's get a move on," I said, refreshed. "You know what Napoleon said, don't you?"

"What?" Hunter said.

"An army marches on its stomach."

Hunter laughed. "Hey. That's pretty good, sir. Did he really say that?"

"I shit you not," I said, stepping into the sunlight.

Around ten o'clock, still far out in the second paddy, we suddenly stopped. I was having second thoughts about my chosen line of work, but hadn't passed out yet. I'd been guzzling lots of water and was still in pretty good shape. *Ha Si* One stood behind me on the dike, and I could hear some busy chatter over his radio. Then the chatter stopped. *Trung-uy* Tri barked a few choice phrases. The lead platoon did a quick right flank march, stepped down into the water, and started wading through the muck heading east.

"There's a canal about three hundred meters to our right, sir," Hunter shouted from behind me as we followed them. "That's where we're headed." The *dai-uy* had decided to forego the paddy-dike route so we could reach the canal bank, a real highway, and make better time, but getting to it was the hard part. For the first time that day, I ventured voluntarily into the muck.

More than a month had passed since planting time, and the burgeoning rice shoots rose from the surface like whiskers on a brown giant's chin. The water wasn't deep, about a foot or so, but I sank into the muck up to my crotch. The stench, a sort of stifling putrescence, filled the air. The next dike was less than fifty yards away. When I reached it and pulled myself up, I stood there, shaking the water from my boots, waiting for it to drain from my trouser legs so I wouldn't be dragging all that extra filthy slime for the next hundred yards. I was simply doing what everybody else was doing. All around me, ARVN were stopping on the dikes and bending over to adjust their trouser cuffs. Or so I thought.

I glanced down to check my boots and saw a leech on my right shin, two inches from the top of my boot. It was huge— the biggest leech I'd ever seen—about three inches long and deep, dark, dirty black-brown. It was wrinkled like an elephant's trunk, and though I couldn't feel it chewing, I knew instinctively that if I didn't get it off fast, it would gnaw an ugly hole through my trousers and start feasting. I flicked it off as quickly as I could with the barrel of my carbine, and it plopped back into the water and disappeared beneath the surface. Luckily, it hadn't had time to work its way through my rip-stop jungle fatigues.

Now I don't know how you feel about leeches, but I've hated them ever since seeing Humphrey Bogart come out of the water with leeches all over him in the movie, *The African Queen*. I turned to warn Sergeant Hunter.

"They're beauts, ain't they, sir," he said, shaking his head.

He was right about the ARVN, too. We sat on the banks of the Snake River for about two hours, doing nothing but waiting for the *dai-uy* to finish his meal and pack up his china. By the time we started moving again, the sun was in the western quadrant.

The Snake was like a big Chinese dragon, and instead of scouring its banks, where the VC might have been hiding, the battalion skipped from curve to curve, leaving in peace whoever might be hiding there.

Around three o'clock in the afternoon, we reached the Bo Long Canal and headed south along its banks to Cai Tac. The canal was narrow—two sampans would have had trouble passing each other on it—but its banks were hard and dry and thick with vegetation. We came to a hamlet, a half dozen tiny hootches nestled along its banks. Pigs and chickens roamed freely about, but I saw no people. Then I remembered the MATA course lore. "When the villages are deserted, or it suddenly gets quiet, that's the time to keep your eyes peeled." Good advice.

I was dragging by then. It was well after three o'clock, and despite the eerie silence and the deserted village, I was just barely stumbling along, trying to make it back to Cai Tac without embarrassing myself or passing out. I couldn't see the rice paddies because of the heavy vegetation that had grown up all along the sides of the canal, and each hamlet was obscured by the thick, heavy, broad-leafed undergrowth that flourished along its banks. All I could see were the empty hootches along the way, and an occasional break in the underbrush, marking a path leading to the paddies on our right. Hunter and *Ha Si* One were behind me, and the *trung-uy* just ahead, but out of sight. A half-dozen ARVN were plodding along with us. Our pace was steady if not swift.

Bam! Pow! Pow! Three distinct firecrackers popped overhead, exploding over my ear. These were immediately followed by the sporadic rattle of outgoing small-arms fire. It sounded like everyone in the lead platoon had opened up at the same time. Without thinking, I ran forward to see what was happening, found a small break in the foliage, and looked out onto the paddy.

About thirty ARVN were charging across it toward a tree line to our left. All of them were running—some firing from the hip—their long, ragged line moving steadily into the wood line. No one was lying in the paddies, and I could hear no cries for help. Suddenly I felt a hand on my shoulder.

"Get down, sir!" Hunter said. "They're shooting at us."

I knew we weren't in danger. Except for the first three pops, the rest of the firing had been outgoing. I did drop to one knee, though, just in case. We watched the ARVN finish their charge into the tree line and listened as the firing petered out. Then, everything was still and very quiet.

Suddenly my mind started racing. That was incoming fire! So that's what it's like. By God, I've been shot at!

Then I felt this sudden rush of pride, knowing that the next time anyone asked me, I could say I'd seen some action. Then it dawned on me—we had just been targets for someone who wanted to kill us—and I began to feel a little light-headed and shaky, so I just waited there on one knee and caught my breath, wondering what to do next. All the nearby ARVN were standing around, listlessly waiting for someone to tell them what to do, too. Nobody seemed worried about anything, so I relaxed and lit up a Camel.

Hunter was listening on the radio. "Just a sniper, sir," he said. "Nobody got hit. They're looking for the little bugger now."

They didn't find him.

Fifteen minutes later, we picked up and continued toward Cai Tac.

A mile short of the highway, I was dreaming about the trucks, a long line of empty deuce-and-a-halfs just waiting for us to emerge from the jungle. The ARVN soldier in front of me stopped so suddenly that I almost bumped into him. The line closed up behind me. I heard someone jabbering ahead, saw some harried looks and some arms jabbing backwards, and the ARVN started backing up. I moved to one side of the path and wondered what could be the cause of the confusion. I asked *Ha Si* One what was going on. He started jabbering, too. I couldn't understand a word. Then he raised his right hand, pointing at something in the air. Something invisible. After shooing it away with his hand, his finger circled back and landed on his wrist. He pinched it and grimaced. Then he slapped it. "Hornets," I figured.

I was right. The entire ARVN column—a full infantry battalion of more than four hundred heavily armed men—had been stopped dead in its tracks by a nest of hornets. We quickly retreated to a better location, made the requisite detour, and that was the end of that.

Delta vegetation is thick, generally low-bush and broadleaf. Palm fronds, banana leaves, giant schefflera, split-leaf philodendra, and ferns of all sizes and shapes brushed against us as we wound toward Cai Tac. I kept losing track of the man in front of me. Every time the column veered, I'd lose sight of him. I was beginning to get angry that I was falling behind when suddenly my shoulder caught on fire.

Something had attacked it. A dozen searing bites ravaged it, burning down my shoulder blade and arm. I cringed, slapping at it, trying desperately to sweep away the burning pain. Then I saw them—there, on the wide green leaf still waving in the air from my passage. The leaf was covered with ants—big, fiery, red ones, almost translucent. I'd never seen any like them. A dozen or so had brushed off the leaf and onto my shoulder as I'd passed by, and they'd let me have it in spades. I don't know how many bit me before I swept them off my shoulder, but there were hundreds on the leaf. Edified, I left them alone. I warned Sergeant Hunter by pointing them out. He winced, sympathetically that time, but said nothing, and we continued slowly southward. My shoulder continued to burn for five minutes, and I'll never forget those ants.

As we closed on Cai Tac, I saw villagers again. Some of them were armed, which made me nervous at first, but Sergeant Hunter said they were local militia, and friendly. How could he tell? I wondered. Whatever, the more we saw, the better we felt. When the ARVN started smiling and chattering and laughing together, I relaxed, too. Then we broke out of the thick vegetation, and I saw the line of empty trucks parked along the highway. We were done.

I felt good about having made it. Certainly relieved. I was, most likely, the happiest man in the column. I was still functioning, too, which amazed me. My first long paddy walk was done, thank God, yet I couldn't help but wonder how the next one would end.

Chapter 4

A Paddy Rat's Diploma

> *Every generation, it seems, must
> learn its own lessons from its own
> war, because every war is dif-
> ferent and is fought by different
> ignorant young men.*
> —SAMUEL HYNES,
> *The Soldiers' Tale*

Some places tell you that you shouldn't be there. That's the way it was in Saigon, with the bottle smashing against our bus's window, all the sandbagged bunkers and barbed wire, and the firefights outside the capital at night. And later, in Bac Lieu, with the *dai-uy* groping his new wife in the bistro. And finally, in Vi Thanh, where I ran into all kinds of unpleasantness. But those of us blinded by the fervor failed to see it.

I'd been in Vi Thanh less than two weeks when the itch began. It started after supper—just a friendly little tickle down my spine at first, like poison ivy, but in a place I couldn't reach. I wasn't sure what it was, but ruled out heat poisoning. (After two weeks in the tropics, I thought I was acclimated.) I tried to ignore it, but the itch got worse, intensifying steadily, until by eight o'clock, it was driving me nuts. It had spread, too—from the back of my neck and shoulders down to my waist—a relentless, all-consuming, unbearable itch, and it offered no respite. Desperate, I sought help.

Sergeant Quinlan, the team medic, was drinking coffee in the mess hall. A young E-5 with pallid skin, he was quiet and well liked. When we'd met earlier, he'd described himself as "a part-time pill-pusher, psychoanalyst, and surgeon."

"I need your help, Doc. My back is driving me crazy."

"You strain it or something, sir?"

"No. It's an itch. The worst I've ever had."

"Got a rash?"

"I don't know. I can't see. Maybe. It's like poison ivy, but worse. Much worse."

"You probably got the fungus-amungus," he said. "Let's take a look-see."

I almost ripped my shirt off and turned around.

"Oooweee, sir. You got the fungus all right. How'd you get it on your back?"

I wasn't sure. We'd been on another paddy walk that afternoon, east of Vi Thanh, up by an old Buddhist temple, an ancient Annamite ruin that had long since been recaptured by the jungle. As usual, we hadn't found anything. On the way back, though, we'd stopped near a hamlet sitting all by itself out in the paddies. Instead of crossing the rice paddy to search it, *Trung-uy* Tri had his mortar team simply lob a few rounds of 60mm high explosive into it.

"Reconnaissance by fire," Sergeant Hunter had said, angry and disgusted.

I had been leaning with my back against a tree, a tall one, covered with vines, strangely hairy ones, like the legs of a tarantula.

I told Sergeant Quinlan about the vines.

"Fuckin' A, sir. You shouldn't a gone an' done that," he said, shaking his head.

"What have I got?" I asked.

"I don't rightly know," he said. "Some kind of fungus. Cap'n Callahan had a case last month, all over his legs, an' he was hurtin' for a few days, that's for sure."

Callahan was the regimental staff adviser, a big man who played volleyball like there was no tomorrow. "Can you do something for the itch?" I pleaded.

"Well, sir, if we had a case of clear nail polish, we could spread it all over your back to seal off the air. That would do it. But all I got is tincture of benzoin. It'll help, but it ain't as good as fingernail polish."

"Anything you got will be fine with me," I said.

I followed him back to his quarters in the NCO shack. Sergeant Jeffries was there reading his *Stars and Stripes*. The doc wasted no time and swabbed my back with tincture of benzoin. The first cool draught of it quickly turned to fire, and the itch seemed to sear away. Then a general numbness spread all over the affected area, and the burning faded.

"That should do it for a little while, anyway," Quinlan said. "There's more where that came from if you need it. Drop by anytime."

"Thanks," I said. I did, several times, but the worst of the itch was over. A week later, it was, for all intents and purposes, gone, and I forgot about it.

Except for my first paddy walk, and a few other unpleasant moments, my recollections of the Mekong Delta have suffered the ravages of time. Suffice it to say that our ARVN friends weren't in any great rush to win the war. In fact, our battalion went out only once every four or five days. During August, for instance, we conducted four paddy walks, one road-clearing operation, and one agonizingly slow canal-clearing operation—motoring up the Can Tho Canal in LCVPs, World War II vintage landing barges, providing security for the rock boats, motorless arks that carried crushed rock in their holds. We spent a half day on the firing range, too—something Captain Moore had been urging his counterpart, the *dai-uy*, to do for several months. But seven days of work in a thirty-day month didn't seem to me like that much effort for a "tiny nation struggling bravely for its independence."

When ARVN wasn't working, we weren't either, and the real challenge was how to cope with all the boredom. I learned to play volleyball with reckless abandon. Everyone else did. It was a vital part of our daily ritual, and after supper, every evening, the games would get more and more lively. There were few other diversions—certainly no tennis club like the one I'd seen at Ca Mau. The only socializing was with members of the team, and sipping brews with the boys grew old fast. My fellow lieutenant, the army pilot, seemed to live in his L-19, his single engine Bird Dog observation plane, and Captain Moore spent most of his free time with the regimental staff in the ARVN compound, endeavoring, I assume, to motivate them to higher levels of endeavor (an exercise in frustration he most thoughtfully took upon himself). Sergeant Jones didn't like the Viets, so he didn't socialize at all. Whatever carousing I did was with Sergeant Hunter.

We had free run of the town, but not a hell of a lot to do there. I visited the barbershop once (and will never forget its shifty-eyed proprietor wielding his straight razor just inches from my jugular; I wondered with his every deft stroke if he was VC). I would drop off rolls of film (black-and-white only) at the local pharmacy (any similarity between it and those in the States being purely coincidental), and pick up the photographs a week later. And one long, dull afternoon, Hunter and I decided to drop by the local gin mill for a *Ba-Mui-Ba*. The town's only pub consisted of a dingy, open-front, gray-wall room with several rough-hewn picnic tables inside. Its primary offering was lukewarm beer. That particular day it was crowded to overflowing with gawking middle-aged males. We tried to enjoy our beers, but the Viets were so shocked by our presence, so nervous we were there, that all they could do was stare at us. We quickly quaffed our brews and departed. So much for showing the flag.

That brings me, finally, to those few unavoidable occasions when we partook of the local cuisine. We'd been told by the brass at MACV to go native. If our Vietnamese hosts offered us chicken heads and rice, we were supposed to eat them with gusto. If they served duck-blood soup, we were supposed to slurp it up with a smile (even though it tasted like liquid chalk). And, when little Johnny ARVN offered to share his cold rice ball with us (which he carried around in a sort of grape-leaf wrapper), we couldn't turn up our noses at it without offending him. Eat and enjoy it we must, even when it was reeking with *nuoc mam*, a pungent, tangy sauce comprised, primarily, of rotted fish. *Nuoc mam* was to Viets what salt is to Americans, kimchi to Koreans, or garlic to Italians. In other words, the Vietnamese put it on almost everything they eat. Being a good soldier, I followed MACV's directives, and it didn't take me long to contract a virulent case of the national malady, to wit, dysentery.

So commonplace was dysentery among the members of the team that its arrival in the rookie was acknowledged with more amusement than concern. I was lucky, too. My case was bacillic dysentery, not amebic dysentery. My case, however, was perniciously persistent. The prescribed remedy was Kaopectate, ruefully referred to as "GI cement." I drank several bottles of the stuff the first week I had the disease. It might have helped, but I doubt it.

During the second week, my colon was cramping almost constantly. I was draining away, rectally, day after day. During the worst episodes, I spent most of my time just sitting in the latrine. It was a clean latrine, though, with two showers and three white porcelain sinks along the wall, and three commodes, and a doorway on the left—built by the French, I'm sure, long before the VC evolved.

One particularly helpless afternoon, I was sitting on the toilet, reading the latest copy of *Stars and Stripes*, when I heard a pair of sandaled feet pitter-pattering along the walkway outside. The latrine door burst open, and an old woman, the oldest of the compound's cleaning maids, bustled in.

"Chao, ong," she said, smiling. Her teeth were rotted and her gums blackened by betel nut, a locally grown narcotic the Viets chewed like coca leaves.

I returned her greeting with a nod and tried to keep some semblance of composure—not that she cared, Viets think nothing of their natural bodily functions—but I was still young, WASPy, modest, and obviously suffering from a Bostonian's puritanical sense of common decency and proper social behavior, which had never, in my limited experience, included defecating with members of the opposite sex.

She bustled over to the toilet next to mine, turned around, dropped her black pajama bottoms, and squatted over the commode.

I returned to my *Stars and Stripes*. "MARINES KILL 600 NEAR DA NANG" blared the headline.

A gush of effluence splashed loudly into the john beside me. I heard the old woman grunt and then the tinkle of her urine. I tried to disregard it. Then she farted. I thought of the old *ba* I had seen my first day at Bac Lieu. She had been taking a crap off the end of a platform behind her hootch, and the "shit fish" in the little pond underneath it were jumping out of the water to catch her offering. Then I wondered if my own stool would ever solidify. Two more wet drizzly blasts punctuated the stillness. I felt a giggle welling up in me, but then my own sphincter cramped again as if a fist were squeezing it, and I fought desperately to hold it back. The newsprint blurred, and I bit my lip. I stared at the sinks across the tiled floor, and the cracked mirror on the wall, and the bug-encrusted strip of screen above it, and the red-tile ceiling overhead.

Another deluge splashed into the old *ba*'s commode, followed by an almost surreptitious sigh, another satisfied grunt, and a long pristine moment of absolute silence. Then the old woman rose abruptly, pulled her pants up, and flushed the toilet. Thank God she did that, at least. I glanced at her. She flashed her rotted teeth at me. I nodded politely. She grunted good-bye and left.

Now that's something I can tell my grandchildren, I thought, letting my sphincter relax.

War is hell.

August flowed into September.

For lack of anything better to do, I asked to fly with the pilots on their long, lonely flights to the boondocks and back. Flying had always intrigued me. As a youngster, I'd studied all the aircraft manuals and silhouette spotting guides I could find, and took no small amount of satisfaction in being able to identify every plane I saw. Watching the huge, six-engine B-36 Peacemakers and the incredible Flying Wings as they cruised over my home in Nahant, Massachusetts, was a thrill I still remember. And my first flight, when I was thirteen, in a

Piper Cub. Before I started jumping out of planes, flying had been a dream of mine. Had Yale offered an air force ROTC program, I'd surely have joined it.

But from Vi Thanh, I only made two flights. The first, with the air force FAC, involved an hour's flight south. We watched three VNAF A-1E Skyraiders bomb the shit out of a supposedly VC farm, a cluster of huts beside a small cultivated field, nestled in the V of a river. Skyraiders were single-engine propeller planes that carried a disproportionately heavy bomb load. They plastered the farm with 250-pound bombs and left. If the farmer wasn't VC before the raid, he certainly was after it.

My second flight, with the army lieutenant, was a short hop north to reconnoiter the target area for an upcoming operation. We were on our way back, about four hundred feet up, making our approach to Vi Thanh over the Can Tho Canal, when I heard a dull *pop* and something *thunked* the wing outside my window.

"Someone just shot at us," the pilot said.

"Roger that," I said, trying to sound calm, but I was asking myself what the hell I was doing up there in that stupid little thin-skinned L-19, and deciding simultaneously never to go up in one again unless I absolutely had to.

We landed without any difficulty, and Sergeant Jeffries greeted us at the airstrip.

"You got new orders, sir," he said, waving a piece of paper at me as his jeep rolled to a halt. "Up to that new airmobile division in II Corps. How do you like them apples?"

"When do I leave?" I asked.

"ASAP," he said. "Back to Bac Lieu first. Then Saigon and USARV and then a place called An Khe. (He pronounced it "Ann Key.") That's way the hell up there, sir. I looked at a map when these came in." He waved the paper in his hand.

"Does Captain Moore know?" I asked.

"Not yet. He's up at regiment. He'll shit when he hears about this." Jeffries shook the orders again. "You're a lucky man, Lieutenant. I'd give my left nut to be going up there with you."

I wasn't sure I'd go quite that far.

Glancing at the orders, I saw "Immediate Reassignment" and "Proceed to US First Cavalry Division (Airmobile), An Khe, II Corps, Republic of Vietnam." It was no joke.

I'd read about the 1st Cav's expected arrival. We all had. It was big news in *Stars and Stripes*. But II Corps was three hundred miles north of Saigon, a whole new, totally different world, and I'd just gotten used to the Delta. I was having trouble grasping the significance of the news.

The 1st Cav, or Air Cav, was the old 11th Air Assault Division, an experimental unit that had been stationed at Fort Benning, Georgia, when I'd been with the 82d. We'd played war games against it in South Carolina—field exercises lasting a month, designed to test the concept of air mobility. I'd been a battalion adjutant then, just a second lieutenant staff officer traveling comfortably with headquarters. I'd never had to confront "the other side," but I'd not forgotten two aspects of the 11th Air Assault. The first was its incredible mobility. With its own complement of helicopters, its infantry could pick up and fly almost anywhere, showing up in our backyard when we thought they were miles to our front. I'd almost been "captured" once. The second was its vulnerability, and this thought began to haunt me as we drove back to the compound. Whenever the Air Assault's helicopters had flown over our location, we could have easily— had the games been the real thing—blown them out of the sky. They would have been even easier targets coming into a landing zone. After all, helicopters weren't the fastest aircraft in the world, and they had to hover while landing. I had seen a helicopter crash, too, back in college. An H-13, one of those little two-seat Plexiglas bubble jobs, had flipped over and crashed in flames during an air show. The pilot had been killed instantly. One tiny error, one minor misjudgment at the controls, and his ship had gone down. Any thoughts I had nurtured about signing up for the army's flight program had been extinguished with that blazing fire on the runway of that air show. And there I was going to join the 1st Air Cav and fly around in those slow, hovering, tricky, little, thin-skinned helicopters, just like the 11th Air Assault's ships in Carolina! I wasn't particularly thrilled with the prospect.

"You lucky son of a bitch!" was Captain Moore's reaction. "That's great, Larry. Just think what this can do for your career." His unabashed exuberance put me off. It was genuine, though. Captain Moore was a good West Pointer.

By suppertime, I'd come around. My new orders were a break. During the last six weeks very little had happened. I could have spent the whole year in the Delta, rotting away with the itch or dysentery or boredom. God knows I wasn't wild about the ARVN. I wouldn't miss them at all. And working with Americans, in an American unit, that was the clincher.

When I left for Bac Lieu the next day, I was feeling pretty good about things.

"Keep your ass down, sir," Hunter said as we shook hands. He wasn't smiling.

"Good luck, sir," Jones said.

Two brave and capable men. I knew I'd miss them both. Sergeant Jeffries drove me to the airstrip. He was a really sharp NCO, too, one of the best I'd ever seen. I wondered fleetingly if I'd ever see him again as we shook hands and said good-bye.

Back at Bac Lieu, Colonel Spellman had arranged a farewell party for the two lieutenants he was losing to the 1st Air Cavalry Division. Peter Speers, whom I'd met briefly at Can Tho, was the other man selected to infuse into the American unit. We would fly to Saigon together the next morning, transfer out of MACV and into USARV (U.S. Army Vietnam), and then join the Cav at An Khe (pronounced "Ann Kay").

Speers and I both arrived in Bac Lieu just as the party was starting. Forty officers had gathered, and though their presence probably reflected their penchant for a party more than the significance of our departure, I was vaguely flattered by the turnout. Colonel Spellman made a short but gracious speech about losing us to the powers that be.

"If the army's priority is to take up the burden of the war," he said, "so be it." Prescient words in September of 1965. He wished us Godspeed and gave us Paddy Rat Scrolls, souvenirs of our service with the 21st ARVN Division. Then, we all got drunk.

After a slew of congratulatory farewells from men I hardly knew, I retreated to the relative privacy of the transient officers quarters and read my Paddy Rat Scroll. It had been presented to me rolled up like a diploma and tied with a red and yellow ribbon, clearly to be framed and hung from an office wall.

The citation was penned in calligraphy and surrounded by a sea of aquamarine. Mekong Delta scenes—a boy on a buffalo, an ancient pagoda, a rice paddy—floated in the corners like clouds in the sky. The division's "Brasso Patch" logo hovered overhead in all its glory. "Loyal Order of Paddy Rats" was inscribed in capital letters—a mock headline etched in yellow bamboo. The citation read as follows:

Having braved the rigors of service in the steaming jungles of South Vietnam and, having been shot at by various and sundry Viet Cong, out and out bandits, as well as some friendly forces and, having consumed copious quantities of Kaopectate and GI Cement after partaking of the native cuisine, and having spent many days dog-tag deep in the rice paddies pursuing the enemy and being pursued by leeches, and after being unduly harassed, embarrassed, be-littled and persecuted by Saigon Commandos and strap-hangers, and after playing nursemaid to reporters, Senators, and other personnel endeavoring to become experts,

Be it known that 1st Lieutenant Samuel L. Gwin, Jr., Infantry, 097564, is designated a counter-insurgency expert and first class paddy rat.

Given under my hand this 11th day of
September, 1965.
J. R. Spellman
Colonel, Infantry, 21st V.N. Div. Senior Adviser.

So true, so true, I thought, smiling.

I had just graduated—from only a primer course, though, only the basic test. The next day, I would fly up to Saigon, then to An Khe where the Cav was, and the real war. I wasn't quite sure how I felt.

BOOK TWO

The Cav

Chapter 5

Coming into An Khe

I have seen much war in my lifetime and I hate it profoundly. But there are worse things than war; and all of them come with defeat.

—ERNEST HEMINGWAY,
Men at War

Getting from Bac Lieu to An Khe took three days. We had to pass through Saigon to process out of MACV and into USARV, which was easily done in the new tent city that had sprung up around Tan Son Nhut airfield since I'd been there last. Then we ventured into the city for some fun. After my six weeks in the bush, Saigon seemed as tame as Boston. The culture shock I'd experienced on my arrival in country had completely dissipated. I don't remember what else I did on that second trip through Saigon, but the transition was painless, and Speers and I had no trouble finding a flight north the next morning on a C-123 air force cargo plane heading directly to An Khe in the Central Highlands.

"We're coming into An Khe," the crew chief yelled over the engine's steady drone. I gave him a wave of acknowledgment and reached down to check my gear. It was tucked under my seat—a MACV jungle pack, my B-4 bag, and weapon. The aircraft began its steep descent—something I was getting used to.

Almost immediately after we leveled off, the landing gear screeched on the runway. The pilot threw his engines into reverse, and they shrieked in protest as we slowly jerked to a halt. We'd been two hours in the air. Not bad for a 250-mile trip.

The C-123 turned and taxied back up the runway. I unbuckled, got up, and stretched. I felt the aircraft turn again, and the rear cargo door started lowering itself to the runway.

I grabbed my pack, swung it over my shoulder, picked up my B-4 bag, and followed Speers out of the aircraft, nodding thanks to the crew chief as he waved good-bye.

Stepping out of the plane, I was momentarily blinded by the sunlight. The air was stifling, too—ovenlike—drier than in the Delta, where the monsoon had begun to manifest itself with regular afternoon downpours. The sky here was blue and almost cloudless.

A deuce-and-a-half truck was coming toward us from the end of the runway, and behind it, lounging in the high grass, was a gaggle of American GIs. It looked like a platoon.

That was comforting, because the airstrip was just a perforated steel mat resting in a lush green valley surrounded by gently rolling hills. Tall grass, bushes, and stands of small shade trees carpeted the high ground around us. In the distance, past the end of the airstrip, I could see some low mountains to the west. They were covered with jungle and looked foreboding.

"Not much here," Speers said, shouting over the engines. He wasn't just whistling Dixie.

Standing there, almost all alone, by an airstrip in a valley without any idea of where to go or how to get there was slightly disconcerting. I nodded to him and started walking off the airstrip. When we reached the edge, we dropped our gear in the tall grass and looked around again. The only friendlies we could see were the men at the end of the runway, and the guys on the deuce-and-a-half, who were now off-loading cartons of C rations from the plane. I glanced past it to the high ground, four hundred yards away. Silhouetted against the sky was a long single file of heavily-armed men—Americans, thank God—coming down the ridgeline. They turned out to be a company from the 101st Airborne Division which had been securing the airstrip. Was I glad to see them!

"Here comes someone," Speers said.

I turned around and saw him pointing toward a jeep with two men in it speeding down a narrow dirt road that ran from a wood line on the other side of the field to the airstrip. We watched it come barreling toward us, a rooster tail of dust billowing behind it. The jeep screeched to a halt right beside us. The driver was a MACV sergeant wearing an OD baseball cap. The man riding shotgun had an M-2 carbine on his lap.

"What brings you to our little corner of the world, sir?" the sergeant asked.

"First Cav, Sarge," Speers responded, casually returning his salute. "Can you help us out and give us a lift to where they're at?"

"No sweat, sir. Can do. Just let me pick up the mail. Any other passengers on board?"

"Nope," Speers said. "We're it."

While the MACV guys were getting their mail, I walked over to see what the men at the end of the runway could tell us. As I approached, I was struck by how grungy and exhausted they looked. They were sprawled haphazardly in the tall grass, their shirts off and their equipment drying in the sun, the scruffiest bunch of GIs I'd ever seen. One of them got up as I approached, and met me twenty yards from the group. He was a lieutenant with a 101st patch inked in black on the left shoulder of his jungle fatigues. We shook hands.

"Got a cigarette?" he asked. I obliged him.

We stood in the hot sun, smoking and talking. He told me that his men had been out in the field for weeks, trekking around, looking for Charlie, staying on the move. They'd been out too long, he said. Several of his men had malaria.

"It's the pits out here," he said. "The pits!" Then he spit into the grass.

I asked him if they'd seen anything.

"No," he said. "But they're out there. You can hear 'em."

I asked him where the 1st Cav was.

He pointed to a small mountain about five miles west of us. "See that hill?" he asked.

"Yeah."

"That's Hong Kong Mountain. It overlooks your base. There's just an advance party there now, clearing brush and stuff. We're providing security."

Good, I thought, feeling safer than I had five minutes before.

I thanked him, gave him the rest of my cigarettes (I had more in my B-4 bag), and walked back to Speers and our gear. Things were looking up.

A few minutes later, Speers and I were riding in the back of the MACV sergeant's jeep through the town of An Khe. It seemed like a small city, really, with a number of stucco buildings along the main road through town and lots of tin-roofed shacks down the side streets and alleys. We drove past a province/district headquarters, too, which housed the sergeant's MACV team, but no one was around. What surprised me about An Khe was the number of street vendors squatting by the roadside, displaying the usual inventory of American cigarettes, booze, clothing, even jungle fatigues and jungle boots. It reminded me of Saigon, where I'd stopped once to purchase a black leather shoulder holster for my Colt .45. I think it cost five bucks. Little did I know, though, driving through An Khe, how precious those items of clothing would be to the 1st Air Cav troopers who came off the troopships in their old-style cotton-twill fatigues, so much hotter and heavier and slower to dry in the sun. Jungle fatigues and jungle boots would soon be worth their weight in gold, and I had a pair of each.

We drove through town without stopping and continued westward for another mile or two before we saw the impressive front entrance to the 1st Cav's base. It was marked by a big wooden sign, ten feet high, with the soon-to-be-ubiquitous 1st Cav horse-blanket patch painted on it and guarded by 1st Cav gun jeeps. They had M-60 machine guns mounted on them and were manned by 1st Cav MPs. They looked STRAC, tough, and imposing, and I couldn't help but feel a sudden surge of pride in arriving at my new outfit, an American Army division with a proud history and an intriguing concept of combat air mobility, as yet untested.

The MPs waved us through, and as soon as we entered the base, I noticed that the road we were on improved markedly. It turned into a smooth, well-graded, carefully drained, winding dirt highway, and it was obvious that some American Army engineers had been hard at work. The surface of the road had been sprayed with a light coat of oil, too—to keep the dust down. You could smell it, but it wasn't offensive, and the road was in very good shape.

We continued to drive through sparsely covered terrain, slightly hilly and marked by deep gullies and small ravines. Oncoming jeeps and deuce-and-a-halfs with GIs in them passed by us every hundred yards or so, and it was really good to see all the Americans. The road took us to a group of open-flapped general purpose tents with a small FIRST CAVALRY DIVISION IN-PROCESSING CENTER sign outside, and that's where the MACV guys dropped us off.

We thanked them, watched them turn around and drive back down the road, and then signed in.

My first disappointment was that we were both assigned to the 3d Brigade. All I knew about it was that it wasn't the 1st Brigade, the division's Airborne brigade. Being ex-82d types, we were counting on an Airborne slot, not a tour with a "straight-leg" outfit, and the news was disheartening. The 1st Brigade was all filled up, we were told. So much for jump pay. The good news was that a jeep was already on its way to pick us up. Efficient Americans, I thought.

A lone jeep picked us up and drove us half a mile farther down the road—what turned out to be the inner perimeter road that circled the division's giant helicopter pad, affectionately referred to as the Golf Course. There was an outer perimeter, too, but that was Indian country. We turned to the right, and fifty yards later arrived at the 3d Brigade headquarters.

We were greeted by the brigade S-4 (supply officer), a

major. He was part of the brigade's advance party, and terribly overweight. The brigade executive officer, Lt. Col. E.C. Meyer, was the advance party's CO. We'd meet him later. We were shown a tent to throw our gear in, introduced to several of the officers who'd arrived with the advance party, and told we'd meet Colonel Brown, the brigade commander, when the main body closed in, which was expected to be in a couple of days. The main body of the division was either still en route, or waiting aboard their troopships, moored in Qui Nhon Harbor. The S-4 wasn't sure.

The brigade HQ had a couple of tents pitched, I recall, including one for Lieutenant Colonel Meyer and one for the tactical operations center, or TOC, but what struck me about the place was the number of small flags stuck in the ground, marking the proposed sites for each of the HQ sections when they arrived. What I also remember clearly about the 3d Brigade HQ, even after all these years, was the fifteen-gallon lister bag that hung from a wooden tripod outside the TOC. Cool, clear water was available to us, within an easy walk's reach. Yes, the 1st Cav knew how to do things.

We had nothing to do until the main body arrived, so, except for meeting Lieutenant Colonel Meyer (very briefly) and hearing him tell us that we'd both been assigned to the 2d Battalion, we had nothing to do except wait around and try to look busy. I think I wrote a few letters that week, but that's about all. I also remember sleeping well at night, with the cool air of the highlands providing much better sleeping weather than we had down in the Delta.

The terrain of the highlands was very different from that of the Delta. The climate, too. First of all, the dry season had begun. The monsoon rains had come and gone, the ground was warm and dry, and you could sit comfortably on it. Secondly, the local terrain was heavily vegetated, but it was scrub jungle, not the heavy triple-canopy stuff that we found when we began to scour the countryside. Thirdly, the humidity was almost bearable that month, and though the temperature hovered in the 90s, the evenings were cool enough to warrant a sleeping bag.

I also remember hearing an occasional firefight erupting around the perimeter at night but taking some comfort in the fact that it was the 101st out there, not some leg outfit. We were safe.

Our sense of anticipation increased from day to day, as we awaited the arrival of the division's main body. It arrived on September 15, I recall, and when the great day came, we weren't disappointed. From early morning until late in the afternoon, the entire base camp was abuzz with the comings and goings of Hueys and Chinooks and Flying Cranes, and vehicles and trucks of all sizes, all filled with American GIs, a welcome sight for sure. The whole area was transformed in a couple of hours from a relatively bucolic quietude to the hurly-burly of a busy American Army base, with troops striding purposefully from place to place, with no time to lolly-gag or stand around with your hands on your hips, and most of them were as apprehensive as I had been my first day in country, wondering what was going to happen next, where the enemy was, and when we would be tested to the max. Speers and I were told that the 2d Battalion's adjutant would pick us up the next morning and escort us to our new billets. With the prospect of finding out who I would be working with for the next ten months weighing heavily on my mind, I hit the sack early that night.

Capt. George Johnson, the S-1, or adjutant, of the 2/7th (the 2d Battalion of the 7th Cavalry Regiment), was the first man in the battalion to make our acquaintance. He arrived bright and early, walked into the GP tent where we were waiting, introduced himself with a warm smile and hand-shake, and guided us to the 2/7th's TOC, wherein waited Lt. Col. John D. White, the battalion commander.

Speers and I followed Captain Johnson as he walked along a path that had already been beaten between the two head-quarters, about a hundred yards from each other. While walking behind the adjutant through the waist-high grass and scrub brush that separated the two HQ's, I could see hundreds of American GIs working on a hillside to my right. They were busy setting up pup tents, clearing brush, digging bunkers, and generally doing all the things one would expect a newly arrived American infantry battalion to do.

What I didn't know at the time was how the battalion's area was organized, but I learned soon enough, and this is as good a time as any to describe it.

Looking up, or generally north, from the division's interior road, the battalion's base camp was comprised of an area that covered two slopes or hillsides separated by a dry, stepped rice paddy. The troops were quartered on the right-hand slope. The battalion's HQ tents were pitched on the lower part of the left-hand slope, with the five company HQ tents one behind the other behind them. Separating the two hillsides was the dry rice paddy, with its levels or steps working upward to what turned out to be the battalion mess hall tent, where the food was prepared. The division's outer perimeter, later called the Green Line, lay fifty yards behind it, but the mess hall was protected from direct enemy fire by the crest of the high ground beyond it. The organization of the battalion's base camp was all very well thought out and had been marked in advance by the advance party that had put those little red flags in the ground.

We followed Captain Johnson along the path, past groups of GIs cutting brush, crossed the lower part of the dry rice paddy, and stopped outside the 2/7's TOC.

"Wait here," the captain said and disappeared into the tent. When he reappeared, he waved us in, and we walked in and reported formally to the battalion commander, coming to attention and saluting.

Colonel White was a tall, thin man, almost gaunt, with a crew cut that was peppered with gray. He motioned for us to sit down on two small wooden crates, the only pieces of furniture in the tent except for a large blackboard with a map tacked onto it. He then delivered an easily forgettable welcome-aboard pep talk and began to tell us about the battalion's mission. He left me cold, frankly. He was a poser, I thought, a man who was trying to make an impression on us, not one who inspires confidence, and he seemed old. He was a veteran of the Korean War. In a nutshell, I didn't like him. He asked us what we'd been doing in Vietnam, then didn't seem interested in hearing what we had to say. After tolerating us for a few minutes, he asked us what we wanted to do in the battalion, what jobs we wanted. Speers said he had experience in supply. I heard myself requesting an XO's slot in a rifle company.

I didn't want a staff job. That would have been the pits. I'd been a platoon leader before, in the 82d, and it was a second lieutenant's slot anyway, so I didn't want that, either. But I did feel qualified to be the executive officer, or second in command, of a rifle company, so I volunteered for it, and though I've never been the same since, I've never regretted doing so. I was still young, after all, probably crazy, and clearly naive. I wanted to serve with troops, and I wanted to see some action. That's what I'd been trained for.

The colonel said he would take our requests under advisement, then told us we were being assigned to the battalion staff as liaison officers until the dust settled and the battalion had finished the first phase of its mission, setting up the base camp. In the meantime, we were to observe the goings on, get to know as many of the officers as we could in the next few days, keep our eyes and ears open, and be patient. With that, he dismissed us, and we wandered back to the brigade HQ area to retrieve our gear. So much for them apples.

For the next two weeks, then, I wandered around the battalion base camp, getting to know the lieutenants and trying to learn the scoop. What I learned wasn't encouraging. The 2d of the 7th was a mongrel.

The worst thing about the battalion was its apparent lack of esprit de corps. First, it wasn't an air cavalry battalion by a long shot. It had been, until just a few weeks before its departure on the United States Ship *Maurice Rose*, a mechanized infantry battalion, the 2d of the 9th, formerly with the 2d Infantry Division in Korea. Second, when it had been ordered to join the 1st Air Cav, the battalion had been terribly under strength, so its ranks had to be filled in a hurry—from every available source. Accordingly, the men I met didn't seem to know each other well. That was my impression, anyway. Third, when I asked what airmobile training they had had, they all laughed. It boiled down, basically, to none, a single short ride on a Huey for each man in the battalion. In a nutshell, morale sucked.

Of the six hundred or so men in the battalion, I recognized only two. One was a lanky red-haired captain named Mc-Carn. He'd been a company commander in my battalion in the 82d, and he'd lost two of his people in a live-fire exercise at Fort Bragg. (An artillery round had fallen short on his position.) McCarn was the battalion's S-4, or supply officer. The other guy was a first lieutenant named Henry Thorpe, whom I vaguely recognized from Ranger School. He told me when I first saw him that he'd dropped out of our class during the mountain phase of training because he had scratched his eye on a bramble bush. He'd been evacuated, he said, but had returned to finish with another class. Thorpe was the CO of Delta Company, sometimes called the support company, a hybrid outfit consisting of an antitank platoon, a reconnaissance (or Recon) platoon, and a mortar platoon. Hank had a droll sense of humor, bordering on the disrespectful, and it was clear from the outset that he didn't like the colonel very much. I remember sitting around Hank's HQ tent, sipping coffee, and hearing him wax loquacious about how the battalion had been formed, packed up, rushed through training, and shipped lock, stock, and barrel to Vietnam—all in the space of three months.

Two out of six hundred left me with much getting to know to do, so I spent as much time as I could with the lieutenants. I was particularly impressed by 2d Lt. David "Pat" Payne, a platoon leader in Alpha Company, and 1st Lt. Don Cornett, the XO of Charlie Company—two great guys with positive attitudes and a fun sense of humor. They were Rangers, too.

There were very few Rangers in the battalion. Hank Thorpe was one. Pat Payne and Don Cornett were two more. Jim Lawrence, the Recon Platoon leader, was another. But the most impressive guy I met was Rick Rescorla, a platoon leader in Bravo Company. A former sergeant in the British

Army, he was something of a British soldier of fortune, and he'd taken a commission in the U.S. Army and volunteered for Vietnam because it was the only war around. Though I didn't get to know him until later, he was already somewhat of a legend in the battalion (and it wasn't long before he justified it).

I guess I was lucky to have had some time in country, and I didn't mind sporting my jungle fatigue shirt, with its MACV patch on the right shoulder, signifying that I'd already had a combat tour. In the land of the blind, the one-eyed man is king.

Another thing I noticed was the number of overweight NCOs in the battalion. A unit's backbone is its NCOs, its noncommissioned officers, the sergeants and corporals. They're the ones who get things done, who kick ass and take names, who translate the officers' wishes into action. Without good NCOs, a unit might as well pack up and go home, and it seemed to me that there were too many fat sergeants in the outfit. But despite the extra blubber, the NCOs were good. They were experienced and tough. Many of the older ones had fought in World War II and Korea. The senior NCOs in particular—the first sergeants and platoon sergeants—were superb. Combined with some thoughtful and motivated lieutenants and some experienced and competent captains, they ultimately made the battalion what it was.

And finally, there was one cohesive force that held the battalion together—an almost single-minded detestation of its commander, John D. White. It wasn't long before I learned why.

Chapter 6

The Court-martial

I trust the quiet coldness of the experienced fighters, I like their knowing that words are wasted in this business.
—KATHERINE ANNE PORTER

While the 1st Cav's advance party was clearing the Golf Course and marking the division's unit boundaries with little colored flags, a brigade from the 101st Airborne Division had been responsible for our security. In other words, after a long day's work, we could rest. Being an old salt, at least in the sense that I'd had almost two months in country, I felt safe under their protection and slept comfortably, enjoying the hard dry ground and the cool night air of the highlands. While the 101st was guarding us, the perimeter was relatively quiet. Only occasionally did we hear a shot fired in anger.

When the division's main body arrived, though, and took responsibility for the perimeter, things changed. Understandably, the newly arrived troops were anxious. For the first time since the end of the Korean War, 1st Cavalry troopers were experiencing the dread of sitting in a foxhole at night, staring into the pitch-black darkness, listening for the telltale sounds of an approaching enemy bent on their death or destruction. Furthermore, the Air Cav troops had been stowed in the holds of various troopships as they sailed across the Pacific. The 2/7 had come over on the United States Ship *Maurice Rose* and had been preparing for action as soon as they came ashore at Qui Nhon. That's what they expected.

Flown from there to An Khe, then assigned their own slice

of the division's territorial pie, they had dug in along the perimeter line, scooping out foxholes from the hard rocky earth, clearing fields of fire along the five hundred yards of the battalion's sector, and tying in their fields of fire with those of our adjacent units. And then, during those long first nights in country, they manned their positions, sitting in their holes, silently waiting for the enemy to strike. Whether he was out there or not, we weren't sure. Suffice it to say that having been conditioned to think there was a Viet Cong behind every tree, the men were reluctant to wait for Victor Charles to sneak up to their foxholes and slit their throats. So, whenever something moved in the tree line, from fifteen to fifty yards out depending on where one's foxhole was, the troops would open fire.

During the week after the division's main body arrived at An Khe, firefights of varied length and intensity broke out every night around the perimeter. And the division suffered casualties—mostly self-inflicted. One story circulated that a man had thrown a grenade at a sound to his front. The grenade caught on an overhanging branch and dropped back into his foxhole, killing him and his buddies. Harry W. O. Kinnard, the 1st Cav's commanding general, was not happy with this, of course, and passed the word down that he didn't want to hear about any more self-inflicted losses.

Colonel White, in his wisdom, conceived of a foolproof plan to prevent further casualties. He immediately issued an order to the effect that no one on the line could load their weapon.

Brilliant.

Unless you've spent a night in the field, waiting for the enemy to attack, you'll never understand the growing and unspeakable terror that grips you with each and every noise to your front. Unless you've waited in a foxhole late at night expecting the enemy to charge, unless you've sat alone, or with a buddy, staring into the pitch-black darkness, your ears attuned to any and all sounds or movements, your imagination working overtime, conjuring up the most horrific scenarios of masses of enemy troops, knives in their teeth, slithering ever closer to your obviously exposed position and bent on your immediate demise, you will never appreciate the utter stupidity of that order. Assigned to the battalion staff, I could only imagine the chagrin of the line officers—the commanders of troops on the line—who had to pass that incomprehensible order on to their men.

Fortunately, because most Americans are smart enough to question orders like that, it didn't take long for three young troopers in Charlie Company to pack up their kits, climb out of their foxholes, walk past their company commander, and proceed to brigade headquarters to protest the insanity of Colonel White's order.

Unfortunately, they were immediately advised to return forthwith to their positions on the line and to obey all subsequent orders, no matter how stupid. The three young troopers balked. They refused to go back on line unless they could load their weapons. The brigade sergeant major then ordered them to return to their unit to await further instructions, and this they did. The following day, they were court-martialed for dereliction of duty, refusing a direct order, disrespect, and desertion. And that's where I come in.

"Court-martial!" I said. "What do you mean, court-martial?"

Having just been advised by Captain Johnson, the battalion adjutant, that I had been designated as the assistant trial counsel for the court-martial of those three hapless troopers, I was fighting off a sudden case of shock.

"Don't worry," the captain said. "Jim Bell is trial counsel. He's already done most of the work. You're just backup."

Jimmy Bell, whom I'd met briefly, was Bravo Company's XO, a short, cherub-faced, quiet guy who stayed in the background and didn't make waves. A good guy, but not a hard charger. Whatever his personality, he was senior to me, and therefore responsible for preparing and presenting the case. And for that I was frankly grateful. First, I'd never acted as a trial counsel in a special court-martial. (Defense counsel and member of the court, yes, but not trial counsel.) Second, having just joined the battalion, I didn't know the men in it.

Third, I would have found it very difficult not to let my own personal feelings interfere with the thoroughness and impartiality of an investigation. I was, in short, appalled by the patent absurdity of Colonel White's order, and certainly sympathetic to the defendants. After all, they'd been perfectly up front about their actions. They hadn't skulked off the line after dark, or skedaddled at the first shot. They'd simply challenged the order in the only way they knew, and rightly so. Or so I thought.

"Who's defense counsel?" I asked.

"Don Cornett." Don was the XO of Charlie Company. That figured. Take care of your people. The defendants were his men.

"And when's the trial?"

"Tomorrow afternoon."

"Tomorrow afternoon!" I said, aghast. Back in the 82d, we'd always had several weeks to prepare for a court-martial. "What's the rush?"

The captain just shrugged his shoulders.

I couldn't believe that the poor bastards were going to be court-martialed for refusing to comply with an absurd order, and that the trial was going to be expedited faster than any trial I had had experience with before, but I didn't know the captain well enough to voice my honest opinion, and that was that. I was appalled, though, and equally shaken, for now I had been suddenly thrust into the uncomfortable position of being one of the two men responsible not only for the proper presentation of the case, but also for seeing to it that the poor guilty bastards received a fair trial.

"What really happened, do you know?" I asked.

"They left their positions," he said simply. "They got up, walked away from their positions—telling Captain Kahalnick to go fuck himself, I might add—and showed up at Colonel Brown's tent."

Captain Kahalnick was Charlie Company's CO.

"And?"

"And the brigade sergeant major ordered them to get their young asses back here."

"Who's on the court?" I asked.

"Major Gill is presiding, and captains McCarn and Baker."

Major Gill was the Battalion S-3, our operations officer, a big, red-haired guy the lieutenants referred to, not always respectfully, as Barney. He'd been a jock at West Point, I'd heard, and at least had a sense of humor. Captain McCarn, whom I'd known from the 82d, was a good, fair man. Captain Baker was the S-2, intelligence officer. I didn't know him at all.

"Anything else I should know?"

"I don't think so," the adjutant said. "Jim's done most of the interviewing, I understand, and Don's apparently ready to go, so I don't think there's much for you to worry about. You'd better check with Jim, though, and take it from there."

"Yes, sir," I said, turning to leave. I think I said it sarcastically. It was a little premature for me to be sarcastic, especially with the adjutant, but I just couldn't help myself.

Now the Army has its own system of justice. They call it military justice, but it works. Its keystones are the officer corps and the assumption that officers are, generally, fair-minded and thorough. The other keystone feature is its framework, its three levels of courts-martial. First and foremost is the summary court, comprised of a single officer, usually the company commander, who metes out justice as he sees it. These are short, quick, efficient affairs, sometimes even informal, and generally limited to minor infractions, like short periods of AWOL (absence without leave), or other slight infractions, and the sentences handed down by the court are limited to relatively minor punishments like fines, loss of pay, a drop in grade, or extra work. Summary courts-martial resolve the great bulk of the army's discipline problems.

Next in line is the special court, consisting of at least three officers who are convened to hear cases of considerably greater significance. Convened by order of the battalion commander, they can try almost any matter, except, I think, treason and capital cases. They require the impaneling of a court, i.e., three or more officers who will act as jury in the case, and the appointment of both a defense and a trial counsel. The latter serves as the prosecuting attorney, but has the added responsibility for seeing to it that all facts and evidence relevant to the case, of whatever import, are brought to the attention of the court. Colonel White had ordered that a special court-martial be convened to hear the matter at issue.

And finally, there is a general court-martial, with all the trappings of a criminal trial, except that the court, comprised of five or more officers (or enlisted men if requested by the defendant), acts as the jury in the case, and a law officer, similar to a judge in criminal trials, makes rulings of law. General courts-martial are convened only by order of division, and generally hear matters of only the greatest importance, including capital crimes. These are the kinds of military trials that you see in the movies (*The Caine Mutiny* and *A Few Good Men* come to mind), and they require a degree of sophistication and a commitment of time and effort unavailable to a line battalion in a combat zone.

I found Jimmy Bell in his tent.

"I've done everything I think we have to do," he said, almost sheepishly. He'd interrogated the three defendants. "They didn't deny anything," he said. He'd interviewed our three witnesses: the defendants' squad leader, their company commander, and the brigade sergeant major. Jim had also advised Don Cornett of all the evidence and testimony we were going to present at the trial.

Jim had done all the work. No doubt about it. I was impressed.

After conferring with him, though, I got my helmet, rifle, and web gear, and took a walk up to the Green Line to spec out the defendants' position. I was hoping it would give me some ideas, or at least shed some light, on the case.

The distance from the battalion base camp, where we all slept, to the top of the hill where the perimeter access road sliced diagonally through the undergrowth separating the base camp from the Green Line, was only a couple hundred yards. Beyond the crest of that hill, though, the ground sloped downward again, leaving our base camp in the enviable position of being protected from direct fire from anywhere outside the perimeter. This incredible blessing wasn't fully appreciated yet, especially since we'd not yet been out in the field, but it's important to realize that heading up to the perimeter was a distinct climb, and negotiating the perimeter access road took one from the relative safety of the rear to the absolute front line of the division's still tenuous position in the Central Highlands of Vietnam.

Out on the Green Line, everything was different. While the troops had spent most of their time cutting and hacking trees and brush and cutting fields of fire so they could see the enemy if he attacked, we had yet to make any appreciable dent in the jungle. While occasional clearings sloped down into the much denser undergrowth to our front, there were also clumps of brush and grass within fifteen meters of our outermost line of foxholes, so the troops' reaction time to an enemy assault would have to be very short if one came.

The afternoon was sweltering, the air hazy and acrid with the smoke from scores of brush fires smoldering in the heat. Along the line, as far as I could see, a ragged row of foxholes and makeshift bunkers punctuated the high ground. About one in ten were manned. All of the other troops were out in the blazing sun, shirtless, cutting and hacking and piling brush onto the brush fires.

I turned right, walked fifty yards or so, and stopped at the Charlie Company command post, where two specialists fourth class were lounging in the shade. I asked them where the defendants' positions were. They pointed down the line, letting me know that the three men had been in Sergeant Camber's squad, and that I'd be able to find someone there who could show me their exact positions. I thanked them, and continued down the line.

It sloped gently, in some places imperceptibly, from right to left. Tree and sapling stumps had been cut off roughly at shin level—after all, you wouldn't want to make it too easy for the enemy to sprint across the open ground—and much of the debris had already been cleared away. It was hot, dirty work, though, and I felt a sense of relief not to have been assigned to any brush-cutting details (not that week, anyway), but the results of the hard work were becoming evident, and it wouldn't be long before there was barbed wire and other, more sophisticated, defensive barriers established along the entire perimeter. At that juncture, however, things were pretty rough.

When I got to the vicinity of where I thought I was supposed to be, I asked the first NCO I saw where I could find the defendants' positions, and he took me right to them. I was immediately struck by the presence of a shallow ravine that snaked from the dense tree line to the front, right past the lip of the defendants' foxhole. The distance from the foxhole to the tree line was less than twenty meters. Their position was just a listening post! I estimated that it would take a charging man less than five seconds to reach the foxhole from the tree line, and that if he came stealthily up the ravine, crawling silently, he would be able to toss or drop a grenade into the poor defendants' foxhole without being seen or heard.

I thanked the sergeant and headed glumly back to the rear. I'd learned nothing from this little exercise except that you wouldn't have caught me dead out there at night without a loaded weapon.

I slept terribly that night.

The trial convened the following afternoon in the operations officer's briefing tent, adjacent to the tactical operations center, at the base of "Headquarters Hill." Remember, I had only known those people for a week or two. Having just joined the battalion, I was a relative stranger. But I did believe in justice, and wanted to make sure that the defendants' rights were preserved, and I had my own impartial views about the colonel's stupid order.

The temperature under the tent's heavy canvas was close to a hundred degrees—certainly hotter for the defendants than for me. They were young men—a specialist fourth class grenadier and two privates first class—and scared. Each of them had been charged with disobeying a direct order, dereliction of duty, disrespect, and leaving their positions on the line in the face of an enemy threat, i.e., desertion. Desertion in a combat zone was punishable by death.

Whatever decision was handed down, the three young men faced the possibility of a firing squad, and they were understandably grim as we filed into the tent.

I was almost immediately put off by the opening remarks of the presiding officer of the court—Major Gill. He said something like, "Okay, let's get this matter out of the way as fast as we can. Lieutenant Bell, you may proceed."

Jimmy Bell jumped through all the required hoops, reading the defendants their rights, presenting them with the charges, then calling the first witness.

As the hot afternoon dragged on, and the witnesses came forward and testified under oath, it became clear that what I'd heard, and what Jimmy Bell had told me, had in fact transpired. The squad leader got up and told his story. The company commander verified that the men had indeed walked past him, and when advised to return to their positions, had told him, in no uncertain terms, to go fuck himself. He testified to this without rancor, perhaps with even a modicum of chagrin, considering the circumstances. Jimmy Bell's final witness was the brigade sergeant major, who repeated what he'd said to the defendants, then informed us gratuitously that they had honored his request to return to their company area, and had done so without fanfare.

Jimmy Bell then rested his case.

All during this line of questioning, Don Cornett had remained quiet. When it came time for him to present his case, he had only one witness: the first sergeant of one of the battalion's other line companies.

Now first sergeants are renowned in the army for being the "Top Kick," the "First Soldier," the senior NCO in the unit, and usually he's the toughest man in the company. The first sergeant holds the company together, sees to it that the Old Man's will is done, and makes sure that things run smoothly day to day. The first sergeants in the 2d of the 7th were an impressive lot, especially to a young lieutenant like me. And this one, First Sergeant Eliot of Bravo Company, was no exception. He was a veteran of WWII and Korea, an experienced combat veteran with several awards for valor under fire, all of which Don Cornett brought out in his simple line of introductory questioning. Then he popped the $64,000 question.

Would the first sergeant, in his professional opinion, blame the three defendants for doing what they had done in light of the order prohibiting them from loading their weapons?

The first sergeant's answer was simple. "No, sir," he said.

With that, Don rested his case.

Jimmy Bell had nothing else to add.

So, with little hesitation, Major Gill adjourned the court. When he did, though, he said something to the effect that we shouldn't wander too far away because he didn't think the court's deliberations were going to take very long.

And he was right.

In less than half an hour, the word came down that the court would reconvene, and we filed back into the tent.

I felt terrible for the defendants. It was clear that they had done what they had been accused of doing and that they faced some very stiff sentences. But it was also clear that they had some justification for what they had done. Whether it would mitigate the severity of their sentences remained to be seen.

With all of the participants back in the tent, Major Gill called the court back into session.

"At the outset," he said, "the court has decided to drop the charges of desertion. We don't believe the circumstances warrant them, and we've dismissed those counts as to each defendant." He looked up and stared at the three glum troopers. They didn't seem to comprehend what he'd said. Then, he continued.

"As for the remainder of the charges, the court, by vote of at least two-thirds of its members concurring, finds the defendants guilty as charged of all counts and specifications."

Oh Jesus, I thought. They were going to get the max.

"The defendants having been adjudged guilty of all counts

and specifications, the court has decided that each defendant be punished as follows . . ."

The major paused dramatically, looked up at the defendants, and continued. "Each of you is hereby fined the sum of fifty dollars."

Was that it? I was stunned.

"Gentlemen," the major continued, "you are dismissed. Return to your unit immediately.

"This court stands adjourned."

And that was it.

I don't recall the three defendants' reactions. I assume they were very relieved and most appreciative of what Don Cornett had done for them. I do remember my own reaction, though. I felt good. Really good. I left the tent knowing that the system had worked, that justice had been served, and that maybe, just maybe, there was hope.

That evening, the colonel's order was rescinded, and as the days melded into weeks, and the men became accustomed to the sights and sounds of the night, fewer and fewer shots were heard around the perimeter, until at long last, you could get a full night's sleep without disturbance.

Chapter 7

The Exploding Man

This, then, was the life I knew, where death sought me, during which I was transformed from a cheeky youth to a troubled man, who, for over thirty years, repressed what he could not bear to remember.

—WILLIAM MANCHESTER,
Goodbye Darkness

We'd been cutting brush on the Green Line for weeks, or what seemed like weeks, and our efforts were beginning to show. Amazing what a battalion of machete-wielding infantrymen can do to a small swath of jungle. We weren't the only ones hacking away at it. Everyone was. But we were on the Green Line, the division's outer perimeter line, and ours was priority work, so everyone turned out every day, the troops sweating under the scrutiny of sergeants, the sergeants grumbling under the supervision of officers, and the officers chafing under the heel of Colonel White, who was, in his own way, trying to impress the Big Six himself, Harry W. O. Kinnard, commanding general of the 1st Air Cav.

The heart of the 1st Cav's base was the Golf Course—a huge helicopter pad—just an open, grass-covered, stump-riddled field. At any one time on it sat hundreds of helicopters—OH-13 scout ships, which looked like bubble-eyed mosquitoes; UH-1D Hueys, which would take us into battle like taxis; CH-47 Chinooks, which could carry a full platoon of combat-ready infantrymen; and the giant CH-54 Sky Cranes, which could fly away with any of the foregoing aircraft dangling underneath its belly. There were gunships, too, aerial rocket artillery ships (ARA), medevacs, and C & C ships (command and control). There was also a long repair line.

Around the Golf Course were arrayed the division's supporting units—the aviation guys, an artillery brigade, some combat engineers, quartermaster, finance, and ordnance types, medical detachments, and, of course, division headquarters. Around those units, manning the Green Line, were the Cav's own reconnaissance battalion (the 1st of the 9th), and the eight infantry battalions, the maneuver battalions, roughly five thousand men in all, busily digging in. We were the grunts, the men who did the fighting, the guys who closed with and killed the enemy, and we were proud of it. But the choppers were our most valuable asset, and we were getting ready to test them against an unknown enemy, so we had to make sure they were safe.

Our orders were deceptively simple: prepare the base camp for a long stay. Sounds easy enough, but you have to understand the situation. First, the 3d Brigade's section of the perimeter faced north, as precarious a position as any, I guess, exposed, as it was, to the most likely avenue of approach for an enemy attack—the densely covered plateau running from the distant mountains of Kontum Province and the Laotian border. Second, the heat was almost unbearable. The temperature hovered in the hundreds, and the humidity greeted us each morning with an almost drenching sweat that clung to us all day. Third, my brand new brethren were itching for a fight. After months in a troopship, I might have been, too, but we had other work to do. Fourth, we were pressed for time.

Accordingly, Old John D., in his quest for recognition and praise, insisted that every man jack, "every swinging dick" as he put it, get out there and work on the line. So every morning after breakfast, the troops would grab their brush hooks, entrenching tools, axes, machetes, and saws, and march out onto the perimeter to cut and hack and pile brush on the fires that smoldered like garbage dumps all around us. And the men who had been on the line, who had spent the night sitting in foxholes, staring into the darkness with all their senses keyed for enemy infiltration, they also got up, ate their C rations, and reported to the officer in charge of the brush-clearing details to cut and hack at the undergrowth, all day, every day, until a visible dent could be seen in the jungle to our front.

Slowly the trees were all cut down and their branches lopped off and tossed onto the brush fires. Later, we would stake down rolls of concertina, set barbed-wire foot snares, and dig intricate defensive positions, but in the early phase of our brush cutting, all we did was clear fields of fire and burn everything.

On that particular day, I was assigned to supervise the right-flank detail. The troops were out on the Green Line, scraping the area clean. Off in the distance, to the right, we could see men from our sister battalion, the 1st of the 7th, men I'd never met, working on their own section of the perimeter. I could see them clearly, a couple of hundred meters away, small clusters of them with their own officers and their own sergeants, doing the same thing we were—with one exception.

I was standing with a radio operator and the first sergeant of our right flank company, two men I would soon know well. It was midmorning. The heat, as usual, was close to a hundred, and the humidity stifling, if not unbearable. I observed the troops to my front, good men all, working as steadily and hard as they could considering the time and place and conditions. I looked over at the nearest group of our neighbors—the 1st of the 7th guys—and wondered, fleetingly, if their morale was as low as ours, if their food was as bad, how their officers were, or their training. I saw a group of men working around a big brush fire, the kind you start up in the morning with a can of kerosene and nurse all day with brush. A gray wisp of smoke rose begrudgingly from it.

I saw, in the distance, a man with a five-gallon can— perhaps it was a number-ten can, open at the top, perhaps not—I saw the man take the can and toss something from it onto the fire, and then the man exploded in a roiling ball of flame.

"Oh, my God," I said, already heading for that blazing pile of brush. As I ran to the site, other men were running there, too. By the time we arrived, someone had already radioed for help. It was on the way, I was told. Certainly, without that help, it would be too late.

The man, a lieutenant, impatient to get the fire burning hotter, had tossed an open can of gasoline on it. God knows how many years he had to suffer the consequences of that momentary lapse in judgment. When I arrived at the scene, he was lying facedown, his arms outstretched, fully conscious of what had happened. His shirt had been burned off his body, and his back was covered with charred bits of cloth. The hair was singed off his scalp, and his lips and face were puffy and blistering. Great blisters of burned skin had already peeled off his back and were hanging from his arms and shoulders.

Two 1st Battalion men knelt helplessly at his side. One was holding his hand. I saw a wedding band on his ring finger.

The burned man's eyes were open. He was conscious, but going into shock. He knew the gravity of his mistake and his condition. He also knew help was on the way. Whether it arrived in time to save him I don't know. What I do remember, though, is that he lifted his head slightly, blinked his eyes, licked his blistered lips, and said, "Oh, shit."

"Hang in there, man," I said, feeling about as useless as you can and wondering how someone who had been burned all over the top half of his body could still be conscious. He nodded. He didn't seem to be in pain. Perhaps he was too close to shock. Both, I knew, would come with a vengeance later.

I looked up and saw a Red Cross jeep coming toward us as fast as it could across the stump-studded field.

"I've got it now, Lieutenant," an older sergeant said to me, kneeling at the burned man's side. I didn't know him, but his eyes told me he cared. I nodded and backed away.

"There's nothing we can do here," I said to my radioman,

and we turned away and walked wordlessly back to our position.

I looked back only once. The jeep was slowly retracing its way back from where it had come, with the burned man, still face down, on a stretcher on the hood. A handful of shirtless GIs walked gravely beside it, holding the stretcher in place.

In recalling that scene, I've often wondered why it remains so clear in my mind. I'd seen wounded men before, a couple anyway, but they'd been ARVN, South Vietnamese troops, and as I'd watched their makeshift stretchers bouncing by, and the swarthy little men in them with their feet blown off or their chests crushed and bleeding, I'd felt as if I were watching a newsreel or a movie. They were just ARVN after all, Vietnamese soldiers who'd been in the wrong place at the wrong time—no one I really knew or cared about—far removed from me.

That was then, down in the Delta. But there, in the Central Highlands, I had just seen an American Air Cavalry lieutenant burn himself up, a lieutenant like me, and it shook me to the core.

Little did I know what a harbinger it was.

Chapter 8

Getting Our Feet Wet

*I knew from my year as a training
officer that the infantry always
got the best of the recruits, and
this was the best of the infantry,
drawn from civilian ranks before
the Tet Offensive, before public
opinion had turned against the war.*
—NATHANIEL TRIPP,
Father, Soldier, Son

We headed out on our first operation on October 1, 1965.
The battalion's mission was to air assault into the lowlands
east of An Khe Pass, seize positions along Route 19—the
road from Qui Nhon to An Khe—and clear the area of Viet
Cong. We would lift off from the Golf Course by company.
Bravo Company would seize An Khe Pass, the high ground
that dominated the lowlands to the east. Alpha Company
would leapfrog over Bravo and assault a landing zone (LZ) at
the base of the pass. Charlie Company would leapfrog over
Alpha and seize key bridges along Route 19. Delta Company
and the battalion HQ would come into Alpha's position after
the LZ was secured. I was to accompany Maj. Henri "Pete"
Mallet, the battalion XO. We'd be flying in with Alpha Company as advance party for the battalion HQ, and stay with
them until the HQ arrived. It was the battalion's first full-
scale air assault since the 2/7th had formed up at Fort Benning, and everyone was pretty excited. Or nervous, I wasn't
sure. The major was okay, a bit standoffish, perhaps, but I was
glad I had something to do.

So, early the morning of October 1, we joined Alpha

Company, left the battalion's base camp, trudged across the interior road, and clambered up the slope to the Golf Course—a long file of anxious, sweating, Air Cav troopers, everyone armed to the teeth and prepared for several weeks in the field.

Foregoing the flak vests worn by our Marine brothers to the north, we traveled as light as we could, wearing clothes that matched the climate (when we could get them) and carrying only the barest of essentials. The lighter our load, the more food, water, and ammunition we could carry for the business at hand. Fully armed and equipped, the average Air Cav trooper carried close to sixty pounds.

Except for weapons, boots were our most important item. Corcoran paratrooper boots were popular, but had to be privately purchased. The standard GI, or government issue, combat boot was good but cut too low. The trouser cuffs never stayed in. The jungle boot, with its nylon top, leather toe, and cleated Corfam sole, was treasured in the early months before they became standard issue, especially because of their steel inserts, protection against punji stakes. The rice paddies, streams, and muck of Vietnam made jungle boots indispensable, however, and by early '66, most of us had them. We used cushion-soled, over-the-calf-length socks, black or olive drab, and always carried an extra pair. They were versatile, too. C rations could be stuffed into a sock and tied to your harness, leaving room in your pack for more ammo.

Most grunts eschewed undershorts because they chafed terribly and crotch rot was rampant, but I wore boxer shorts, probably because they gave me an additional layer of protection from biting insects and leeches. Undershirts were optional, but made it difficult for mosquitos to get through with their own special brand of "Welcome to the war, boys!" T-shirts got heavy when wet, though, and we usually were.

The grunt's only jewelry were his dog tags—hanging from his neck on a key chain, taped together to prevent jingling, and usually with the ubiquitous P-38 can opener. Dog tags were mandatory. They identified you, dead or alive. They also told medics what your blood type was, as well as your serial number, rank, and religion. (My blood type read "A-Pos" and my religion, despite the fact that I was a confirmed Episcopalian, read "none.")

We all wore fatigues, olive drab, cotton-twill trousers and shirts, with cloth name tags and, in safe areas, rank and unit designation. Later, we were issued jungle fatigues, cut from a much lighter rip-stop nylon fabric that dried faster than twill. Finally, most of us kept a soft field cap for quiet times in the heat. They were also the preferred headgear for night work.

As for accouterments, the list is almost endless. Simply stated, each man wore a helmet, carried one or more weapons, and a harness (his web gear).

Our helmets, or steel pots, consisted of a liner, with sweat bands and chin straps to keep them on, an outer steel shell which sometimes deflected shrapnel, and a camouflaged canvas cover, into which we stuck burlap strips or local vegetation to break up the helmet's telltale silhouette.

Individual weapons depended on your position in the squad, your particular skill, and, in rare instances, choice. The rifle—the M-16—was standard issue from the company commander down (hence, the moniker "rifle company"). Except for grenadiers, medics, and machine gunners, everyone carried a rifle. Machine gunners had their hands full lugging the M-60s, and grenadiers, two per squad, carried the stubby but light M-79s, which could launch grenades accurately up to two hundred yards. Some men brandished additional weaponry, like shotguns for the bush, or sniper rifles for static defensive positions. I carried a Colt .45 automatic, in a shoulder holster, just in case. Machine gunners, grenadiers, and the medics all carried .45s, too.

The combat harness was an engineering masterpiece designed by an efficiency expert who'd probably never carried anything heavier than a six-pack of ice-cold beer. It had a tendency to get heavier and heavier as the going got rough. Its basic components were an adjustable web belt, suspenders designed to hang from the shoulders (not the back), and a pack, attached to the belt but held in place, above the buttocks, by the suspenders. To this harness we could attach a number of items. Vital were our two canteens—plastic quart water bottles, one with an aluminum cup—protected by padded canvas covers. Equally vital were our three ammunition pouches, each carrying four twenty-round clips of .223-caliber high-velocity cartridges. (You only put nineteen in the clips, though, to prevent jamming.) We carried extra ammo in our packs. Clipped to our suspenders was a first-aid pouch containing a single field dressing, or bandage. Bayonets and entrenching tools (collapsible shovels) hung from our belts. Despite their weight, those small shovels provided us the means to garner a little priceless peace of mind at night, to wit the oft maligned, but truly sacred foxhole.

Jingling and clinking from all of this, though we taped them for silence, were our pyrotechnics: fragmentation grenades; smoke grenades in various colors (red, green, yellow, and purple); white phosphorous grenades (Willy Peter); claymores; trip flares; hand flares to signal with or to illuminate the night sky. Other items were individual choice: weapon-cleaning equipment, map and compass, flashlight, binoculars, bug juice, foot powder, toothbrush, etc.

Finally, we all carried ponchos. They were our home in the bush, our shelter in the rain, our blanket at night, and a stretcher in case we got hit. They were also, for far too many, a shroud.

This was what we carried on our treks into the bush—the armor of a 1st Cav grunt. It was thin, but got the job done.

As we crested the slope to the Golf Course, I was struck by the sight of that high-grass, stump-riddled field. It seemed to be carpeted with helicopters. Bravo Company, which had preceded us, peeled off to the left to board its Hueys, parked in a long line of twenty-plus ships. Alpha Company, with our little advance party in the middle, veered off to the right and walked down the equally long line of choppers designated for us. Each time we passed a ship, a group (or "stick") of six men would peel off and take position next to it. Our Huey was halfway down the line. As the men of Alpha Company peeled off and took their positions by their designated ships, I thought it was all very organized.

The aviation guys—the pilots, copilots, crew chiefs, and door gunners—arrived shortly thereafter, and as they did, I could hear the low drone of the Bravo Company lift ships warming up, preparing to lift off en masse and take them to An Khe Pass. When our pilot and his crew arrived, they immediately started inspecting the ship, which made me feel better. As soon as they finished, they told us to get on board. Our chopper was a Huey "slick," a troop carrier, unarmed except for two M-60 machine guns manned by the crew chief and the door gunner. Slicks had no troop seats or cargo doors, so we scrambled in and sat on the studded floor, finding what positions we could. The pilot started the engine, and while it was warming up, we waited anxiously for our turn to lift off.

It wasn't long—a couple minutes or so—before the engine reached its proper liftoff torque. The noise inside the ship was deafening, the engine's roar making it almost impossible to communicate with fellow passengers other than by hand-and-arm signals, or shouting into an ear. As we got ready to lift off, the ship seemed to shake, quake, and vibrate from the strain of its pulsing engine. Then off we went, lifting straight up at first, about ten feet, then lowering our nose so we could get some forward lift speed. As we did, I was looking out and around the ship, and the sight of the Golf Course filled with choppers took my breath away. Our long line of Hueys lifted off one behind the other, swung gently east away from the helipad, then formed up into assault formation—a company flight, with four platoons in a V of four ships each, echeloned to the left, and four ships trailing—twenty ships in all, carrying 120 infantrymen. Looking out the door, I could see Hueys all around us, filled with grim-faced men. It was a hell of a thrilling sight. Then I started wondering what we'd run into when we hit the LZ.

We flew east for fifteen minutes at an altitude of a thousand feet, following Route 19 to the An Khe Pass. By the time we'd reached it, Bravo Company was already on the ground, taking up positions in the hills around the pass.

After we passed over them, our formation seemed to dive into the lowlands of the broad coastal plain. We swooped down to treetop level and swung sharply to the right, heading south to our own LZ. I could see it out the door, a large expanse of lush green open ground, surrounded by tree lines and hills. As our ship flared its nose for a landing, the downdraft from the rotor blades flattened the grass underneath us, like hair parting on a scalp. We touched down. I jumped out, hit the ground, sprinted five yards away from the ship, then dropped to one knee in the grass. I could barely see over it. Almost immediately, the ships lifted off together, then roared off and faded into the distance, leaving 120 of us on the ground, kneeling in the tall grass, waiting for something to happen. Luckily, no one was there; in Air Cav parlance, the LZ was cold.

Before the choppers' roar had faded, Alpha Company troops were spreading out and moving toward the edges of the LZ. I could hear the shouts and commands of the men around us as they moved to secure the area. Our advance party followed them, heading south away from the highway and into the tree line and the higher ground on the edge of the cold LZ.

The entire operation, from liftoff to assault, had taken less than thirty minutes. The prospect of covering twenty miles on the ground in that kind of terrain and heat would have been unthinkable in a conventional straight-leg outfit. I was beginning to think that airmobile was the way to go.

Long story short, the battalion's first operation went like clockwork. As impressed as I was, though, I couldn't help but wonder what lay ahead.

Two days later, after we'd moved another five miles or so down Route 19, I was summoned to the battalion commander's tent. The colonel, looking haggard and gaunt, was sitting in a canvas chair. He looked up as I reported.

"Gwin," he said, "I've taken your request for assignment under advisement and have decided to send you to Alpha

Company as its executive officer. Your new company commander is a captain from the 1st of the 7th, Captain Sugdinis. He joined us last night to take command, and he's there now, expecting you."

"Thank you, sir," I said, wondering why a captain from another battalion had come over from the 1/7 to command one of our companies. What had happened to the former CO? I had seen him walking with the colonel the day before, and neither one of them had looked very happy. On the other hand, I didn't care what had happened. I was too elated by my new assignment. I was even beginning to think the colonel wasn't such a bad guy after all.

"I'll grab my gear and head right over there, sir," I said. "Thank you, sir, and Garry Owen!" ("Garry Owen" was the battalion's battle cry, and we'd call it out with gusto every time we'd salute a superior.)

"Good luck," he said, waving me away.

It took me less than fifteen minutes to get my gear and make my way through the scrub brush that separated the two headquarters. Alpha Company was providing security for battalion HQ, and Alpha's command post, or CP, was less than two hundred yards away. It consisted of a small gray tent set up in a bowl-like depression surrounded by high ground, a hundred yards south of the highway. I could see a few GIs lounging around the tent, and three or four others inside. One of them was on the radio. It turned out to be Captain Sugdinis.

He came out of the tent and greeted me with a firm handshake and a warm smile.

"Hi!" he said. "I'm Joel Sugdinis. Welcome aboard."

About five feet ten inches tall, maybe less, he was stocky, almost compact in an athletic way. He had closely cropped light brown hair, a round face, a strong jaw, and gray-blue eyes, like a wolf's. They crinkled when he smiled, which was often. I liked him right off.

He escorted me into the tent and introduced me to the headquarters group: our first sergeant, Frank Miller; our communications sergeant, an E-5 named Rodriguez; and two of our radio operators, Sp4s. Larry Sargent and Denny Wilson. I recognized the first sergeant. Frank Miller was a hulking presence, six feet three inches at least, with a sort of perennial scowl on his face that was only occasionally broken by a gap-toothed smile. He was going bald, too, like a monk, and for some reason he reminded me of Rasputin, or what Rasputin must have looked like at some point in his life—a dark-eyed, glowering presence, lurking in the palace at St. Petersburg, striking fear into the hearts of his minions. It turned out, though, that there wasn't a better first sergeant in the battalion, and we were lucky to have him. I grew, early on, to respect his judgment and to enjoy his company and sense of humor (and later on, to love him like an uncle), but at first blush, he made a very gruff impression.

After handshakes all around, the captain took me outside and explained briefly how the company was deployed, pointing out the platoon positions and areas of responsibility. Then we found a quiet spot in the shade, sat down, and he told me what he expected of me.

First and foremost, I was to be ready at all times to step into his shoes should he be incapacitated, so I had to stay apprised of the company's situation whenever we were out in the field. Secondly, he wanted me to see to it that everyone in the company had everything they needed to get the job done, food, water, ammunition, equipment, medical supplies, etc. And lastly, whenever we got orders to move by chopper, he wanted me to manifest the company, i.e., figure out, based on how many men we had and how many ships were coming in, who would go where, which platoon would take which helicopters. At first, I thought the task would be insurmountable, but later, after a couple of hours of practice, and several weeks of on-the-job training, I could manifest the company in my head, get the word out, and stay flexible for any last-minute changes. What he didn't tell me at the time, and what I learned later, was that the XO would also be responsible for calling in medevacs for our wounded. I got very proficient at doing that, too, unfortunately. Much more so than I wanted.

The captain was an excellent teacher. His clear and patient guidance prepared me in two hours for operations the other lieutenants had been training for, supposedly, for months. He was, in short, one of those men who simply inspire confidence. He'd been with the 1st of the 7th when it had been part of the 11th Air Assault Division. He'd had a prior tour in Vietnam, too, so he knew what he was talking about. He was a Ranger, a West Pointer, and a consummate professional committed to his job. He was also full of zest.

Suffice it to say that by the end of the afternoon, I was one young happy lieutenant. Not only did I like him, but I was also convinced that he cared, really cared, for the men—for their welfare, for their comfort, and their safety. In short, we were blessed.

My first few weeks with the company are a blur. We continued moving down Highway 19, clearing it as best we could. In the process, I got to know the platoon leaders, platoon sergeants, and as many of the men as I could. A second lieutenant named Mantegna had our 1st Platoon. Second lieutenant David "Pat" Payne, clearly the best of the bunch, had the 2d. Second lieutenant William Sisson, fondly referred to as "Willi Z," had the 3d. His platoon sergeant was an E-7 named Charles Eshbach, a genuine piece of work. He was an old soldier, a Korean War veteran, and bleary-eyed most of the time. Rumor had it that he carried vodka and orange juice in his canteens, but there wasn't a better field soldier in the outfit, and he kept things together in the 3d Herd. Second lieutenant Jack Hibbard was our Mortar Platoon leader. I think he'd been the XO before I arrived—I'm not sure—and he wasn't very pleased with my arrival.

Two nights after I'd joined Alpha Company, after a platoon leaders' briefing in our little gray tent (which, by the way, we never used again), Willi Z got lost. Three platoon leaders returned to their CPs and checked in by radio. All but Willi Z. The captain kept calling, but the message from Sisson's CP was the same for over an hour: "Three-six hasn't returned yet."

It was late at night, pitch-dark, and the area wasn't secured. (That is, we didn't know if there were VC around.) I could see the captain getting more and more concerned. We all were. At one point, he turned to me and asked for a cigarette. He didn't smoke, at least I didn't think he smoked, and his request surprised me, but I gave him one of my Winstons. (I had changed my brand to Winston. They had a filter tip. Camels, filterless at the time, would dissolve on your lips in the jungle humidity.) The captain lit up and began to smoke, puffing quickly, barely inhaling. Five minutes later, he asked for another, and as the tension mounted, he asked for yet another. The longer we waited, the antsier he got. He began pacing back and forth inside the tent—one hand holding the radio handset, the other holding his cigarette. Like many of us, he held the cigarette between his thumb and first two fingers, the burning end cupped in his palm. I noticed his ring finger flicking back and forth, back and forth, over the cigarette. Back and forth, back and forth. It was just a nervous habit, really, but it turned out to be a completely reliable barometer of his anxiety level.

Willi Z finally stumbled into his CP, called in, and sheepishly explained that he'd gotten temporarily disoriented while making his way from our HQ to his own CP, less than two hundred meters away. This, for the uninitiated, is an easy thing to do, but lieutenants aren't supposed to get lost, and we were all embarrassed for him. We breathed a sigh of relief and hit the hay (all but the men on watch). The captain never said anything about the incident. Not that I heard of, anyway. It would have been an egregious breach of leadership to chew a young lieutenant out in public, and I think the captain just let it go as a lesson learned the hard way. Again, I was impressed.

The battalion continued the operation for another week, at least, clearing the highway so that the Korean Tiger Division could move in and take responsibility for pacifying the area north of Route 19. We found out later that the operation was really just a shakedown cruise, something to get our SOPs down, our standard operating procedures, something to give us a chance to get to know each other and to work together. In that, I think it succeeded.

But it wasn't just a training exercise. There were occasional helicopter forays and platoon-size patrols, one of which resulted in the company's first casualties. SFC Ben Johnson was killed and another man wounded when a booby trap exploded on a trail. I wasn't there, and didn't know them, but I remember the look on the captain's face when he came back from that bloody hillside trail. He wasn't the same for days.

Chapter 9

"Cover Me, Barney"

*There was nothing heroic here,
we were being pushed by old men
with self-serving ideas, pushed to
the brink of death just to glorify
old men.*

—NATHANIEL TRIPP,
Father, Soldier, Son

Returning from Route 19, we worked on the perimeter for a week, did some Chinook ladder training, and conducted platoon-size patrols on the plain north of the base camp, by then called Camp Radcliff. The patrols stayed out for several days, setting up different positions every night, and moving during the day. This gave the platoon leaders a chance to work with their people, the troops some much-needed on-the-job training, and me some flying time. I accompanied the Hueys on their resupply runs every evening, dropping off marmite cans of hot chow to the troops in the field. Nothing exciting happened, though, until we got orders to prepare for a company-size air assault into the Vinh Thanh Valley, a.k.a. Happy Valley, about six klicks northeast of An Khe, to seize and clear an LZ just south of a village, and to secure it for a 105mm howitzer battery that would fly in right behind us to support additional air assaults farther north. As the word spread, and we prepared for the operation, our adrenaline began to pump. There were bad guys in that valley, and it was going to be the first air assault for Alpha Company under its new CO and XO. We wanted to do it right.

Captain Sugdinis made an aerial reconnaissance of the village we were supposed to seize, and returned to give his operations order the night before we went. We'd be picked up by the choppers on the Green Line, which by then had been mostly cleared of undergrowth and formed a natural and convenient pickup spot for most of our future operations. All we had to do was saddle up, walk to the Green Line, and climb on board the ships when they arrived.

According to our standard operating procedures, Captain Sugdinis always accompanied the troops in the first lift so he would be on the ground if something untoward happened. His two RTOs (one on the battalion net, one on the company net) traveled with him, of course, as did our artillery forward observer (the FO) and his RTO to call in artillery if we needed it. The company medic or commo sergeant filled out the CO's stick. I usually flew in with the last lift, along with my two RTOs and the first sergeant. That way, I could call the captain to let him know that the entire company had closed into the LZ, and he wouldn't have to worry about it.

We used the clock system to consolidate on the LZ, with twelve o'clock being determined by the direction of flight. Whether the company assaulted en masse, or by platoons in separate lifts, the first platoon in would exit its ships and seize the terrain from ten o'clock to two o'clock. The next platoon would exit its ships and move to positions from two to six o'clock. The third platoon in would cover the terrain from six to ten o'clock. The rest of us, the HQ group and the mortar platoon, would set up inside the perimeter. That was the way we tried to do it, and it usually worked. A perimeter could be formed within minutes of our assault, with each platoon having a clearly specified area of responsibility as soon as it landed. As I said, it usually worked that way.

That trip we'd be going in with twenty or so ships in one fell swoop—hitting the LZ in strength—and it was going to be exciting.

That evening, after his aerial recon, Captain Sugdinis called the platoon leaders and platoon sergeants into our tent and issued his op order. It sounded something like this:

"Enemy Situation: There are suspected Viet Cong units in the Vinh Thanh Valley, but the Battalion S-2 has no specific information regarding our objective, and I didn't see any-thing suspicious on my reconnaissance flight this afternoon.

"Friendly Situation: There are no friendly troops in the area. After we land, though, a 105 battery is coming in to fire support missions for insertions farther north. We'll be the first on the ground, though.

"Mission: Our mission is to air assault into Vinh Thanh Valley, seize the village there, search, and clear it, and secure our LZ for the artillery battery that will be coming in right be-hind us. We will provide security for that battery until we re-ceive further orders.

"Tactical Plan: The 3d Platoon will be the lead platoon for this operation, taking positions from ten to two o'clock. First Platoon will take the two to six portion of the LZ. Second Pla-toon will cover the six to ten portion of the perimeter. Mortar Platoon, with one tube, will set up in the vicinity of my HQ.

"Logistics: Each man will carry a basic load and three days' rations. RTOs will carry an extra battery. Mortars will carry twenty rounds.

"Command and Communications: I'll fly in with the 3d Platoon and set up in the middle of the perimeter. The XO will come in with the Mortar Platoon and join me on the ground when he can. Normal communications SOP. When we're in the air, though, don't call me unless you've got something hot to report.

"Are there any questions?"

It's amazing to me that after thirty years, I can still rattle off a five-paragraph field order and not have to think twice about it.

On the morning of November 5, 1965, Alpha Company lifted off from the Green Line and headed east, then north, flying at a thousand feet. The exhilaration of flying in a com-pany formation, seeing ships to my right and left, all filled with troops I knew, is hard to explain, especially since we were heading toward God knows what. At a thousand feet up, though, you don't have to worry about somebody taking a pot shot at you from the ground. You can just sit back and look out the door and admire the view around you. You try not to think about what you'll find on the LZ because you'll know soon enough, and worrying about it won't help any, so you sit there, deadpan, looking out the door, or glancing at your ship-mates, and wait to see what happens. My company RTO con-tinuously monitored all radio traffic and kept me advised of anything important, so all I had to do was sit there, stay cool, and jump when the ship hit the ground. I also had to be ready to take over if the Old Man got hit in the assault. First Sergeant Miller was with us that day, and he was as steady as they come, so for the first ten minutes in the air, we just sat there, looking out the door, and letting our adrenaline flow.

As we veered to the north, I saw mountains to our left and right, and the wide flat valley below us—a broad sandy plain, studded with palm trees and clumps of thick vegetation. I was thankful we weren't assaulting the mountains, as steep and heavily vegetated as they were, with their razor-backed ridge-lines thrusting into the valley. They could have been crawling with bad guys, and we'd never know it until we landed. The mountains were strangely beautiful, though, enshrouded in an almost purple mist, but foreboding, to say the least.

The village of Vinh Thanh was nestled at the foot of one of those heavily vegetated, haze-enshrouded, razor-backed-ridgelined mountains, but securing the LZ south of the vil-lage was our only concern that day. We didn't have to worry about the mountains.

As we flew into the valley, our formation dropped to treetop level. The terrain below us turned to green scrub and palm trees. The roar of the ship's engine, the wind rushing through the cargo bay, and the drone of the formation all around us blocked out the din of the LZ prep—artillery and ARA (rocket "artillery" fired from helicopters) that preceded us into the objective—but we knew it was going on.

We were flying so low by then that the Huey's landing struts were brushing the tops of the palm trees, and that made me nervous as hell. We were going ninety knots an hour, and if we hit one of the trees and crashed, it would be all over but the shouting. But we got used to flying and learned how important it was. Though in range of small-arms fire, we were going so fast that nobody on the ground would be able to get a shot off quick enough to do us any harm. At least that's what we'd been told.

I was scouring the ground as it flashed below us, looking for signs of life, but I couldn't see anything suspicious. Then the LZ hove into view.

We thundered in, twenty ships swooping in simultaneously, and the din was horrific. When we landed, things got confused.

The LZ was a large sandy clearing just south of the village, and as the ships came in for the landing, the downdraft of their rotors caused a sandstorm. As we hit the LZ and jumped out, sand was swirling around us in a violent billowing maelstrom, and with the *wop wop wop* of the rotors, and some of the men shouting, and the general noise and confusion, I had the distinct, albeit momentary, impression that the LZ was hot, that we were receiving small-arms fire from somewhere in the village, and my heart jumped into my throat.

The formation lifted off and swung away to the west, leaving us kneeling in the open sandy plain—easy targets for anyone who wanted to shoot at us—so our little XO team moved quickly to the right toward three o'clock. Through the still swirling dust, a bunker loomed to our front, a bunker with an aperture like an eye socket staring straight at us.

"Grenade that bunker!" I yelled to one of the mortar guys with us, jabbing my finger at it. The rest of us knelt there and covered him with our M-16s, and I watched (with some amusement, now that I think of it) as the poor guy, his eyes wide with fear, began to stumble forward through the sand, fumbling for a grenade as he did so, tearing it away from its harness on the dead run, almost falling while he pulled the pin, then tossing the live grenade into the bunker as he ran by its aperture. We hit the dirt. The grenade exploded with a muffled whump, and when I looked up, a cloud of smoke and dust was drifting out of the aperture. Sergeant Miller fired a few rounds into it, just to make sure, and we picked ourselves up and continued forward, moving past the now-neutralized bunker and taking up positions on the right edge of the perimeter. There we waited while the company spread out and seized the rest of our objective.

Over the company radio I could hear Willi Z reporting to the captain that his lead squad had seen several villagers, some of them armed, running from the village toward the mountains. The village, however, was deserted. Then, suddenly, it got quiet.

I moved forward with the others to Captain Sugdinis's position, and plopped down beside him. He looked at me with a grin on his face and shook my hand.

"That was fun, wasn't it," he said.

"Shades of Audie Murphy," I said. "Was the LZ hot?"

"I don't know," he said. "I don't think so. Sisson said he'd seen some villagers hightailing it out of the village toward the high ground, but nothing else. They're clearing the village now. I'm waiting to hear from the other platoons."

All around us on the far edges of our perimeter, I could see our men spreading out and taking up positions. We formed a huge circle, almost five hundred yards in diameter. After a few minutes, all the platoons called in to report that they were in position, had found nothing, and taken no casualties. We settled in and waited.

Within minutes, the deep steady drone of another formation of ships resounded from the valley behind us. I rolled over and saw a flight of six big, two-engine Chinooks, with 105mm howitzers dangling from beneath their bellies, heading toward our position. On and on they came, thundering into the southern half of our perimeter, and as they did, another violent sandstorm was kicked up to swirl around them, obscuring them in a cloud of whirling dust. I just lay there and watched in fascination as the big ships roared in, hovered for a second, then slowly lowered their precious guns to the sand. Their cargo straps went slack and fell away from the bellies of the ships. Then the Chinooks sort of backed away, like graceful hippos bowing after a waltz, and lowered slowly to the ground. Through the maelstrom of sand and dust, I saw the rear cargo ramps coming down, and out of the ships streamed the gun crews, like tiny ants, and some jeeps pulling pallets of ammunition, and the fire-direction guys, all setting up in the hot swirling sand. Then the big ships slowly lifted off, all together, obscuring the gun crews again in the maelstrom of swirling sand. The Chinooks turned gracefully to the west, then thundered off together like a herd of flying buffalo.

The artillerymen worked like frenzied ants, rushing around their guns and laying them in for registration. It wasn't long before the first gun barked out a round, the report booming behind us, and the shell whooshing overhead like a freight train.

"Five minutes," the captain said after the first round roared overhead. "Not bad."

Those guys knew what they were doing.

The other guns were quickly laid in and fired their own registration rounds, and for the next twenty minutes or so we lay there in the sand with the hot sun beating down on us, feeling suddenly exhausted from all the excitement. But things had gone just fine.

Sometime later, Willi Z called and said they had a problem. They needed someone who could speak Vietnamese. We didn't have an interpreter with us, so the captain told me to go see what they were talking about.

I picked up and headed to the village, my two RTOs with me, and when we got there, I could see a number of small thatch-roof hootches, just a tiny village really, with GIs in position along its southern edge. Though I thought I'd heard some firing from the village when we'd assaulted, it was still and quiet.

Willi Z and Sergeant Eshbach were standing near the doorway of a hootch. They had a woman with them. As I approached, I noticed she was pregnant. Sergeant Eshbach said they were having trouble understanding what she was saying, and they didn't know what to do with her.

She was a pathetic sight, really, that poor pregnant woman, her face etched with fear. She was so scared that she vomited, I recall. She tried to stifle it with her hand, but a trace of grayish drool was oozing down her chin. Maybe it was from her contractions, I thought, something to do with having her baby. She was very pregnant, indeed, so pregnant that she hadn't been able to run away from the village with the others when we'd landed. She'd just gone underground, hidden in a bunker underneath her hootch, and had come out when the troops had searched it. She was the only Viet they had found in the village.

I tried to calm her with what little Vietnamese I could think of, but she just looked at me, her dark eyes wide with fear, and vomited more drool again. Then she started shaking, and I got the impression that she was really in the early throes of childbirth. I felt terribly badly for her, but knew she was harmless and could deliver the baby herself. I told her we wouldn't hurt her. She didn't understand what I was saying, of course, but after I pointed to her hootch and indicated that she should go back there to have her baby, she turned and waddled away uncomfortably, her hand still raised to her mouth.

That chore done, I returned to the CP, and there we waited in the hot burning sun.

We'd dug a hole or two for our CP and set out a bright orange panel to identify it from the air, when we got word that Colonel White was coming into our position. Minutes later, a lone C & C ship approached from the south, flew into our perimeter, and landed right on the panel.

The captain jogged immediately to the ship, ready to report to the battalion commander as soon as he exited, but the Huey just sat there, its engine winding down, its rotors slowing gradually, its doors still shut. When the rotors had lolled to a stop, the door slid open.

Inside, I could see Colonel White, with his earphones still on, and the cargo bay crowded with men and communications equipment. Two grim men with radios on their backs, the colonel's RTOs, jumped down from the ship, shielding their eyes from the sun as they looked around to see where they were. The colonel was fumbling with his earphones, trying to take them off. He finally managed to do so and thrust them impatiently at the pilot. Major Gill, the Battalion S-3, then jumped out. He, too, looked around, said hello to Captain Sugdinis, and moved to the side of the ship. Then the colonel got out, stiffly, painfully.

"Captain Sugdinis, CO of Alpha Company, reporting, sir," the captain said. He didn't salute. We didn't salute in the field. It gave the officers away, made them targets.

Instead of acknowledging Captain Sugdinis's report, the colonel turned back to the ship, reached in to get his helmet, and placed it on his head. Then he did the same thing with his combat harness. As he slipped it over his shoulders, I noticed that it looked almost new. Then he turned around and finally looked at the captain.

"Is this LZ secure?" the colonel asked, loud enough for all of us to hear him.

"Yes, sir," said the captain.

Then, as if he hadn't heard him, or was ignoring him, or didn't believe what he had heard, the colonel turned around and reached back into his C & C ship for his M-16. When he turned back to face us, he was holding it at high port arms.

I was lying in the sand, just watching.

The colonel slowly turned to Major Gill.

"Cover me, Barney," he said. Then, with his rifle at high port arms, he began to "high-step" toward the rear of the chopper, lifting his feet high above the ground and putting them back down, toe first, as if he were trying to step over some imaginary trip wire, or not trigger a mine. As we watched, somewhat aghast, the old colonel tiptoed slowly to the rear of the chopper, holding his rifle at high port arms, and scanning the sand dunes around him for enemy troops.

Without a word, Major Gill scowled at us, then turned to the captain and sort of rolled his eyes, and the two of them fell in behind the colonel and his RTOs, and they all trooped off together.

I was dumbstruck.

"Move it," growled the first sergeant to the captain's RTOs.

They jumped up, swung their radios onto their backs, and jogged off to catch up with the captain. I watched the colonel and his little entourage walk single file slowly toward the village.

Disturbed by what I'd seen, I went back to my position, lay back down in the sand, and waited for something to happen.

Ten minutes later, we heard the dull muffled whump of a grenade exploding somewhere in the vicinity of the village. I froze, wondering what had happened. Then the radio crackled. It was Captain Sugdinis.

"Gilligator Five, this is Gilligator Six. Over," he said, calling me by my call sign.

"This is Gator Five, over," I responded.

"This is Gator Six. Did you hear anything?" he asked.

"Affirmative," I answered.

"Disregard it," he said. "We're just grenade fishing. Out."

The old colonel, whom I now considered senile, was playing the game of war, getting in some hard-core "combat time," experiencing the thrill of throwing a live grenade into the water. The thought of it made me sick. It would have been funny if it weren't so pathetic, and I knew then that if that old man was going to lead us into battle, we were in for a very long tour.

Half an hour later, the colonel's entourage returned as it had come, with the captain and his RTOs just traipsing along behind it. The colonel got back in his ship, the engines started up, it eventually took off, and we breathed a sigh of relief. But none of us who had seen that strange vignette could be anything but horrified at the prospect of that old colonel leading us into combat.

BOOK THREE

Baptism

Chapter 10

Xray

*We few, we happy few, we band of
    brothers.
For he today that sheds his blood
    with me
Shall be my brother . . .*
    —WILLIAM SHAKESPEARE,
        Henry V

Almost immediately after we returned from Happy Valley,
Lt. Col. Robert MacDade came down from the division G-1's
office to replace Lieutenant Colonel White as our battalion
commander, and we all breathed a sigh of relief. Maybe God
had intervened. The change of command ceremony was a
short, perfunctory one, with only the battalion staff, company
commanders, and guidon bearers participating, and a few curious onlookers like me standing by. Under a blazing midday
sun, with most of the troops up on the Green Line clearing
brush, I watched Ole John D. hand the battalion's many-
streamered colors to our new CO, step back, salute, and for
all intents and purposes fade into oblivion. Actually, he replaced MacDade as the division G-1, and we'd hear from him
again, though much later.

Outwardly, Lieutenant Colonel MacDade was a singularly
unimpressive individual. A phlegmatic man with an aquiline
nose, reddish brown hair, and a prominent Adam's apple, his
eyes seemed to bulge like a chicken's. He appeared new, if not
reluctant, to command, but quietly took charge and began to
familiarize himself with the way we did things.

Fortunately, the battalion had spent most of the previous
month in the field, patrolling the scrub-covered plains north

of An Khe and getting our SOPs down in the hot dry sand of Happy Valley. Although we found nothing of significance or concern, we were getting much-needed training in the basics of airmobility. The troops were getting accustomed to boarding and disembarking from Hueys, flying in and out of landing zones, setting up perimeters, and patrolling. That is, we were getting acclimated, getting used to the jungle, getting ready for what lay ahead.

Captain Sugdinis and I were pleased with the company's progress, especially with our headquarters team, which seemed to be getting along well. First Sergeant Miller, as I've said, was first-rate. Sergeant Rodriguez and Sp4. Larry Sargent, the Old Man's RTOs, were solid. My RTOs, Sp4. Denny Wilson and PFC Tom Costello, were both smart, capable, and, if initially shy, certainly good-humored guys, and I felt lucky to have them with me in the field, a sentiment that strengthened as our experiences together intensified. Hank Dunn, a cheerful artillery lieutenant from Georgia, joined us from div arty as the company's forward observer. All in all, Alpha Company's morale seemed to improve day by day.

The new battalion commander quietly observed, circulated, and gave sotto voce orders, but despite our hopes for improvement, not that much seemed to change. Then, quite suddenly, less than a week after he took charge, the housecleaning began. Maj. Henri "Pete" Mallet, the battalion XO, was promoted upstairs to brigade, and a short, barrel-chested spark plug of a guy named Frank Henry took his place. Major Henry was an aviator (and, unbeknownst to me, the former aide to General Kinnard), and he knew exactly what choppers could and couldn't do. He was also a great guy, with a sense of humor and a twinkle in his eye, and I, for one, was delighted that he'd joined us. The S-3, Barney Gill, shipped out for Saigon to be the senior MACV recreation officer. His shoes were more than adequately filled by Capt. Jim Spires, an intense, taciturn, dark-browed West Pointer with a crew cut, graying at the temples. He, too, was a Ranger and had come from MACV. Finally, Capt. John "Skip" Fesmire, a big, handsome, happy-go-lucky guy, arrived from somewhere to take command of Charlie Company.

At our level in Alpha Company, we lost our 2d Platoon leader, David "Pat" Payne, who'd earned the honor of heading up the Recon Platoon, the battalion's long-range patrolling unit. (Jim Lawrence became Delta Company's XO.) Second Lieutenant Gordon A. Grove, a redheaded ex-Marine with a round face and a gap-toothed grin, came over from Delta Company's Antitank Platoon to take Pat's place. Sporting a faded "jarhead" utility cap, a memento of his prior Marine service, Gordy Grove went about his chores with such a dogged determination and such a positive attitude that we couldn't help but like him.

With that transfusion of new blood and talent, the line companies continued their daily brush-cutting routine with a little more élan, if not enthusiasm, and by then a clean swath almost a hundred yards wide had been cut around the brigade's section of the Green Line. All the stumps had been sawed off, hacked down, or blown away. Chinooks had flown in and lifted the largest of them out. All the brush had been burned. Triple rolls of concertina wire were then strung out and staked down in concentric circles around the position, and the foxholes and bunkers were deepened and reinforced with sandbags. Our perimeter-clearing chores were almost done.

Soon after all of these changes in command, word filtered down from headquarters that the division commander, Maj. Gen. Harry W. O. Kinnard, would be visiting the battalion to address its officers on what was happening west of Pleiku. Recent reports of the VC siege of the Special Forces Camp at Plei Me had indicated that there were large enemy units in the area, and rumors had circulated that the 1st Brigade had made contact with soldiers of the People's Army of North Vietnam or PAVN—North Vietnamese regulars. We were looking forward to hearing what the general had to say, and he didn't disappoint us.

We were milling around the battalion's tactical operations center at the base of Headquarters Hill when two jeeps roared up the interior road and halted in a cloud of dust. Someone called us to attention, and we watched General Kinnard dismount from the lead jeep and walk over to us. He was a short, trim man, impeccably dressed in pressed jungle fatigues and spit-shined jungle boots. His closely cropped gray hair was hidden beneath an olive drab baseball cap with two black stars on its crown. He wore dark glasses, too. Aviator style. The general stopped, returned Lieutenant Colonel MacDade's salute, and told us to be at ease.

He took off his glasses and began to speak. "Gentlemen, we've been in country for almost two months now, working on our base, digging in, familiarizing ourselves with the terrain and climate. We've undertaken a few search-and-destroy operations, spreading out and working eastward to the coast, securing our lines of supply, and flushing out local VC. In this respect, we've accomplished our initial objective of setting up for prolonged operations.

"But the real mission of this division is to find the enemy, fix him in position, and destroy him, and I'm here today to let you know that we are beginning to do just that."

He pulled an OD handkerchief from his trouser pocket and began to clean his glasses.

"As you know, the 1st Brigade has been sweeping the area south of Plei Me Special Forces Camp. During their search, they have made contact with large numbers of the enemy— not just scattered groups of VC, but Main-Force units. We are receiving daily reports of increasingly heavy contact and will be committing additional forces—the 3d Brigade included— in the very near future."

He inspected his glasses, stuffed his handkerchief back into his pocket, and glanced over at the tall, sandy-haired colonel standing to his right.

"Colonel Bellamy's staff is preparing operation orders for you right now."

The tall colonel nodded gravely. The men around me began to stir.

"This is just the kind of mission the division was designed for. You'll be glad to hear that the 1st Brigade is finding airmobile tactics ideal for the terrain and the situation before them. They have captured or recovered large caches of enemy equipment—heavy equipment—weapons, ammunition, stockpiles of food and medical supplies. Our mobility has enabled us to maintain contact with the enemy once we've found them, and our patience is beginning to reap considerable rewards.

"I came down here to wish you good hunting and good luck in the next few weeks. I know you'll do your best when the time comes. And you can be assured that we will support you from here as best we can."

He scanned our group intently one more time.

"Thank you, gentlemen," he said.

Colonel MacDade called us to attention and saluted. The general returned his salute, turned around, and strode back to his jeep, his entourage close behind him. They got back in their jeeps and drove off in another cloud of dust.

The colonel's voice broke the silence. "That is all, gentlemen," he said.

"Dismissed."

We dispersed slowly, most of us subdued and introspective. I headed back up the hill towards the company area, wondering what awaited us west of Pleiku.

Three days later, the battalion embarked in a convoy of trucks for Pleiku. When Alpha Company went, we went without two of our platoon leaders: Jack Hibbard, who'd been evacuated with malaria, and Mike Mantegna, who told Captain Sugdinis he was ill. That meant our first platoon and mortar platoon would be commanded in the field by NCOs: SFC James L. Fisher and PSG Harold L. Braden, both experienced platoon sergeants. Bill Sisson and Gordy Grove were fine, though, and both had outstanding platoon sergeants, Charles L. Eshbach and William A. Ferrell, a kind and softspoken Tennessean who most of us referred to as Pappy. Morale was good, but we were understandably anxious.

Our convoy took the only road open to Pleiku—Route 19 through the Mang Yang Pass. I knew it to be the same highway that had been the site of one of the bloodiest battles of the French Indo-Chinese War, memorialized in Bernard Fall's excellent book, *Street Without Joy*, and I was, to put it mildly, apprehensive. In 1953, the Viet Minh had ambushed a French armored column—Group Mobile 100—on that very same stretch of highway. The Communists had completely overwhelmed it. They had swarmed over it like ants. The French tanks had lowered their machine guns, and were shooting the fanatical attackers off each other, but one by one, the Viet Minh neutralized the vehicles with satchel charges and grenades. The French had screwed up royally, I thought. They'd fallen into a trap and let themselves get hammered. Maybe they'd been overconfident.

Well, we weren't. Each of our deuce-and-a-half trucks was heavily sandbagged to protect it from mines. The troops sat back-to-back, facing out, with their weapons at the ready. Every truck I saw looked like a porcupine, bristling with rifles and machine guns. I rode in the back of Captain Sugdinis's jeep, feeling naked as a jaybird as we passed through the narrow, jungle-covered ravines along the route. Three sandbags was all the protection we could muster for our jeep and still have power for the trip. Fortunately, we were traveling with friends.

At regular intervals along the route, recon jeeps with mounted M-60s would roar past us to take positions. Wherever the road allowed it, they would careen to a halt, weapons pointing into the jungle, grim men peering into the dark shadowy vegetation, ready to return fire. OH-13 scout ships buzzed overhead, fearlessly dodging the treetops. Higher up, gunships circled like wasps hovering for an attack. Luckily, they weren't needed. Not that afternoon anyway.

We reached Pleiku in the late afternoon. It took us five hours to cover ninety miles. The outskirts of the city were dirty, uninviting, and apparently deserted, except for small groups of raggedy children who lined the road, cheering us with their arms outstretched and begging for cigarettes, candy, or food. Cries of "You numba one, me numba ten" reminded me of the kids in the Delta. But we were in Pleiku, the capital of a province on the Cambodian border, where the war, for us, had started.

I'd read about it the year before—a VC sapper attack on the U.S. advisers' compound in Pleiku. The VC had snuck onto the airfield and blown the barracks apart with satchel charges, killing a score of Americans and bringing the blood of the conflict into American homes. And we were back where it had started.

Pleiku was the biggest city in II Corps (pronounced "two corps"), and II Corps headquarters—a huge white-columned building—rose from a hill on the western outskirts of the city. Two tall flagpoles, one flying the saffron-and-red striped Vietnamese flag, the other the Stars and Stripes, added an almost antebellum touch to their compound. It was there, at the base of the hill, that we bivouacked for the night.

On November 12, 1965, we flew into the Ia Drang Valley of the Central Highlands and began our search.

Water was going to be our biggest problem, I thought, unless we settled in next to a stream or a river, but my map showed few of those, and none in the immediate area. We had landed in the early afternoon, sent out patrols, and started digging in, but we were already running short of water.

Our LZ, code-named Atlanta, was small and remote, a quiet, strangely beautiful place, covered with plush green, shin-high grass. But trees loomed all around us—forty or fifty feet high—and they'd restricted our landing to only six ships at a time. They were hardwood trees, too, with small leaves like elm or ash or beech. The heat, as usual, was intense.

It was November 14. Alpha and Delta companies were providing security for the battalion headquarters. Bravo and Charlie companies were elsewhere, searching for PAVN. I'd impinged on the generosity of Jim Lawrence, Delta Company's new XO, for a couple of extra jerricans of cool, clear water, and was heading back to Alpha's CP. I could see the HQ people in the woods to my right, digging in for the night, and could hear the thunks of shovels breaking ground and the occasional scrape of steel against rock—all a part of the nightly ritual for infantry digging in the field. Captain Sugdinis was out walking the perimeter, I thought, checking the company's defenses and coordinating the tie-ins with the Delta Company people on each end of the line.

I was crossing the LZ with the two jerricans when I saw Captain Sugdinis striding briskly from the direction of battalion headquarters toward our company CP. When he saw me, he raised his right fist and pumped it up and down, the signal for me to hurry, and pointed to our CP.

When I got there, he was on the radio. He looked at me, his face grim. "The 1st Battalion's made contact," he said. "Bravo Company's already been detached to it. They're going in tonight to reinforce. We're going in tomorrow morning, at dawn."

Jesus Christ, I thought. That was fast. "Where?" was all I could ask.

"Five klicks west of here. Off our maps. New ones are on their way from brigade. As soon as they come in, I want you and the first sergeant to piece them together and distribute them to the platoons. And get all the water you can."

My mind was racing, my adrenaline beginning to pump.

"What kind of contact?" I asked.

"They're taking casualties. That's all I know. We'll monitor their radios tonight. Right now I've got to check the perimeter." He motioned to Sergeant Rodriguez and Larry Sargent, who'd been listening intently. They reached down, slung their radios onto their backs, and followed Captain Sugdinis into the brush.

Going in the next morning at dawn! Jesus! This was it! This was what I'd been wondering about since I'd signed up, and the next morning we were going to hop into our Hueys and fly into a shoot-out. The prospect was terrifying, but we had to carry on. No reason to panic. There was nothing we could do until the chopper came in with the maps.

I looked at the first sergeant. He'd been digging his foxhole, and his olive drab T-shirt was soaked with sweat, but his eyes were calm and steady.

"That didn't take long, did it?" I said.

He shook his head gravely, and went back to his digging.

I thought about the men in our company, all the new guys, the young, untried troops, and the ones I'd gotten to know. I couldn't worry about them, though. They'd be okay. I had to worry about the things I had to do. Manifest the company for the lift, piece together the maps, order a resupply, clean my weapons, dig a hole, rest up. Jesus, slow down, I thought. There was little for me to do just then but dig my hole and wait for the chopper.

As if on cue, the *wop wop wop* of an incoming Huey, still far away, broke into my reverie. Must be the maps, I thought, gearing up for the short walk to battalion. Mike Kalla, our new S-2, would give me the maps, and I'd ask Captain Mc-Carn, the S-4, for more water.

That night, we listened to the radio and tried to piece together, from the few garbled transmissions we could catch, what was going on at LZ Xray, where the 1st Battalion had made contact. Xray was just a little too far away for us to receive clear transmissions on our PRC-25s, but we caught occasional snippets, and they told us that some definitely "heavy shit" was going on. I didn't sleep well, and every time I woke up that night, I saw the captain listening intently to the radio. He'd served with the 1st Battalion. He knew Colonel Moore, its commander. Those were the captain's friends at Xray, and he was concerned.

Justifiably, it turned out.

I woke up at first light with a dry mouth and a headache. We all had them because we were all dehydrated. Talk over breakfast was sparse. The captain had issued his op order for our assault into Xray the night before, and with little more than that on our minds, we ate our C rations, filled in our foxholes, checked our weapons, and got ready for the incoming choppers. Everybody was apprehensive, needless to say, but calm and resigned to their fate.

Battalion informed us shortly after breakfast that there

would be a delay on our assault. The LZ at Xray was too hot. So we sat back down and waited. Some time later, the captain took me aside and asked me to make sure that everyone on each lift boarded the ships when they came, and to be sure to call him when I landed at Xray. I assured him I would.

Around eight o'clock, I think it was, we received word that our choppers were on the way, and shortly thereafter, the company appeared in the tree line around the LZ for pickup.

The first wave of six choppers arrived on cue. Captain Sugdinis's team boarded with Willi Z and the 3d Platoon, and they took off in a thunderous roar. It was going to take those ships about twenty minutes to make the round trip to LZ Xray and back. The second lift would take the 1st Platoon and most of the 2d. The rest of Grove's men would go in the third lift with us and the Mortar Platoon. Three lifts of six ships each, twenty minutes between lifts, and we'd all be in the fray.

It turned out that Captain Sugdinis and the 3d Platoon landed at LZ Xray right after a large PAVN force had smashed into the positions held by the 1st Battalion's Charlie Company. The North Vietnamese had broken through the line but then had mysteriously pulled back. While the Old Man was reporting to the 1st Battalion CO, our 3d Platoon had literally plugged part of the gap in the 1st Battalion's perimeter. The 3d Herd had seen some scary stuff.

Back at LZ Atlanta, we had no clue what was happening at Xray. We just waited near the pickup zone, thinking about what lay ahead. About twenty minutes after the first lift departed, it returned—intact, thank God. It swooped into our little LZ and picked up the second lift. After it departed, I looked at who was left. Sergeant Braden and his Mortar Platoon and a squad from Grove's platoon had gathered near our headquarters. They were looking, expectantly, at me, so I made a short speech—something to the effect that we were going into a hot LZ. "Look to your squad leaders," I remember saying. "Follow them. Watch what they do. Do what they tell you, and you'll be okay." Everyone was listening.

I recall vividly, even today, the powerful rush of pride I had talking to these men. Here they were, about to fly into serious combat for the very first time, and everyone was ready to go. No slackers in this group! I remember how strongly I felt about them, how responsible, how paternal, for lack of a better word, and I'll never forget the looks on their faces as they listened to me, as if they were looking to me for some comfort, some faint glimmer of hope regarding the outcome of our flight into that battle. I then said something like "Carry on, Sergeant Braden, and good luck to you all," and we broke up into our separate six-man sticks, took our positions around the LZ, and waited for the third and final lift.

It, too, returned in good order, thank God, and as the six Hueys thundered into our LZ to pick us up, I saw the separate sticks of Alpha Company infantrymen running toward them and boarding them just as they landed, and I was doing the same thing but thinking what a sight I was seeing—U.S. combat infantrymen, boarding the choppers that would take them into battle, into an LZ they knew was under fire, to help their brothers out, nobody hesitating, nobody flinching, everyone scared yet running hard to make the pickup as smooth as they could. It was quite a sight.

I scrambled aboard my ship, flashed a thumbs-up to the crew chief when we were all in, and turned to survey the LZ as we took off. The six ships lifted off together, and the grassy field was empty after they did. Everyone was up.

Our Huey seemed to rise straight up, like an elevator in a forest, and I remember the tall trees with the vines entwined around them. When we lifted above the treetops, I turned to see where we were going. A column of gray smoke rose from a spot on the distant horizon—LZ Xray—less than five miles away.

"How's the LZ?" I asked the crew chief, yelling the question.

He hesitated for a second, spoke into the intercom, then yelled back, "Light sniper fire."

I passed this on to the men in my stick: First Sergeant Miller, Denny Wilson, Tom Costello, and two guys from the mortar platoon. The expressions on their faces didn't change.

We covered the five miles in short order, flying at five hundred feet. Columns of smoke lay dead ahead of us, rising from the side of the Chu Pong Massif, a mountain that dominated the LZ. The closer we got, the more smoke we saw. Clouds of it were billowing from the base of the mountain, and much of its northern slope was obscured by it. Suddenly we dove down to treetop level and swooped into a large open field, a savannah of dry grass the color of wheat, dotted with clumps of small trees. I was looking for GIs, but couldn't see any. At the far end of the LZ, about a hundred meters ahead of us at twelve o'clock, I noticed a large black burn scar in the grass. I learned later that it had been left by an errant napalm canister that had come very close to incinerating the entire 1st Battalion command post.

Then we hit the LZ.

I jumped from the chopper's left door, heading toward the mountain, took a couple of steps into the waist-high grass, and dropped to one knee. There was a lot of noise around us—not just the roaring of the engines, but the sounds of artillery and mortar fire, the crunch of falling bombs, and something else, but I couldn't tell what it was.

Just as our chopper was starting to lift off, a specialist fourth class named Don Allred from the mortar platoon, seemed to pop up out of the grass right in front of me.

"I'm hit, sir," he yelled, pointing to his shoulder. I'll never forget the look on his face—a mixture of pain, fear, astonishment, and hope.

There was a four-inch gash in his triceps, and muscle tissue bulged from it like raw chicken meat, but the wound was clean and surprisingly free of blood.

"Stay down! You'll be okay," I yelled at him. "Patch him up, Top," I yelled at the first sergeant. Jesus! I thought. That was fast.

The choppers were lifting off, and we hunkered down in the tall grass, unable to hear anything over the roar of their straining engines, unable to see anything in the tall waving grass except the men in our team. As the ships lifted away, though, we started to hear the *pop! pop! pop!* of rounds crackling overhead and sporadic bursts of small-arms fire all around us.

The LZ was hot, and it was grazing fire!

"Stay low!" I yelled, reaching for my radio's handset.

Artillery and air strikes were pounding the high ground at nine o'clock. The mountain was getting blasted, but that was fine with me because it loomed over us, a malevolent mass of heavy vegetation, dominating the LZ. Pound it, baby. Pound it good, I thought.

While the first sergeant was bandaging Allred's wound, and the rest of the team was lying low in the grass, I called Captain Sugdinis.

"Gilligator Six, this is Gilligator Five. Over."

"This is Gilligator Six," he answered. "Over."

"This is Gilligator Five. We're all in. Over."

"This is Gilligator Six. Roger that," he said. "Three-six's group has already been detached from my control. They're at nine o'clock right now. The rest of us are at twelve o'clock, in reserve. Work your way up here, but keep your head down and take your time. Over."

"This is Gilligator Five. Wilco. Out."

And that's how we talked on the radio, no matter how bad things got.

I glanced at the first sergeant. He'd finished bandaging Allred.

"Stay with us," I yelled to Allred. "We're moving to twelve o'clock. When we get there, you'll be able to get a ship out of here. Do you understand?"

Allred nodded.

"Okay," I yelled to the team. "We're moving to twelve o'clock. That's where the captain is. Short sprints is how we'll do it. Stay with me and stay low!"

With that, we began working our way forward, sprinting in short bursts of ten or so yards, dodging left and right through the high grass. We passed a small group of GIs clustered in a circle around a scraggly little tree. First Battalion guys, I figured. They were filthy and exhausted, but otherwise okay.

"Keep your asses down," one of them said to us as we passed by, "or you'll be sorry."

Sorry my ass, I thought. You're the sorry bastards who got so fucked up we had to come and bail your asses out of trouble. I didn't say that, of course, but that's what I was thinking. Except for that cluster of 1st Battalion grunts, we didn't see anyone until we reached the Old Man's location.

About halfway there, the captain came back on the radio making a net call (a call to everyone on our company's frequency) and announced to us with unabashed pride that Four-six had drawn first blood.

"Look to the trees," he added. "That's where Four-six got his man. Look to the trees for snipers." With that, he signed off, again.

We picked up and continued zigzagging to his position.

About a hundred yards later, we broke into a clearing—not a clearing really, but the tall grass had all been beaten down around it—and on the other side of the clearing I could see the 1st Battalion's command post, a big anthill covered with brush. There were several trees around it, and some Americans behind it, talking into their radios.

The clearing was littered with the carnage of combat. Broken weapons, abandoned equipment, and ripped-open ammo crates were strewn in the grass. Cartons of C rations and boxes of ammo and grenades were stacked in piles near the anthill. Then, to the right, I saw a dozen or so poncho-covered bodies—dead Americans laid out in a row—their boots askew under their rubber poncho shrouds. It was a sad, unnerving sight. Then I saw Captain Sugdinis about twenty yards to the right of the 1st Battalion's CP. He was lying in the grass, resting on his elbow. My eyes went back to that row of dead Americans, and I realized, at last, what had been going on at Xray.

I sprinted across the clearing, past the shattered and broken weapons, past the piles of discarded equipment, past the empty ammo crates, past that row of American dead, and plopped down next to the captain.

"Glad you made it," he said, and we shook hands.

* * *

He briefed me on what was going on. We were basically
pinned down in a perimeter at the base of a jungle-covered
mountain that was crawling with PAVN. They'd been
pressing the LZ since early morning, and some, it was feared,
had infiltrated into the perimeter. Just then, though, we were
in a standoff. The mountain was being pounded by air and artillery, and though incoming fire occasionally crackled overhead, it seemed to be diminishing. I learned then that one of
the 1st Battalion's rifle platoons was still outside the perimeter, cut off and surrounded, and that Colonel Moore was
trying desperately to orchestrate the men's rescue. They had
been cut off since the beginning of the fight, and were still apparently fighting just west of the LZ, near the base of the Chu
Pong. Our mission was to remain in place as the 1st Battalion's reaction force, and to be available to plug any holes if
the PAVN broke through. For about an hour or so, it seemed
like they might just do that. But until we were called, there
was nothing for us to do but lie back in the grass and wait.
And that's what I did. Lie back, wait, and watch what was
going on around us.

I remember the first sergeant digging a hole, doing it from
a prone position, and thought that was smart. But except for
that, all I can remember is watching in fascination as air
strike after air strike was called in to blast the mountain with
high explosives and napalm, and watching with unbridled admiration as Colonel Moore, the 1st Battalion's CO, did his
thing.

He was standing behind that big anthill, calmly talking on
the radio, his helmet off and his hair sandy red. He had an old
army twill fatigue shirt on, with a red 7th Division hourglass
patch on its right shoulder, his unit in Korea. Around him
worked his staff, captains mostly, none of whom I knew, but
most of them were on the radio, calling in artillery and air
strikes on the mountain. There didn't seem to be any panic or
desperation in the way they were conducting themelves, but
all of them were in deadly earnest and doing what they could
to control the action. Fierce firefights broke out sporadically

around our perimeter and rounds occasionally popped overhead, causing everyone to duck, but otherwise, there was no
cause for alarm.

At one point that morning, I crawled over to Hank Dunn,
our FO. He and his RTO were sitting near the colonel's anthill
with their backs to a tree. A burst of incoming fire caused us
to dive into an empty foxhole. Hank then handed me his
camera and told me to get a picture of him and his RTO. I took
a picture of him, he took a picture of me, and then another
burst of incoming fire caused us to scramble back into the
hole. We were giggling as we did it, giggling at the absolute
absurdity of taking pictures of each other while a battle was
raging around us. I'm still appalled that we did that, now that
I think of it, but men do some strange things in combat.

Later that morning, the 2d of the 5th—a full battalion of
American troops—came overland into our perimeter from
the east. I remember watching as the commander of the
column, filthy, sweaty, and exhausted from the trek, walked
over to Colonel Moore and shook his hand. (It was Lt. Col.
Bob Tully, CO of the 2/5, and a friend of Colonel Moore's.)
While they conferred, the men in the column simply dropped
to the ground in place. They were filthy and exhausted, too,
but there were lots of them, and I knew then that we'd be okay.
Then the leader returned to his men. They picked themselves
up and moved off past the CP, heading toward the western
edge of the perimeter to relieve the cutoff platoon.

With the arrival of that fresh American battalion of five-
hundred men, my tension dissipated, and as the afternoon
came and went, I actually began to feel comfortable with the
situation.

Late in the afternoon, the survivors of the cutoff Lost Platoon came stumbling into our perimeter. They were filthy beyond description, all with the thousand-yard stare, absolutely
exhausted, yet strangely proud. I watched in awe as they
stumbled in, carrying their dead and wounded with them.
When they arrived at the battalion CP, they were literally
staggering, but they refused help from strangers, and
wouldn't allow anyone else to touch, or carry, their dead.

Their leader broke away from the platoon and reported to Colonel Moore. The colonel spoke with him for a minute or two, and the leader came back and issued some orders to the platoon. They picked themselves up again and stumbled to a spot within fifty yards of where we were lying. Then, when they knew they were safe, they relaxed. They either collapsed in the grass or stumbled around shaking each other's hands. It was a sight I'll never forget, those proud exhausted filthy men, so happy to be alive, so tired, yet ready to do more, if necessary.

While I was watching the lost platoon returning from its twenty-four hour ordeal, Captain Sugdinis was receiving orders to move Alpha Company to the northwestern sector of the perimeter. When he came up and told me that we were moving to positions on the perimeter, I got a sick feeling of panic at the prospect of moving out, moving toward the enemy, and I was scared. But that's what we had to do, so we picked ourselves up from the tall grass and moved to our new location.

We didn't have to move very far. Our new CP was situated near a large anthill about a hundred meters north of the battalion CP, and that's where we started digging our foxholes, orienting them to the southwest, while the Old Man placed the platoons into their new positions on the perimeter.

I remember how hard the ground was. It was so studded with small pebbles and held together by the roots of the tall grass that it was almost impossible to dig in. We dug and scraped and dug and scraped, but it still took us several hours just to dig two small foxholes. The RTOs set up in one. The captain and I shared the other, our radios within reach. As we prepared our positions for the night, Gordy Grove and Pappy Ferrell dropped by to pick up C rations and extra ammunition. They were in good spirits, and we chatted for a while. We were all relieved, I think, that the day had gone as well as it had. Though we'd lost tactical control of our 3d Platoon, we knew that they'd been attached to Bravo Company, whose CO, Capt. Myron Diduryk, was outstanding. Bravo Company had suffered casualties in the fight, but we didn't know how many. No one in our 3d Platoon had been killed, though, and only one man, Sergeant Merida, had been wounded. Otherwise, the only casualties we'd suffered were Specialist Fourth Class Allred and another man from the Mortar Platoon, whose name eludes me. Both had been evacuated. And finally, except for all the digging going on, it was quiet around the perimeter.

On the bad side, we knew that the 1st Battalion had suffered heavy casualties. They'd been in one hell of a fight—that was clear—but apparently it was over, and the equivalent of almost two more battalions had come in to reinforce them—Bravo and Alpha Companies from the 2/7, and the entire 2d of the 5th. The rest of the 2/7 was due in the next day.

As dusk settled over us, it got very quiet. Eerily quiet. Captain Sugdinis put out the word to stay at one hundred percent alert that night. All night. We expected an attack, and his order made sense, but we would suffer for it later.

The captain and I shared a foxhole. We crouched in it all night. I dozed off at some point, and he let me sleep. He told me years later that his legs started to shake and he couldn't stop them from shaking. I don't remember that at all, just the fact that he'd let me sleep, and how much I appreciated it.

We waited and waited for the enemy to attack. Staring into the darkness, I could see the tall grass in front of our foxhole, and beyond that the outline of the trees a hundred meters farther on, and beyond that the great dark looming hulk of the Chu Pong Massif. The sounds of the night fueled our anxiety—the croaking of tree frogs, the clicking of gecko lizards, like sticks of bamboo banging together, the drone of myriad insects, and the occasional screech of a monkey. They were eerie enough to keep anyone wide awake, but I dozed off, again.

I was awake, though, at 0400 when the southern edge of our perimeter suddenly seemed to erupt in a massive firefight. The whole southern half of the perimeter opened up, and though most of the firing was outgoing, rounds from attacking PAVN were popping overhead and whizzing past us. It felt like a blanket of lead, and it pressed us into our foxhole.

Then the artillery started whooshing in overhead from behind us, crashing into preregistered defensive fires at the base of the mountain.

The captain grabbed our radio and pulled it into the hole with us, and we were able to listen to it and hear Colonel Moore conducting the fight, getting reports from Captain Diduryk and the other company commanders on that side of the perimeter, and encouraging them to keep the fire coming, to keep pressure on the attacking force, to keep the artillery coming in.

The first PAVN attack began at 0400 and petered out about half an hour later. About an hour after that, they came back and hit us again, this time with a Main-Force battalion. The same thing happened. We clobbered them, pouring artillery on their heads, and breaking up their attack as soon as it reached our perimeter.

As dawn broke, the enemy attacks faltered. We'd fought them off—easily, it seemed—especially from where we were on the other side of the perimeter. But we'd been there, ready to do our part if the enemy attacked our positions, and we'd heard the incoming fire popping overhead, and the wall of steel that had come from our artillery, and we'd heard the fight being orchestrated by Colonel Moore on the radio, so we felt part of it. And we had been.

That morning, at 0600, we tried a new tactic, firing a clip or two into suspicious areas around our perimeter—places where a sniper might be hiding, or clumps of bushes where an enemy squad might be hiding. At a predesignated time, everyone on the perimeter would start firing, and we would rake the fields of fire to our front. We called it a "mad minute," and it was something we started to do on a regular basis, especially if we'd made contact, or were still in contact with PAVN. So that morning we fired our first mad minute, and I've read reports that a large group of enemy was so surprised by it that they jumped up and ran away. I don't remember that happening, though, or even hearing that it happened.

Later that morning, long after the mad minute, Colonel Moore's men and the men of Bravo Company and our 3d Platoon conducted sweeps a couple of hundred yards out from the perimeter and back. The sweeps were designed to police up the battlefield, to find missing 1st Battalion troopers who'd been killed or wounded in the previous day's fight, or the fight of the fourteenth, which had been horrendous, and to collect enemy wounded and their weapons. Though we on the southwestern edge of the perimeter didn't participate in those sweeps, we could hear the sporadic rattle of fire as they took place, and at one point, I think, the colonel ordered everyone to return to their foxholes so artillery could sweep the area clean again.

During the sixteenth of November, then, the men of the 1st Battalion continued to police the battlefield and care for their dead and wounded. At some time during the day, the rest of the 2d Battalion arrived, whether by chopper or by foot, I can't recall. Charlie Company, Delta Company, and Headquarters Company all closed in, relieving, in effect, the men of the 1st Battalion. Later that afternoon, the entire 1st Battalion, along with Bravo Company of our battalion and the 3d Platoon of Alpha Company, were picked up and flown out of Xray back to Camp Holloway at Pleiku for a much-deserved break, leaving the 2d of the 5th and the rest of the 2d of the 7th manning the perimeter.

Again, we spent the night on full alert.

Chapter 11

Albany

*Prolonged combat can wreck the
personality.*
—JONATHAN SHAY,
*Achilles in Vietnam: Combat
Trauma and the Undoing
of Character*

Nothing happened that night—no probes that I can remember, no attacking hordes of PAVN, no Main-Force battalions charging out of the darkness, no incoming fire of any
kind. Except for sporadic requests for illumination and the
mad minute we fired at 0600, it was eerily quiet all night.

On the morning of November 17, we dragged ourselves
out of our foxholes, dusted ourselves off, and stumbled
around sleepily doing the things we usually did in the field,
like brew coffee or make cocoa or eat sliced peaches or heat a
can of scrambled eggs or toast some bread or wolf down
some ham and lima beans.

The captain was called to battalion for a briefing, and the
rest of us just lollygagged around our CP, resting as best we
could and swapping stories of what we'd heard about the fight
we'd just been in. One of the best involved a sergeant in the
lost platoon. Ernie Savage was his name. The platoon had
been cut off and surrounded and had been fighting off PAVN
attacks all that first afternoon (of the fourteenth). Their platoon leader had been killed, then their platoon sergeant, then
their ranking squad leader. By the time Ernie Savage, an
E-5, took charge, they had lost more than half of their people,
and all but two of those remaining had been wounded. At
one point, Sergeant Savage's section of the perimeter was

125

overrun. While he was lying there, two PAVN soldiers walked right up to him. He aimed his M-16 at them and pulled the trigger, but nothing happened. He'd run out of bullets. He just waved at the two PAVN and gave them a great big smile, and while they were trying to figure out what he was smiling about and why he was waving at them, he ejected his empty clip, slammed a full one in, and blew the two PAVN away. (Twenty-eight years later, I asked him if that story was true, and he said it was.)

Stories like that circulated around our perimeter and kept our spirits up, but we were clearly exhausted after forty-eight straight hours, more or less, without sleep, and everyone was wondering what was going to happen next.

We lost Larry Sargent—one of the Old Man's RTOs—that morning. He'd come down with a 104-degree temperature that night and was sick as a dog. Malaria, I think. As soon as we discovered how sick he was, the first sergeant escorted him to the battalion aid station, and he was medevac'd back to An Khe. So Sergeant Rodriguez carried the Old Man's radio, along with another man whose name eludes me. Tom Costello and Denny Wilson stayed with me.

Captain Sugdinis returned from his briefing and immediately called the platoon leaders to our CP. I asked him what was going on, and he told me. We'd been designated as the point company for a battalion march out of there. We'd be leaving in an hour. He also told me that Pat Payne's Recon Platoon would be attached to us for the march, to replace our 3d Platoon, which had flown out with the 1/7th the evening before.

When Pat Payne, Gordy Grove, Pappy Ferrell, Sergeant Fisher, and Sergeant Braden arrived at our CP, Captain Sugdinis issued his op order. It sounded something like this:

"Okay, gentlemen. We're leaving LZ Xray. A B-52 strike is scheduled at noon to obliterate this place, and we don't want to be here when it happens. So we're moving in a battalion column to an LZ designated as Albany."

At this point, he showed us his map. Albany was marked with a little blue grease-penciled circle three klicks north of

Xray, and appeared as nothing more than a white dot on the green map, possibly a clearing surrounded by jungle, with no easily definable terrain features for us to guide on to find it (except the Ia Drang which snaked through the valley a couple of hundred meters beyond it).

"So, here's my order," the captain said.

"The enemy situation is presently unclear, but there are definitely PAVN units in the area, so everyone has to stay alert. The terrain, as you know, is high grass, anthills, and heavy vegetation. The 2d of the 7th is moving by foot from LZ Xray to LZ Albany. Their order of march is Alpha Company, with the Recon Platoon attached, followed by Charlie Company, Delta Company, and Headquarters Company, with Alpha Company, 1st of the 5th, bringing up the rear. With the Recon Platoon attached to us, we'll have three rifle platoons, which is good.

"Our mission is to move to LZ Albany and to prepare the landing zone for probable pickup and evacuation back to Pleiku.

"We'll move out on command in a company-wedge formation, with the Recon Platoon on point, 1st Platoon on the right, 2d Platoon on the left, and Mortar Platoon in the rear. Company HQ will be in the middle.

"Every man will leave Xray with two full canteens of water and a clean, test-fired weapon. I also want everyone to take two APC tablets prior to departure. That'll help us all to stay alert.

"Any questions?"

I don't remember there being any.

First Sergeant Miller dispatched our company medic to the battalion aid station to pick up the APCs (aspirin mixed with caffeine). As he left our CP, I noticed that his Colt .45 was filthy with rust, the dirtiest weapon I'd ever seen, and under the circumstances it surprised me. But he was a medic, not a grunt, so I didn't say anything. I remember it, though, and I remember cleaning my own .45 (which I carried in a shoulder holster under my left arm) and my M-16, then test-firing my M-16 into our foxhole just before we departed on our march.

About ten o'clock that morning, Alpha Company, spear-heading the battalion column, left the perimeter and headed north-northeast, guiding just to the left of a small hill on the distant horizon as we went. Leaving the perimeter, I was sur-prised at how pristine it looked, how unspoiled the ground. I was hoping to see lots of dead PAVN soldiers strewn around the place. Artillery had been falling all around us, and the stench of death had grown increasingly horrible as time pro-gressed. It had, in fact, permeated the air since we'd landed in that hellish place, but I hadn't seen a single enemy corpse at LZ Xray, and when I didn't see any on the northern edge of the perimeter, I was disappointed.

As we moved out of Xray, we found ourselves in surpris-ingly clear terrain, a sort of scrub forest with small trees, ankle-high ground cover, and very little undergrowth. Visi-bility was good. We were trudging up a gentle, almost imper-ceptible slope, and our route would take us up a ridge that crested roughly two klicks east of Albany. At that point, we'd turn to the west and come down the ridgeline, again an almost imperceptible slope, but the only way we could really be sure of our location.

Navigation was going to be tricky, but our primary prob-lem was the heat.

God it was hot! The men had been awake for more than forty-eight hours, and we were all carrying as much ammo as we could. For the first hour or so, then, as we trekked slowly up that hill through that scrub forest in the Ia Drang Valley, our biggest concern was the heat. Except for the radiomen, who carried the PRC-25s, the mortar guys carried the heavi-est loads. The tube, itself, weighed twenty pounds, and the base plate even more. The ammo bearers carried four rounds each on their packboards. Each round weighed eight pounds, which meant they were carrying thirty-two pounds of dead weight on their backs in addition to their basic load. About two hours out of Xray, one of them collapsed with heat ex-haustion, and Sergeant Braden reported it.

The column halted. The captain called Gordy Grove and told him to send a man from his platoon to help Four-six out.

Gordy picked a Specialist fourth class named Fred D. Elliot to fill the bill, and it turned out to be the luckiest moment in that young soldier's life. A few minutes later, we picked up and moved out again.

We continued up the slope in good order, the troops maintaining their dispersion and the platoons maintaining formation. Then, reaching the top of that gentle ridge, we turned left and headed west-southwest, down the ridgeline, toward LZ Albany. The terrain changed then, as it did even more dramatically later on, but it was still fairly open and visibility was good. I remember passing a huge depression on our right, sort of a saddle filled with knocked-down trees. They'd been felled, or had toppled over, and were crisscrossed all over each other. Luckily, we could circle around them. And later on, we came upon a ragged row of small Montagnard huts. They were old and long-since abandoned, but they rested in a line along the ridge. We stopped there and waited in the shade while Gordy Grove's men checked them out. I remember seeing Pappy Ferrell coming out of one of the huts with a Montagnard crossbow in his hand and a small monkey on his shoulder. He waved the crossbow at me, with a big smile on his face, and I joked with him about collecting souvenirs.

It might have been about this time that we heard the awesome thunder of the B-52 strikes around Xray. I vaguely remember hearing them at some point, and feeling the ground shake, and being very thankful I wasn't a PAVN soldier at Xray.

Battalion ordered us to burn the huts, and I guess we did, but I don't remember that. I do remember that we continued slowly and quietly westward for another hour or so, until we came to a small stream. It was only a trickle, really, but big enough to fill our canteens in, which we did. I also checked my map. There was a stream marked on it, and if this was that stream, we were less than five hundred meters from Albany.

As soon as we crossed the stream, the terrain changed dramatically, and the jungle seemed to engulf us. Tall, triple-canopied trees, festooned with hanging vines and mosses, towered overhead, shutting out the sun. The undergrowth changed from the tall, dry grass and scrub brush of the valley, to the in-your-face, heavy, broad-leafed vegetation of a tropical rain forest. It enshrouded us like the night, and all was obscured in a dim, eerie light. The men in front of me virtually disappeared as if they'd been swallowed by the earth.

Our progress slowed to a crawl. Captain Sugdinis put out the word to tighten up the formation, and we did. Still, we were well dispersed, covering a hundred-yard front, and moving noiselessly westward. As exhausted as I was after three sleepless nights, the prospect of Pleiku kept me going.

The battalion halted again for a short break so that the units behind us could fill their canteens. I couldn't understand why the troops who hadn't seen action, like we had, needed so much time to get their act together, and I was pissed.

When we started up again, I suddenly noticed the quiet. The endless comings and goings of our usual aerial escort had ended some time ago—how long I wasn't sure—and the quiet was unnerving. I couldn't help but wonder where all our choppers had gone, but it was only a fleeting thought, because everything was getting confused and jumbled in my mind. As we trudged slowly westward, I had to concentrate on keeping Costello in sight. He was in front of me, at the time, and my link with command. His packboard-slung radio seemed to fade away then grow again. I was having trouble staying awake. God knows how he was feeling.

Suddenly he stopped and raised his hand, but I bumped into him anyway.

"What is it?" I whispered.

"Recon's captured two prisoners," he said. "They almost walked right over them."

Two prisoners! Two prisoners? How could that be?

Word came over the radio to take another break, so I went forward to see the prisoners for myself.

Less than fifty yards ahead of where we'd been standing, but hidden by the undergrowth, I came across the two prisoners—two scared little men squatting, wide-eyed, on the ground. Sergeant Rodriguez had his rifle leveled at their faces. They were well equipped, these little Viets—khaki uniforms, canvas harnesses, ammo pouches, potato-masher grenades, canvas sneakers, the full load—North Viet regulars, no doubt about it. The captain was examining one of their rifles, an SKS Chicom carbine, with a brownish-orange stock and a bayonet that folded back under its barrel. The weapon was in mint condition. The little buggers were PAVN, no question about it, hard core all the way. I was getting nervous.

The captain handed the SKS to his other RTO. "Give them some water and treat them well," he said. "The colonel's on his way up here to interrogate them."

I studied the two little men—so this is what they look like up close—clean shaven, swarthy, high cheekbones, hair closely cropped on the sides, longer on the top, sort of Dagwood cuts, thin but not emaciated, and scared. More nervous than scared. One was shaking. With malaria, probably. Or was it fear? They gladly drank the water that was offered them.

"What are they doing out here?" I asked the captain. We were three miles north of Xray.

"They're deserters, I think," he said. "There were others, too, but they lit out when they heard us coming." He nodded in the direction we were headed.

Colonel MacDade and his RTOs arrived, with Mike Kalla, the S-2 (intelligence), Captain Spires, the S-3 (operations), and an interpreter, and gathered around the prisoners. Colonel MacDade seemed in a rush, but he always seemed in a rush. I didn't like the way they were all clustering around the prisoners, especially so close to the head of our column, so I backed away from the group, into the underbrush, to check our formation. From what I could see, and the positions of our people, we were still in pretty good shape, formation-wise, but I didn't like stopping here.

And why had these PAVN just quit? Why had they just stayed there and surrendered? It didn't make sense. Not after what we'd been through. Two days of contact, and not a single PAVN had surrendered.

Just then I saw Don Cornett, Charlie Company's XO,

coming forward through the heavy undergrowth. He saw me, came over, and asked what was going on.

I told him as best I could. We had a cigarette and shot the breeze for a few minutes, then he went back to his men. I rejoined my RTOs, and we waited for the word to move. It came, eventually, and we resumed our trek toward Albany.

We had gone less than a hundred yards when the direction of our march shifted slightly to the left, and the pace began to quicken. I recall a sudden sense of urgency, magnified, perhaps, by the fact that I wasn't sure where the landing zone was. But then, in the distance, I could see a clearing, the first one we'd seen in two hours. It must be the LZ, I thought. I was then surprised by the sudden appearance of the battalion commander and his entourage hurrying past me and heading toward the front of our column. They seemed in a terrible rush.

Captain Sugdinis called me forward.

I found him kneeling in the woods at the edge of what appeared to be the LZ—a large grassy field that sloped gently downwards to the left into a depression or swamp of some kind. A large clump of trees, about a hundred yards away, rose from the middle of the field. I was suddenly flabbergasted to see the battalion commander's crowd heading across the open field toward the clump of trees.

The captain told me that the Recon Platoon had already crossed the field to reconnoiter the far side, that he'd sent the 1st Platoon around to the right and the 2d Platoon around to the left to secure the LZ. I couldn't see them because the wood line around the LZ was too thick, but they were there, slowly circling the LZ to secure it for our extraction. With that, the captain rose and followed MacDade's party into the open, and I, in turn, followed.

The field was fine for an LZ. The grass was only waist-high, and the ground fairly flat. High trees surrounded the field, but I estimated it could still take up to eight ships at a clip. We'd be out of there in no time.

When I reached the clump of trees in the middle of the field, I noticed more open ground beyond it. The clump turned out to be a small grove, sort of an island in the field, studded with saplings, clumps of thick underbrush, and several big anthills, six feet high, at least. We'd made it, I thought, collapsing into the high grass. Costello and Wilson and the first sergeant plopped down beside me.

God I was tired. My whole body ached. My mouth was dry. My head hurt. But we'd made it.

The rest of the company closed in behind us. Sergeant Braden's mortarmen staggered into the small stand of trees and dropped to the ground, exhausted. Captain Sugdinis sat calmly in the grass behind us, handset to his ears, waiting for reports from our flanking platoons. First Sergeant Miller was lying on his side, chewing a piece of long grass and staring at the ground. Several other troopers, evidently from the headquarters company, straggled in behind us.

Brrrrrrpppp! Brrrrrrpppppp! A couple of quick bursts of small-arms fire erupted from the jungle to our left, where the 1st Platoon had disappeared. It must be the PAVN stragglers, I thought. I sat up, but couldn't see anything in the tree line across the field.

Pop! Pop! Pop! Several rounds broke the air overhead. Instinctively, I ducked back into the grass. They were followed by an answering burst, from the left, across the field, then some more shots from the right, where we'd just been. Then, as if on cue, the entire jungle suddenly seemed to explode in an incredible crescendo of small-arms fire, as if everyone had opened up around us with every weapon they had, and firecrackers started popping overhead.

I sprinted to a tree on my left. The firing swelled around us. The air was alive with rounds crackling overhead. People were shouting, but I couldn't hear them because of the noise. And it kept getting worse. *Crack!* A chunk of bark burst from the tree trunk right in front of me, leaving a gash in the wood just inches from my face. Jesus, that was close! I had to get back to my radios, find out what was happening. I sprinted back to Costello and dove into the grass. Tom was lying face down now, almost hugging the ground, his handset pressed to his ear. Wilson lay next to him, his eyes wide with fear. The captain was crouching behind a big anthill now, just past us on the edge of our clump of trees, holding both handsets to his ears, listening intently. I low-crawled to him behind the anthill.

The firing was raging around us now. As the noise grew, so did the confusion.

"First Platoon's surrounded and taking fire," the captain yelled at me through the din.

From behind us and to our left, in the middle of the clump of trees, I could hear someone shouting "Cease fire! Cease fire!" But none of us were firing. None of us could tell what was happening. The whole jungle had just erupted in a monstrous firefight, and nobody knew what was happening.

The captain's face contorted. His eyes darted back and forth. The firing ebbed momentarily, then picked up furiously again.

"First Platoon's taking casualties," he yelled. "So is 2d."

The headquarters guys were still screaming "Cease fire! Cease fire!"

"Second Platoon's taking fire from Charlie Company," the captain yelled. Then, into the handset, "What's your position, Two-six?" His brows knit in consternation. "Negative! Negative! Throw smoke. Affirmative!" Then he yelled into the other handset—the battalion net—"Negative, negative! My Two-six reports incoming fire from behind him! Roger. Wilco." Then, into the other handset, "Cease fire, all units. Cease fire!"

The shooting continued all around us, unabated, rolling back and forth in the jungle, swelling down the column, incoming rounds still crackling overhead.

I popped up and down again, quickly, but couldn't see anything. Bullets were exploding overhead like wildfire.

"First Platoon's surrounded," the captain said, looking at me in desperation. "Four-six, throw smoke for One-six . . . One-six, look for the smoke!"

"Roger," Sergeant Braden said. "Throwing smoke . . . smoke is out."

We watched for the smoke. It was red.

"Do you see it, One-six?" the captain asked. He was getting desperate. "Smoke is out. Red smoke. Do you see it? Come to the smoke!"

The firing swelled again, all along the tree line and deeper in the jungle where the rest of the battalion was spread out behind us.

"He says he can't see the smoke!" I heard the captain yelling, helplessly. "He says all his people are dead or wounded. That they're being overrun!"

Whump! A loud, sickening *whump* erupted from the jungle to our right, down in the low ground, the swamp, down where the 2d Platoon had gone. Mortars! They had mortars! They were dropping rounds on Grove's position! The first round was followed by another, and another, and the ground shook with each concussion. The rounds kept crunching in, four, five, then six, landing to the right, just below us, their sound muffled by the swamp.

Joel was trying to raise Gordy on the radio, but nobody answered. "I've lost contact with the 2d Platoon," the captain said to me, helplessly.

I'd never seen the look on his face. The firing picked up furiously to our front. Chaos, absolute chaos, from where we'd just been. Hundreds of small arms blasting away at each other. Grenades exploding. Men screaming or shouting hysterically. Worse than anything I'd ever heard, anything I could have imagined. The mortars suddenly stopped, thank God, but the firing continued furiously all around us.

"I've lost the 1st Platoon!" Joel said, shaking his head, his eyes wide with shock and disbelief. He glanced helplessly at the battalion CP behind us. "I've lost two platoons," he said, again. His jaw sagged. In the two months I'd known him, I'd never seen such anguish. I couldn't believe what was happening.

I jumped up and looked across the field, back where we'd come from.

Three men were struggling across it, GIs, coming right at us. One of them was a captain I didn't know, one was the battalion sergeant major. The third man, behind them, was very small, almost hidden in the grass, a private first class. He was staggering behind them, clutching his stomach, holding in his intestines. He had a bad stomach wound and was holding in his guts!

Behind him there was movement in the trees. Men in uniforms, strange uniforms, mustard-colored shirts with floppy hats. PAVN! Jesus, they were PAVN! Twenty, thirty, forty men, moving upright through the trees on the far side of the field where we'd just been!

We were cut off from the rest of the column!

The firing continued to swell. I heard Colonel MacDade's voice again, still screaming "Cease fire! Cease fire!"

His head popped up from the grass behind his anthill.

"No! No!" I screamed at him. "Look over there! They're PAVN. You can see 'em in the tree line. Look! They're all over the place!"

I'm sure he saw me, but his head dropped back in the grass.

I turned and waved at the figures coming toward me. "Over here!" I yelled as loud as I could. "Over here!"

The captain staggered past me into our position. He was wild-eyed, breathing so hard he could hardly speak. "Oh, man, that was close," he said, dropping to his knees, totally spent. He muttered something incoherently, then asked me for water.

"It's going to be a long day," I said, ignoring his request. I pointed to MacDade's position. "The CP's over there."

He got up and stumbled over to the battalion HQ anthill. By that time, MacDade had stopped screaming "Cease fire."

The sergeant major lurched past me, puffing hard and shaking his head. The man behind him had just a few more yards to go—a young private I'd never seen—still holding in his intestines, bulging from a gash above his belt.

He stumbled into the perimeter. "Attaboy," I said. "You made it. Good man."

"Are the choppers on the way?" he asked, his eyes glazed.

"Yes," I lied. "They're on the way. Lie down over there and get some rest. You'll be okay."

He staggered past me and keeled over into the grass.

I glanced at the sergeant major, partially hidden now by a small bush on my right.

Kaboom! Something exploded. Something behind us. I whirled around, my rifle raised, but nobody was there.

"I'm hit!" cried the sergeant major. Somehow I knew he had been. Someone had snuck up behind us and shot him in the back!

"Where is he? Did you see him?" I screamed. "Did you see anyone?" I was getting hysterical. "Tell me where he is so I can shoot the son of a bitch!"

"I didn't see anyone," the sergeant major said. "Help me. I've been hit."

I didn't move. I was staring at the terrain behind us, scanning every tree, bush, log, gully, mound, fern, and twig—every conceivable place that someone could be hiding. I took my .45 out of its shoulder holster, chambered a round, clicked the safety on, then put it back in its holster—all the time scanning the area in back of us, fully expecting to see a PAVN jump up and shoot at us again, but he didn't. Then I turned to the sergeant major.

"Where're you hit?" I asked.

He was clutching his shoulder. When he took his hand away, I could see an ugly three-inch gash under his armpit. Muscle tissue bulged from it just like Allred's wound, but it wasn't bleeding.

"It's not too bad," I said. "Got a bandage?"

He nodded.

"Good," I said. "The battalion CP's over there. They'll fix you up. We're going to have to fight our way out of this, Sergeant Major, wounded or not. Do you understand?"

He nodded again and began to make his way over to the battalion CP.

I turned around and glanced back at our anthill. No one was there! Then I remembered seeing them low-crawling to the other side of the clump of trees. As I turned to where I'd last seen them, I almost tripped over Sergeant Reed, a medic in the headquarters company. He was sitting there, frozen in the tall grass, his eyes wide with fear.

"What the fuck are you doing?" I screamed at him. "There are wounded all around here. Get off your fucking ass and do something!" Then I kicked him in the buttocks. He shook his head slowly, as if coming out of a trance, then jumped up and ran over to the battalion CP. As I watched him, I saw Joel and the others crawling in the grass, snaking their way past the battalion's CP anthill about twenty yards away. I dodged and weaved, sprinting short distances then dropping back down on one knee, until I caught up with them. I passed Major Henry. He was lying in the grass on his back, with a terribly pained expression on his face. I thought he'd been shot, but there was no time to help him. I saw a few more men from battalion headquarters, but they were lying low. I finally caught up with the captain and plopped down next to him.

He'd stopped in the tall grass, but some bushes and saplings gave us cover. We were now facing west, looking at a big open field on the other side of our clump of trees. This must be the LZ, I thought. Across it, there was another line of trees, about fifty yards away. The fighting was off to our right now, but it hadn't let up at all. Everyone around me was lying in the grass, so I popped up to look around.

Suddenly three enemy soldiers charged out of the tree line, heading right at us. There were more behind them, lots more, but my attention was riveted on the three lead PAVN. They were bent low at the waist, carrying AK-47s, and coming right at us.

"Here they come!" I screamed, raising my M-16 and sighting in on the lead man.

I heard the colonel yell "Withdraw!" and thought that was pretty weird because there wasn't any place to go.

I fired single shots, I remember, one into each of the three lead men, and watched them stumble and fall. The first man, still alive, began to crawl forward. I fired another round into him, between his neck and shoulder. I saw it jolt him, and he dropped to the ground again. But then I saw him push himself up from the ground and continue to crawl forward, inch by inch. Aghast, I stood up, switched to automatic, and emptied the rest of my clip into him. That did the trick. By that time, the other PAVN had been stopped, too. They were either lying dead in the open field or fading back into the tree line, just shadows now.

"We're falling back," I heard Joel say. We were out too far in the grass.

Joel and the others worked their way back toward Mac-Dade's anthill, back where we'd just come from. First Sergeant Miller and I kept an eye on the tree line. When I turned to follow Joel, I saw the young private with the stomach wound lying out in the grass. Somehow, he'd managed to crawl out into the field behind us. I ran over to him, slung him over my back, and stumbled back into the perimeter. First Sergeant Miller was covering me as I ran past him, firing single rounds from his M-16 into the tree line, and I'll never forget the steadfast look on his face.

Back inside the clump of trees, I slid the young soldier off my back and laid him gently on the ground. He was going fast, delirious now, calling for his mother, clearly beyond help. There was nothing we could do for him.

The firing continued unabated all around us, but the worst seemed to come from where we had first broken out of the forest. I saw Joel and our HQ team making their way back to the first big anthill we'd stopped at. In the confusion, we were moving back and forth, back and forth, but there was nowhere else to go.

Inside the clump of trees, an island of safety in the middle of a deadly sea, we now had our mortar platoon, some of the battalion headquarters group, and our headquarters team. I could see our mortar tube where Sergeant Braden had set it up, and I remember worrying that the PAVN would see it, too, and come for it. They were everywhere, it seemed. All around us. The only place I hadn't seen PAVN was when the sergeant major had been hit and I had scanned the trees behind him. I had no idea where the recon platoon had gone, other than the fact that they were supposed to be on the far side of the LZ.

By that time, we'd crawled back to our old anthill and were oriented back toward where we had first exited the jungle. The captain was crouched behind the anthill. His RTOs were kneeling on either side of him, looking back across the open field. The first sergeant was to my right, lying prone in the grass, covering our rear, the area behind me where the sergeant major had been hit. I was also in the grass behind the anthill, using the mound as cover. I could still see groups of PAVN moving in the tree line across the open field.

We were surrounded. That was clear.

Suddenly, several long bursts of automatic fire erupted from the far side of the landing zone, back where we'd just been, where we'd stopped that PAVN rush. The firing marked the return of Pat Payne's Recon Platoon. I heard men yelling, and saw several others sprinting into our perimeter from the southwest. A few more straggled in behind them. I thought they were dragging their wounded. The Recon Platoon had somehow managed to work itself back into our little perimeter from their position in the woods on the southwestern edge of the LZ. As they did, men in our perimeter were cheering and yelling and providing them covering fire. When I looked back at Joel, he was talking to Pat on the radio, telling him where to set up. Things were looking up.

The firing was still heavy in the jungle from where we'd come, but with the Recon Platoon back inside our perimeter and oriented to the west, the mortar platoon oriented to the north, and our HQ group oriented to the northeast, I felt a little better. I remember lighting up a cigarette, and then another one for Joel. We smoked them behind the cover of our anthill and discussed our situation, deciding that the little grove or clump of trees was going to have to be our last ditch perimeter, sort of a triangle, with our anthill, MacDade's anthill, and a third anthill near Sergeant Braden as its corners. If we could consolidate our defenses, we might still have a chance.

"Yeah, good," Joel said. "Now, what about a way out?"

We had both been thinking about that—a bug-out route, a last resort, a way to escape encirclement with as many men as we could. The only place I had not seen enemy troops was the area I had scanned when the sergeant major had been shot. I pointed it out to the captain—a narrow gully leading down and south, away from the worst of the fighting. Joel agreed that that's where we'd go if we had to.

"Somebody's coming!"

I looked across the field. Emerging from the tree line near the low ground a hundred yards away was Gordy Grove. The familiar pattern of his camouflaged helmet was unmistakable. We shouted at him and waved. He turned around and beckoned to someone behind him—I couldn't see who it was—then began to jog across the field. In the high grass, he seemed to be floating. His shirt was open, and his harness swung loose behind him, but otherwise, he looked okay. A hundred meters past him, I could still see enemy soldiers. Why they couldn't see him, I'll never know. Halfway to our position, Gordy turned again and beckoned to the people behind him. I was sure that the PAVN would see him and cut him down, but they didn't. He turned again and continued to our position.

As he got closer, I could see figures in the grass behind him—two men, one crawling on his hands and knees, the other with his arm dangling uselessly at his side.

"Over here! Over here!" we called, and the three men staggered into our perimeter.

Joel shook Gordy's hand. I shook Gordy's hand. He looked awful.

"Over here," Joel said to the wounded, pointing to his position behind the anthill. I recognized Sergeant Evans, a squad leader, and O'Brien, a machine gunner. Evans had a gash in his shoulder. O'Brien's left thigh was wrapped in a blood-soaked bandage. Neither had a weapon. They looked pale and exhausted, aghast but relieved to be there.

Grove was distraught. "I've gotta go back," he said. "Bring the others out. VC all over the place. Up close, both sides, everything all mixed up." He was shaking his head, his eyes wild, flicking back and forth from Joel to me. "I need some men to take with me."

"Hold on, Gordo," Joel said. "Slow down. Get your wind back. Now, once again, what's the situation there? Where's your radio?"

"Smashed. Mortars got it."

"Where's everyone else?" the captain said.

Gordy looked at me, then at Joel, then back across the field. "Everyone's dead or wounded so's they can't move. Radio's smashed. We're the only ones who could make it. I need some men and stretchers. Have to go back and get the others out!"

"I'm not going to let you go back out there," Joel said, firmly.

He wouldn't get me to go out there, either—not in a million years.

Gordy was stammering now, as if he hadn't heard. "One or two still there. I came to get some help. Got to get 'em out."

"Negative," Joel said. "I won't let you go!" He yelled the words, right into Gordy's face.

"Permission to ask the colonel," Grove said, undaunted.

"Go ahead. Ask. He's over there," Joel said.

"Stay here," Gordy barked at Evans, then turned and ran over to where Joel had pointed. Evans and O'Brien, the only apparent survivors from our 2d Platoon, settled in with their backs against the anthill, and lit up cigarettes. Sergeant Reed appeared out of nowhere and began to work on them. I watched him administer morphine to Evans. He'd been wounded before, on our first operation down Route 19. He looked okay, happily smoking his cigarette. Joel looked over to me, shook his head, and turned back to the anthill.

Several rounds popped overhead, and we cringed again. I dropped to the ground.

This couldn't be happening, I thought. It was worse than any nightmare I'd ever dreamed. In fifteen, maybe twenty minutes, we had been cut off and surrounded, lost two of our four platoons, half of our people, more than fifty men, and God knows what was happening to the rest of the battalion. They'd been strung out behind us when PAVN opened fire. They must be spread out, pinned down, and totally confused right now. And the firing hadn't let up at all. We were getting the shit kicked out of us!

Gordy came back. The colonel wouldn't give him any men.

What did he expect?

"Stay here, Gordo," Joel said. "Stay here with us. There's nothing you can do. Don't feel bad. I've lost two platoons."

Those dirty bastards, I thought, suddenly scrambling to the top of the anthill. It was sandy and dry but covered with plenty of grass and brush. I poked the barrel of my M-16 through it and looked out across the open field. Through the tangle of twigs and grass, I could see PAVN moving in the tree line, about two hundred meters away. Well within range. I saw one man, wearing a gray khaki shirt and a floppy hat, standing in the high grass near a thicket. I took a deep breath, steadied myself, lined him up in my sights, and slowly squeezed the trigger. My rifle bucked, and the little man dropped out of sight. I found another target, took aim, and fired. This one jerked sideways, as if he'd been yanked by a rope. I found another, lined him up, and fired. This one exploded in a cloud of gray smoke. My round must have hit a grenade. I saw another, his head just barely visible. I aimed again. My heart was pounding. Sweat was trickling down my cheek. My front sight was blurring in and out of focus. I fired, but the man didn't flinch. I took more careful aim, squeezed the trigger again, and this time he dropped like a sack.

I continued sniping until I'd fired a full clip—nineteen rounds. Then a loud *crack* exploded by my head, and I realized how exposed I was and slid back down behind the anthill.

Gordy Grove scrambled up where I had been and began to fire away, in two- and three-shot bursts, muttering to himself. I remember sitting there for a moment, coming slowly out of my rage. Joel was kneeling by the side of the anthill, firing his M-16, too. I saw a puff of dust erupt just inches from his knee. He saw it, too, ducked back behind the anthill, looked up, and saw me staring at him. We both rolled our eyes and shook our heads. Sergeant Evans was out of it now, his eyes glazed. The cigarette he was trying to smoke kept sticking to his lips. A morphine surrette dangled from his shirt. O'Brien had crawled to the aid station.

I began to worry about ammunition. Spent cartridge casings lay strewn all over the place, and we were all firing up a storm. We'd have to conserve ammo if we were going to get out of this mess alive.

Grove came down from the anthill, and Specialist Fourth Class Elliot, the 2d Platoon man who'd been assigned to carry mortar ammunition, took his place atop the mound.

I couldn't see much from where we were, but sensed we were holding our own. No PAVN had rushed us since we'd stopped that first charge, but they were still visible in the far tree line, and could come at any moment.

Suddenly two more of our people dashed into our makeshift command post—Sergeant Temple (Rother A.) and Sergeant Caple (Walter T.), squad leaders from our 1st Platoon—and they looked completely spent. They crashed down next to the captain.

"Where are the others?" Joel asked. "Are there any others?"

"We're it," they said, both shaking their heads.

That confirmed it. The 1st Platoon had been overrun, maybe all dead. Joel told them to report to Sergeant Braden, and without a moment's hesitation, they picked themselves up and dodged over to the Mortar Platoon's positions.

A few minutes later, Captain Spires, the S-3, loped into our position. "We're getting TAC Air," he announced. Tactical air support, bombers, fighters, possible salvation. "It's on the way. The colonel wants to know what the situation is out there." He pointed to the low ground to our front, where Grove's platoon had been.

Joel looked at Gordy. Spires looked at Gordy. We all looked at Gordy. But Grove didn't say a thing.

"What's the situation out there?" the S-3 asked again.

"I dunno," Gordy mumbled, looking away.

Joel intervened. "He said everyone was either killed or wounded—wounded too badly to move," he said. "That was twenty minutes ago."

None of us had heard any firing from the 2d Platoon's positions since Gordy had made it into our perimeter.

"Is it likely that anyone's still alive?" Captain Spires asked. He was pressing the point.

No one spoke, and none of us could look him in the eye.

"Then everyone's dead, you think," he said.

Still, no one spoke.

"Okay," he said. "Be ready to throw smoke. Good luck." With that, he turned and zigzagged back to the battalion anthill.

The firestorm in the jungle swelled again, maintaining its intensity, but deeper, farther into the woods. I heard a different sound, a heavier weapon, much lower and more foreboding, firing from the jungle. Heavy machine gun, I thought, but wasn't sure. It scared me.

The radios soon crackled for everyone to throw smoke, any color. I dodged about ten yards to the left, positioning myself to hurl a smoke grenade into the high grass to our front. When I heard Joel yell, I popped red smoke and threw it as far as I could into the open field to my front. I saw Captain Fesmire, to my left, throw one, too. It surprised me to see him there. What the hell was he doing in our perimeter? The grenades popped and hissed all around us, spewing smoke into the air, marking our position with a ragged circle of red, green, yellow, and white smoke, billowing from canisters, its acrid smell mixing with the haze of cordite.

I was crawling back to our anthill when I heard the first plane. I couldn't tell how high it was, or how far away, but its engine droned louder and louder. Salvation was at hand. I rolled over on my side and peered through the branches overhead. There it was, an A-1E Skyraider, diving toward the far tree line.

Down, down, down it roared, closer and closer. All the firing was drowned out by its roar. Then, about a hundred feet up, it let go of the silver napalm canister it carried under its belly and climbed sharply back up into the air. I watched the canister tumble slowly downward, end over end, then crash into the treetops, breaking apart and exploding in a ball of roiling flame. Blazing napalm rolled into the trees and began to seep downward, slowly, like stalactites of flame. A dozen shadowy figures suddenly rose as one from the jungle floor, PAVN trying desperately to flee, but the flaming jellied gas engulfed them all.

Suddenly I was on my feet, fist clenched, cheering. Everyone around me was cheering, too, laughing, yelling, clapping their buddies on the back—"Oh, man, it's beautiful." "Fry the little bastards!" "Kill the fuckers." "Yeah, kill 'em all!"—venting our pent-up rage at what we had seen.

A second Skyraider followed close behind the first, dropping its two canisters slightly to the left of that first deadly strike. They were right on target, hitting the spot where we'd first exited the forest. Dead on! The napalm burst into the treetops and filtered downward, all in a matter of seconds, engulfing everything underneath it. Bull's-eye!

I sat back down, in numb fascination and horror, and watched as the bombing continued unabated for about twenty minutes. I saw a canister crash into the treetops over the place where the first PAVN rush had come from, where I had killed my first man, and the jungle floor seemed to writhe as at least twenty PAVN, lying hidden in the tree line, tried to flee. A billowing gasoline fireball swept over them all, roiling with thick black, tiger-stripe smoke, leaving the small patch of jungle charred and smoking. I saw the same scene repeated a half dozen times. The napalm was devastating, utterly terrifying, effectively clearing out hidden enclaves of PAVN poised around us. And each aircraft seemed to come a little closer, fly a little lower, and drop a little more accurately. And each pass seared a swath of safety around us.

It was beautiful.

When napalm finally struck what had been the 2d Platoon's position, first one canister, then another, about a hundred yards away from us, it was as if all sound had been blotted out for a moment, as if I'd suddenly gone stone deaf. After the orange-black flameball rolled over the place where our men had been, we sat there, too stunned to move. Then my hearing came back. I could hear the *Pop! Pop! Pop!* of unexpended ammunition burning in the flames. It sounded like popcorn popping on a stove.

I looked up once more. A Skyraider was diving right at us, its propeller coming head-on, the roar of its engines deafening. The jungle behind me was still spitting small-arms fire, all the PAVN guns blazing away at it in defiance. I watched the Skyraider coming right at us, realizing, almost sadly, that it was going to drop its canister right on top of us. I was frozen to the spot, unable to move, thinking what a horrible miserable way this was to die.

The plane released its bomb. I watched it fall away from the plane's belly and begin its ineluctable tumble toward our position. It was coming right at us. I stared at it, mesmerized by its strange sad beauty, the awful fascination of its flight. I watched it tumbling closer, and closer. I could see the rivets in the aluminum along its side as it passed overhead, so close I could almost reach up and touch it. I buried my head in the ground.

It *KAAARRRRUUUMMMMPPED* in a huge ball of flame that seared the air around me. Then I looked up.

As if in a dream, I saw a young PAVN soldier pop up out of the grass—about thirty feet away—and charge right at us. He was trying to flee the fire. Someone screamed, bullets tore into his chest, and, horribly riddled, he crashed headfirst into the grass at my feet. He looked about ten years old.

How many more were out there?

Then that heavy PAVN machine gun barked its foreboding message from behind another large anthill in the wood line. The new weapon's sound was heavy, loud, and deep. Every time a Skyraider made a pass, the heavy gun opened up and fired at the plane. On the last pass the air force made, they dropped a canister dead center on the heavy PAVN machine gun, but its crew kept firing defiantly until the very last second, when they were horribly engulfed in flame. With that last bull's-eye, the air strikes suddenly stopped.

For several minutes—I don't know how long—we lay there, listened, watched, and waited. A wary hush seemed to settle over the field. I looked around. The far wood line looked different now. PAVN had gone, or so it appeared, and the dark green jungle wall was blackened by sections of smoking and withered vegetation. A few small fires still burned intermittently around us, adding their smoke to the haze of cordite and dust that had settled over the battlefield. The haze in the air was acrid, but a new stench began to permeate it—a stench I had smelled before—the stench of death and decaying flesh.

I glanced over at battalion HQ. Major Henry and Captain Spires were standing behind the shelter of the anthill, talking on their radios. Several wounded troopers lay behind them in the grass. Sergeant Reed was ministering to a man with his head wrapped in bandages. The sergeant major was there with his T-shirt still on.

A deathly pall seemed to hover over us. Having witnessed the carnage of the air strikes, most of us were clearly in shock. Some of the men were babbling, others chatting away, thinking the worst was over. I wasn't sure. PAVN was still out there somewhere. They could still rush us at any minute. They could still overrun us.

And what about the rest of our people? Except for Bravo Company, our entire battalion, over four hundred strong, had been out there in that jungle. How many were still alive? How many had we burned? And who was going to help them? The thought made me heartsick.

I looked at the men around me, sitting numbly in the grass, silently staring at the wood line, waiting for PAVN's next rush. Whether it came or not, I suddenly didn't care. I glanced at my watch. It was 1630.

Chapter 12

Aftermath

A puff of wind came up, carrying the stench of who knew how many corpses. Oh, that stink—it ought to be bottled and sold to every president, prime minister, king, dictator, and general for use when he gets an idea in his head to go to war.

—PHILIP CAPUTO,
Means of Escape

While we were fighting for our lives around Albany, the word filtered down from the 3d Brigade TOC at Pleiku that we had run into something bad. How bad, it wasn't clear, and the fighting was so intense and the communications so confused, that Lieutenant Colonel MacDade wasn't able to convey the severity of our predicament to the higher ups. At any rate, Colonel Brown, the brigade commander, alerted units to get ready to reinforce us. Bravo 2/7 was ordered to prepare for a possible air assault into Albany, and the battalion providing security for the artillery at LZ Columbus (the 2/5, with companies from the 1/5 attached) was ordered to send a company overland from LZ Columbus to help us out. It eventually reached the tail end of our column, but only to reinforce Alpha Company, 1/5, which had circled its wagons as soon as the fighting had started. But from where we were, at the head of the column more than five hundred meters away, they might as well have been in Texas.

* * *

At some point after the air strikes, I remember hearing that Bravo Company was on the way in to help us out. Where they'd land was anyone's guess, but if the napalm had pushed the PAVN back, reinforcements might be able to fly into the LZ. After all, we'd done the same thing at LZ Xray just two days before. Stunned by the ferocity of the battle, though, we remained in place, counted noses, treated the wounded, redistributed ammunition, and waited for the next shoe to drop.

Late that afternoon, I remember seeing Major Henry and Captain Spires standing behind the battalion CP anthill and talking into their radios. Then I heard the low drone of a formation of inbound Hueys. What a wonderful sound! But where could they land? The drone increased steadily. Then I saw them, a flight of Hueys coming from the south, from the direction of Xray, about five hundred feet up. They flew to the east of us, past our perimeter, then curved slowly around to the west and back south again, circling the LZ, trying to figure out where to land. I'm not sure, but PAVN must have been firing at them as they circled.

We were hoping desperately that they would land and disgorge reinforcements, of course, but the situation had been so horrendous before the air strikes, it was hard to accept even the remote possibility that they would be able to fly in without getting shot to pieces. I vaguely recall that the flight made one serious attempt at a pass, coming in from the south but not quite making it, and having to veer off again, to circle once more for another try. But another try they made.

I could now hear Major Henry on the radio, explicitly instructing the flight leader to tell his people to fire to the left and exit to the right. Fire to the left and exit to the right. The instructions seemed to echo over the radio net around us. Then the formation came thundering into the LZ—the clearing to the west of us—and the noise and confusion of a formation of Hueys making an air assault into a hot LZ took over. They swept in from the south, eight ships at a time, I think, and the woods to our north seemed to spit enemy fire. The Hueys' door gunners were returning it—raking the far tree line with their M-60s. The noise was horrendous, deaf-

ening, unbelievable. I could see Bravo Company troops jumping from the choppers and sprinting through the grass toward
our location, and as they did I could feel this wonderful exhilaration and sense of awe, salvation, and relief. Having
watched it, I can say without equivocation that it was the
most heroic combat air assault I've ever seen. Certainly the
boldest.

Another flight may have come in behind them. I'm not sure.

Not all of the Hueys made it into Albany, but most of them
managed to do so. All in all, about eighty Bravo Company
troopers came in, along with water jugs and crates of extra
ammo and grenades that were just dumped into the grass. As
the Bravo Company guys closed into our perimeter, we were
all up on our feet, cheering and yelling and hooting and
waving them on, welcoming them into our position. I saw
Sergeant Braden waving a little American flag he had been
carrying with him, and thought that was terrific. I saw Rick
Rescorla, the British soldier of fortune, striding purposefully
into our perimeter checking his M-16. (He'd just killed a
PAVN soldier on the edge of the LZ.) An M-79 grenade
launcher was slung from his shoulder, bandoliers of extra
ammo were crisscrossed on his chest, and he was looking
around, taking it all in, saying "Good. Good. Good. We'll
wipe 'em up now! I hope they hit us tonight. We'll whip 'em
good."

I remember walking up to him, shaking his hand, and
saying something dumb, like "Thanks for coming."

He shook my hand, looked me in the eye, nodded grimly,
and continued past me, intent on his job, but it was clear from
the look on his face that he knew what a mess we were in.

Then Major Henry caught my eye and waved me over.

"Okay, Gwin," he said. "I want you to gather up some men
pronto and bring in that extra ammo over there."

To my horror, he was pointing across the LZ, to the far side
of it, past where the choppers had landed. I could see some
ammo crates strewn in the grass, about seventy yards away,

beyond the spot where I'd killed those first three PAVN soldiers during their first rush at us early in the fight.

Oh my God, I thought. You want me to go out there, where the PAVN troops had been massing before the air strikes? You want me to walk across that LZ with some of my people and bring that shit back? You've gotta be out of your fucking mind!

"Yes, sir," I said, sick with fear.

But there was no time to dwell on it. I called to First Sergeant Miller, Tom Costello, Denny Wilson, and some others, told them quickly what we had to do, and we did it. We moved warily across the open field, slowing as we approached the far tree line, scanning it carefully for PAVN. The first sergeant and I kept watch while the other guys picked up or dragged the ammo crates and jugs of water back across the grass to the perimeter. I hauled a case of grenades up on my shoulder, the first sergeant picked up the last of the crates in the grass, and we both turned and ran as fast as we could behind them. We stumbled and ran and staggered back across the open field and deposited all the water and ammo crates next to the battalion CP.

"Good job," the major said.

Grateful to be alive, we staggered back to our positions. Retrieving that ammo was one of the hardest things I'd ever been asked to do, and after we did it, I think I reached the end of my rope.

Walking back to our anthill CP, I saw Captain Sugdinis talking with Myron Diduryk, CO of Bravo Company, and I went over to shake his hand. When I did, he joked about not being able to leave us alone without our getting into all kinds of trouble, but I don't think it registered. All I remember is how happy and grateful I was to see him.

"I've been relieved," Joel said to me. He said it calmly, as if it made sense, as if he were almost happy that he'd been eased of the burden of command. He had accepted it. "Captain Diduryk is taking over the defense of the perimeter, and we are now attached to Bravo Company." Through the haze of my exhaustion that made sense. We were so fucked up and exhausted after four hours of close-up fighting that it made consummate sense for the fresh troops to come in and take charge.

So, Bravo Company took over. Captain Diduryk had managed to scrape up about eighty volunteers from the bars and clubs around Camp Holloway (where they'd been celebrating their "victory" at Xray). And now, after that incredibly courageous air assault into our sizzling hot LZ, they took on the additional job of defending us. We were there, too, of course, and would help as best we could, but none of us was particularly sharp, or coherent, at the time.

I just stood there and watched as the Bravo Company troops simply pushed our last ditch perimeter out a little farther, still using the cover and concealment of the trees and anthills in our island/clump of trees, but also filling in the spaces between our hasty makeshift positions. Perhaps we just filled in between their positions. I'm not sure. The trouble was that their eighty or so men more than doubled our small force of shell-shocked survivors, and that didn't leave us with that many men to fend off a PAVN battalion. Whatever, I remember the positions of the Bravo Company men and the survivors of our fight were very close and tight all around the clump of trees.

Captain Sugdinis suggested that Gordy Grove and I dig a hole about ten yards in front of where he and Captain Diduryk were setting up, so that's what we did. I remember trying to dig in that unbelievably hard ground. It was just like the ground at Xray—almost impossible to dig in. We were located between the Alpha Company anthill and the battalion CP, with captains Sugdinis and Diduryk right behind us. We dug and scraped and dug and scraped as hard as we could, ending up with barely a two-man fighting hole, maybe six inches deep, but enough to lie down in. As dusk settled around us, everyone was digging in and preparing for the inevitable night attack, and when dark finally came, I remember carefully laying my harness and ammo clips and grenades out where I could reach them, lying down in the shallow hole with Gordy on my right as we faced out, then curling up with my M-16 and falling asleep.

I didn't wake up until dawn.

At first light on the morning of the eighteenth, I woke up, amazed at being alive, equally amazed that we hadn't been attacked that night, and thoroughly oblivious to what had transpired during the eight or so hours of darkness. I looked up over the rim of my foxhole and saw the helmets of men in the foxholes in front of us, less than fifteen yards away. Except for the occasional movement of heads turning left and right, scanning the grass to their front, nobody was moving at all. Everything was eerily still and quiet. As the day began its unavoidable slide into the horrors of discovering what had happened to us, I simply looked over the rim of my foxhole, stretched my cramped muscles, and marveled at the thought of being alive.

I got up, eventually, and stumbled over to Captain Sugdinis's foxhole to find out what had happened during the night. He said that Sgt. James E. Mullarkey, a 1st Platoon fire-team leader, had made it into our perimeter that night. He had been wounded during the initial PAVN onslaught and was lying in the tall grass waiting for help when the PAVN came back that night and found him. A PAVN soldier thrust the barrel of his pistol into Sergeant Mullarkey's mouth and fired a round. The round passed through the back of his throat and exited out the back of his neck, knocking him out. He woke up later that night, realized he was still alive, and crawled into our perimeter. The captain said he'd been evacuated, which meant choppers had been in and out of the LZ that night, but I hadn't heard a thing.

I returned to my foxhole and waited there, heartsick at what had transpired, heartsick at the loss of so many of our men, heartsick at the horrors we'd just experienced. In less than half a day, we'd lost two of our four platoons. Half our people. Sergeant Fisher and all of his men in the 1st Platoon—all except Sergeants Temple, Caple, and Mullarkey. Almost all of Gordy Grove's platoon. And Pappy Ferrell, bless his soul. He was one of the best NCOs I'd ever met. Now he was lying out there somewhere in the jungle, probably dead.

It wasn't long before Bravo Company troops began to venture out from our perimeter to look for survivors. Major Henry was one of the first to lead a party of volunteers back into the jungle and down the long column to see what they could find, and what they found was truly awful. As morning settled in, so did the grim reality of what had happened to the men in the column behind us.

The battalion, roughly four hundred strong when it left Xray, had suffered more than seventy percent casualties—155 dead, 124 wounded. Charlie Company was the hardest hit, losing all but 9 of its 110 men. The Delta Company Mortar Platoon was virtually wiped out. And Headquarters Company had been decimated. Captain McCarn, the battalion S-4, had been killed at the outset of the battle.

Choppers began flying in and out of the LZ, but I wasn't paying any attention to them. Some brought in the brass, who wanted to know what had happened. Some brought in the press, who scurried off immediately and began taking pictures. And some of them brought in our 3d Platoon. They were aghast at what they found.

We spent the entire day at Albany searching for survivors, rescuing the wounded, and eventually bringing in the dead. A ghastly pall hung over the place. Teams of our men and the people who had come in to help us made the gruesome trek down the column, searching for our wounded, carrying them back to the LZ for treatment and eventual evacuation, and trying to identify the dead. I suppressed that day for fifteen years, but flashbacks continue to haunt me.

First of all, an unbelievably horrible stench filled the air—a sickening, ghastly putrescence—the same we'd smelled at Xray, but worse. Much worse. At Albany it filled your nostrils and permeated your soul. There was no escaping it. I smelled the stench of death several times that year, and though I've never smelled it since, I can say without hesitation that I would be able to recognize it instantly. But I pray I never have

to. Death and the smell of burned or decaying flesh surrounded us. In the heat, it didn't take long for a corpse to start
to deteriorate, and there were more than three hundred
corpses around us, and the stench was absolutely sickening.
And we were surrounded by bodies, bodies of our men,
bodies of PAVN, bodies of the three hundred or so poor bastards who'd fought and died for their country. Almost everywhere you looked, you could see bodies lying sprawled
and bloating in the tall grass. Unless someone has walked
a battlefield covered with three hundred or more torn
and bloating North Vietnamese and American bodies, he
shouldn't feel qualified to talk about the "glory of war," because there is none.

At some point early that morning, word came over the
radio that one of our rescue parties had found a survivor from
the 2d Platoon. Sgt. John F. Eade. He'd been wounded in the
legs early in the fight, when the mortar rounds had dropped
on their position. He may have been wounded a second time,
or burned by napalm, I'm not sure, but he'd managed to prop
himself up against a tree. Whatever the case, he was sitting
with his back against a tree when some PAVN soldier found
him, raised a pistol up to his face, and pulled the trigger. The
round entered his eye, passed through his skull, and exited
through the back of his head. The PAVN left him for dead, but
Eade survived. He was conscious when the rescue party
found him. They laid him out on a stretcher and brought him
in. When I saw him, he was lying on his back on the stretcher,
all fucked up, his legs and his head wrapped in bandages, but
he was conscious and smoking a cigarette! He survived, too,
unlike Sergeant Mullarkey, who died some months later, I
heard, from the trauma of his long night of horror.

Finding Sergeant Eade gave us all a little boost, and shortly
after he was brought into the perimeter, I gathered up a detail
of Alpha Company men and ventured out from our perimeter
to search through the heavy undergrowth for more of our 2d
Platoon. We didn't find any of them alive.

We did find a dead PAVN soldier. He was sprawled in the
thick vegetation, and even though there were no visible

wounds on his body, he was clearly dead as a smelt. He'd been an ammo bearer, carrying six rounds of 60mm mortar ammunition in two metal boxes tied to the ends of a bamboo pole. They were lying next to him in the undergrowth. I remember thinking he might be booby-trapped, so we tied a piece of commo wire around his ankle, moved back twenty yards or so, then dragged him and his ammo boxes just far enough to assure ourselves that they weren't booby-trapped. Afterward, we left him to rot, but we brought back what he'd been carrying. We'd searched him, too, found some papers in his pocket, and turned these over to HQ.

There was a large pile of smashed PAVN weapons, equipment, and gear being assembled near the LZ. It grew bigger as the day wore on, and I remember being appalled at seeing how huge that pile of PAVN equipment was—burned and twisted machine guns, wrecked small arms of all shapes and sizes, even several mortar tubes. My guess is that Charlie Company had overrun the PAVN mortars when it had tried to break out of the killing zone of the PAVN attack. The pile of enemy weapons and equipment continued to grow well into the following day as we continued our gruesome task.

Sometime around midday, I heard that Don Cornett's body had been found. I knew he was dead, but confirmation of it was the straw that broke my emotional back, and I remember turning away from the CP after I heard the news, wanting to be alone (though there was no place to go for that), and breaking down. I don't know how long I cried—less than a minute, I guess. It was more like an overwhelming wave of sadness, a sense of loss, an anguish that simply overcame me. I think we all broke down that day. If not actually breaking down, we all suffered a sense of anguish at the unspeakable nature of the things we'd seen. I would venture to say that none of us who were there that day has ever been the same since. Whatever, I finally pulled myself together and continued, as best I could, the job of policing up our people.

I didn't get up the courage to walk over to our 1st Platoon's positions until early that afternoon. I think Captain Sugdinis had gone over there earlier, and had surveyed the situation, and had told me where they were. I remember walking over there and being amazed at how close they had really been to us, so near yet so far away, and I remember seeing Sergeant Fisher's body in the grass, already swelling in the hot sun, so much so that I hardly recognized him. There were PAVN bodies intermixed with those of our men, and it was clear from what I saw that their fight had been a desperate one, short and fierce. It had been catastrophic, too. In retrospect, I think most of the men in our 1st Platoon had been killed in the first few minutes of the fight. Thankfully, the bodies strewn in the grass around their position had been spared the scourge of napalm. None of them had been burned that I could see. Saddened beyond description, I returned to our CP and tried to function, but I think I was basically useless after that.

All that day, the eighteenth, the survivors of the battalion and the men who had flown in to help us, policed up the battlefield. They performed their gruesome task until all of the wounded were found, patched up, carried back to the LZ, and evacuated. After retrieving the wounded, it was time to bring in the dead. That took another day.

Alpha Company found all of its troopers but one—PFC Toby L. Braveboy. When we left Albany, he was one of four men in the battalion who had been listed as missing in action. The anguish we felt not knowing what had happened to him was palpable. Considering the ferocity of the battle, though, and what had transpired, I thought we were lucky. Captain Sugdinis didn't agree, however, and it wasn't until Braveboy was picked up days later, that the captain felt we'd done everything we could. Braveboy (ironically from Coward, South Carolina) had been wounded at the beginning of the battle, shot in the thigh and the hand. He had crawled away from the perimeter, played dead when the PAVN were shooting our wounded, and had escaped and evaded capture for four days until he was able to flag down a friendly scout ship. He was rescued and flown to a field hospital at Qui Nhon, and when Captain Sugdinis returned from interviewing him, he immediately changed our radio call sign from Gilligator to Braveboy.

At midday on the nineteenth of November, Captain Sugdinis called me over and ordered me to catch a Huey out of Albany and fly to LZ Crook, where we were going to be the security force for a battery of 105mm howitzers that night. Tom Costello and I were to act as a two-man advance party and find out what positions Alpha Company's two surviving platoons would occupy when they landed. By that time, I was wondering when things were going to end for us. Everyone was absolutely exhausted, not to mention demoralized, and we only had forty men left to work with. Costello and I flew out of Albany on the next chopper, landed at Crook, and walked our company positions before the rest of the company arrived.

We spent the night of the nineteenth in well-prepared positions around LZ Crook and were flown back to Camp Holloway the next day.

For us, the battle was over.

Chapter 13

Refitting

They had emerged from the wilderness alive but not unscathed. Every last one of them not quite whole. The terrible ordeal had indelibly scarred them.
— TERRY C. JOHNSTON,
Trumpet on the Land

The flight out of LZ Crook to Camp Holloway, the trip back from Pleiku to An Khe, and the drive into base camp in four deuce-and-a-half trucks past the division's band playing the carefree strains of Garry Owen, is basically a blur.

I do remember being met at Camp Holloway by Peter Cadigan, an old friend from my camp counseling days in the late fifties. Peter had joined the army, too, and was working with MACV at Pleiku. He had heard about the 1st Cav's fight in the Ia Drang Valley, had come to Camp Holloway to look me up, and found me with Joel Sugdinis shortly after we'd returned from LZ Crook. Peter offered us the use of his BOQ room to get cleaned up in. Joel opted to get a haircut instead, but I gratefully accepted the offer. The troops who'd survived the fighting were okay, camped out next to the airstrip, getting showers and clean uniforms themselves, and we wouldn't be heading back to An Khe until the next day.

In the privacy and quiet comfort of Peter's BOQ room, I remember stripping out of my filthy, blood-soaked fatigues, then turning to enter his bathroom to take a shower. I was stopped dead in my tracks by a completely naked stranger blocking my way. He was gaunt, unshaven, filthy dirty, and had a terribly haunted look in his eyes. I stared at him, wondering where he had come from. We stood there glaring at each other, neither of us moving, until I suddenly realized I was staring into a mirror. Having lost forty pounds, and not having seen myself full length since I'd come to Vietnam, I hadn't recognized myself. Though badly shaken by that cadaverous apparition in the mirror, I enjoyed the hot shower immensely.

The night we returned to base camp was a surrealistic one. Almost everyone who'd been "in the valley" got drunk.

Prior to the Pleiku campaign, most of us had been spending our off hours helping Jim Brigham, the assistant S-4, build an officers club in the defiladed position beyond a ravine in back of Headquarters Hill. The lieutenants in particular had spent many a late afternoon laying out the foundation forms, mixing and pouring cement for the floor, and erecting the wooden framework for an unbelievably commodious tin-roof shack that served very handsomely as our very own officers club. The NCOs and enlisted men had built their own clubs, too.

So, after everyone had turned in their crew-served weapons and pyrotechnics, the battalion went slightly crazy. We were so happy to be alive and so heartsick at what had transpired that the logical thing for most of us to do was get hammered. And I mean hammered.

Despite our terrible casualties, morale was sky high. We'd taken on PAVN's best and whipped 'em good. We'd killed hundreds of the bastards and held our ground. We'd won—at least that's what we thought—and some of us were still alive. So, we celebrated.

A couple of dim vignettes from that night. When Alpha Company arrived in Vietnam, its 1st Platoon Leader had been a second lieutenant named Patrick James "Jim" Kelly. Jim had contracted malaria and been evacuated to the Philippines before Captain Sugdinis and I joined the company, so I didn't really know Jim then. When we came back from Pleiku, though, Jim had returned from the hospital in Manila. He was at the base camp when we returned from Pleiku, and that's when he learned that almost everyone in his platoon had been killed at LZ Albany. Mike Mantegna, who had taken over Jim's platoon but hadn't gone with it to the field, was similarly stunned by our losses. The two of them couldn't quite fathom what had happened and didn't dare ask. I wonder how I would have felt.

At one point, late that crazy night, I was sitting with Pat Payne and Jim Kelly in my tent, sharing a bottle of Jack Daniels, I think, when Mantegna appeared in the doorway.

"The Old Man is outside," he said. "And he isn't doing too well."

Of course he isn't, you stupid fuck! I thought. He's been out in the field with us, and he's lost more than half of his people. Of course he isn't doing well. What did you expect?

"I'll take care of it," I said, getting up quickly, not wanting the others to see Joel if he was, indeed, incapacitated. I left the tent and went out into the dark night to find Captain Sugdinis.

It was pitch-black outside, and I didn't have my night vision, but I soon found him staggering around outside our tent. He was out of it, indeed, the only time I ever saw him intoxicated, and he'd been having trouble negotiating his way back to our tent. In fact, he'd tripped on one of the tent ropes and stumbled into a ditch. I helped him up and walked him back to our quarters, shoo'd the others out when we arrived, and left him stretched out on his cot for the night. I may even have taken his boots off. I'm not sure.

Twenty-eight years later, at a reunion of the 2/7th in Chattanooga, Tennessee, the first since the Ia Drang fight, Joel Sugdinis had an erroneous recollection cleared up about that night. During his walk from the officers club back to our quarters, he'd stopped along the way. He was sitting with his back to a tree. It was pitch-black, and I guess he fell asleep. When he woke up, someone was pissing on him. For twenty-eight years, he had thought it was me. During our reunion in Chattanooga, however, Mike Mantegna set the record straight.

He asked the captain if he remembered that night.

"No," Joel said.

"Don't you remember waking up with someone pissing on you?" Mike asked.

"No," Joel said. Then he thought about it for a while. "I thought that was Larry," he said.

"No," Mike confessed. "It was me."

I didn't know anything about it, of course, and when I heard the story, I was happy that Mike had clarified things, had owned up to what he'd done, and cleared the air.

"I'm sorry," Mike said. "It was dark. I didn't see you there. I'm really sorry."

After attending to the captain, I went up to the enlisted men's club for a drink. I'd been invited there by some Alpha Company guys to have a drink with them, so I went. When I entered the place, it was total bedlam, with Alpha guys screaming "Alpha Tigers! Alpha Tigers!", and Bravo Company guys answering "Hard core! Hard core!" They'd taken on that call sign during the fight at Xray, and they kept it for the rest of the year. It suited them. Anyway, the EM club was bedlam. After a beer there, I wandered up the hill to the NCO Club. It was equally crazy, so I didn't stay long, but instead stood outside with a beer in hand generously provided by our supply sergeant, Dan Slimp, who was working behind the bar. One of our mortar guys, whom I liked a lot, an E-5 named James E. Hibbitts, saw me, staggered over, and asked me a question I've never forgotten.

"Sir," he said, "can you explain to me why I'm still here, alive, when my best buddy got burned up by napalm?"

I couldn't answer him then and I can't now. If I'd said "blind luck," I might have been close to the truth, but at the time, I didn't know what to say. Fortunately, the battalion chaplain just happened to be diddly-bopping down the trail past the NCO Club at that exact moment, so I flagged him down, waved him over, and suggested to Sergeant Hibbitts that he ask our chaplain. So he did.

The chaplain had an answer, too. I can't remember the

exact words he used, but he had an answer—an answer filled with quotes of chapter and verse, so many that I turned away in disgust, shaking my head at what I thought was total Bible-thumping bullshit, and stumbled back to my quarters to get some sleep. As I walked away, I heard the chaplain expostulating that God was on our side because we were Christians and that God wouldn't help the North Vietnamese because they weren't.

Looking back on it, I'm still appalled by such a simplistic response to such a troubling question.

The following morning, November 22, 1965, we got up and resumed our normal routine (as if anything would ever again be normal for us). As XO, it was my job to gather the personal effects of our KIAs and to pack them for shipment back home. A sadder duty I've never had.

As company commander, Captain Sugdinis had the unenviable job of writing personal letters to the KIAs' next of kin, and though I volunteered to help him, he took it upon himself to write every letter. Thirty-four of them, to be exact. How he managed it, I'll never know. But he did.

I managed to write home, too.

Dear Folks,
Returned yesterday, healthy, but weary. I miss you all very very much. All my love—Larry.

The Thursday after we returned from the Ia Drang was Thanksgiving, and the troops, like all the troops in Vietnam that November, were supposed to get a hot turkey dinner with all the fixings. As they lined up outside the mess tent to receive their turkey dinners, someone called them to attention, and Gen. William Westmoreland, commander of American forces in Vietnam, suddenly appeared in our midst. He climbed up on a stump near the mess tent and beckoned the troops to gather 'round.

I had just come out of Alpha's HQ tent and was standing on the other side of the dry rice paddy, about a hundred yards from the mess hall, but I could look up the hill and see what was happening, so I stopped to watch the show. I saw the general get up on his stump, motion for the men to gather around him, and I heard him make a speech. It was a nice speech, full of praise for the great job we had done, and the great victory we had won. He even went so far as to salute us. "I salute you men of the Seventh Cavalry," he said, dramatically saluting us from his stump. Then he stepped down from it and strode off briskly down the hill, followed by his entourage—the colonels, majors, and other high-grade REMFs that followed him around wherever he went—and they strode off purposefully out of sight, on their way, I assume, to dine with the 1st Battalion.

The men of the 2d Battalion who'd been waiting for their Thanksgiving dinners returned listlessly to their place in line. Unfortunately, the troops who'd already been served their "hot chow," as many of them had, now looked around for a place to sit and eat their cold and lumpy dinners. It was, as usual, a typically thoughtless way to screw up one of the few treats our troops had been looking forward to since coming back from that hellhole in the jungle west of Pleiku, and thinking about it now still makes me angry. Instead of feeling pride at the general's kind words (after all, he didn't have to come down and make that speech), I felt numb. Instead of feeling appreciated and renewed by his pep talk, I felt bitterness and rage. And after he left us, I wondered if he had any idea of what the battalion had just been through.

It turned out that General Westmoreland had no idea what had happened to us at Albany. While Colonel Moore had been able to brief him about the fight at LZ Xray, no one had told him about the debacle we had suffered at Albany. The 1st Cav brass were too embarrassed or ashamed to tell him the truth—the truth being that we'd suffered roughly seventy percent casualties in that fight. It wasn't until the week after Thanksgiving, when he was visiting the 85th Evacuation Field Hospital at Qui Nhon, that he wondered why there were so many wounded 1st Cavalry troopers there awaiting transport home. In his diary, the good general penned something to the effect that it wasn't until he returned from the hospital at Qui Nhon that he began to doubt the accuracy of what he'd been told about the battle. And that's my understanding of the way the 1st Cav brass handled the matter of our "victory" at Albany LZ. They covered it up.

For the next few weeks, then, we did what all combat-blooded units do after they've suffered heavy losses in battle. We refitted. Scores of new men freshly arrived from the States were diverted from their originally designated units and assigned to the 2d Battalion of the 7th Cavalry, which had the dubious distinction of being the unit that had fought the biggest battle of the war to date, and had suffered the worst casualties. Us and the 1st Battalion. Surprisingly, our morale was still high, though those of us who had survived that terrible fight were somewhat subdued in our exuberance and certainly in deadly earnest about training the new men for what we then knew was going to be more bloody fighting in the jungle.

There were additional personnel shifts in our company, too. Jim Kelly replaced Mantegna, who went to Charlie Company. Jack Hibbard returned from his bout with malaria and took charge of our Mortar Platoon. Bill Sisson, I recall, simply lay around all day in his tent with his knee wrapped and swollen. (He had injured it at Xray.)

It wasn't long, though, before we were conducting company-size patrols around the base camp again, and I remember hearing Captain Sugdinis on the radio, riding herd on his platoon leaders, especially Jim Kelly, to keep tighter formations, to keep up with the company, to keep better dispersion among their men. I realized how important it was to do that, but still felt bad about the tongue-lashing some of them were receiving over the radio. Slowly but surely, though, the company got whipped back into shape. The 1st Platoon grew to full strength again, with Sgt. Hale Vannoy, who'd been wounded at Xray with the 3d Platoon, taking over as Kelly's platoon sergeant, and a little pimply-faced tiger of a guy, Sp4. Tony Davida, who'd survived Albany, now acting as Kelly's RTO. (For the next six months, they made one hell of a team.) Gordy Grove stayed on as 2d Platoon leader, with Sergeant Caple, another Albany veteran, taking over as his platoon sergeant. Sergeant Eschbach was, for all intents and purposes, 3d Platoon Leader. And Jack Hibbard, as I said, was our Mortar Platoon leader. Slowly but steadily we worked our way back into fighting trim, and by the time Christmas rolled around, we were close to full strength.

Just before Christmas, we headed out on another battalion operation. We laagered one night at the base of An Khe Pass. We lifted off the next morning, made an air assault into a cold LZ southwest of the pass, and swept the area. We found very little there—no Vietnamese dared show themselves, and all the rice we found was packed into sandbags and flown back to An Khe. The only thing I remember quite clearly was that we had no trouble convincing the troops to dig foxholes.

On December 23, we got the word to return to base camp for a Christmas truce. That was nice. My flight log indicates an extraction from the field and a return to base camp on the twenty-third. It was a short-lived truce. On the twenty-sixth, we embarked on another operation.

I also remember the almost excruciatingly painful disappointment of not hearing the news—which had been rumored since the Ia Drang battles—that the 1st Cav was going to be sent home right after Christmas. I guess every unit (and every man in that unit) since the beginning of the history of warfare has suffered the ravages of the rumor mill, and though I knew they were just rumors, I still believed them. I hate to admit it, but I did. After all, we'd fought a great battle in the Ia Drang Valley, and we'd severely mauled the PAVN, so when we heard that the 1st Cav was going to be rotated home because of the great victory we'd won, I really thought there might be some truth to the rumor. Well, there wasn't, and when Christmas came and went, and we found ourselves still there—not only still there, but just ordered out on another search-and-destroy mission—I suffered a terrible letdown and probably went into a depression. I think we all did.

After our Christmas truce, my flight log indicates a

forty-minute reconnaissance flight on December 26, an air assault into LZ #3 on December 27, and an extraction on December 31, for New Year's Eve. Happy 1966!

Along with my flight log, which indicates every sortie I made during my tour, I have a stack of my letters home, which my mother gave to me before she passed away. Reading them has helped me reconstruct my year in Vietnam. At the end of a short letter to my dad dated January 4, 1966, I wrote, "Things are fine here. We're back up to strength."

Chapter 14

The Day We Shot Us Out of the Sky

That which does not kill me makes me stronger.

—NIETZSCHE

In mid-January, we received orders to conduct a search-and-destroy mission in the Happy Valley, about six kilometers northeast of the base camp. The day before the operation, Captain Sugdinis invited his platoon leaders and me to accompany him on an aerial reconnaissance of the objective. All we had to do was hop on a Huey, fly up Happy Valley, "spec out" a village for an air assault the next morning, and come home. Piece of cake. The weather was perfect, too—clear skies as far as you could see. It was hot as hell, but if you're flying, who cares?

I grabbed my helmet, rifle, map, and web gear, and hustled to the Green Line to catch our flight. As soon as I reached the perimeter, I spotted Captain Sugdinis a couple of hundred meters down the line. He was standing with Denny Wilson in the open, talking on the radio. First Sergeant Miller and the platoon leaders were clustered nearby.

You could do that on the perimeter now—stand around in a group. You didn't have to worry about a sniper taking a pot-shot at you, or a burst of machine-gun fire sending you scuttling behind a rock. The perimeter line was our turf, carefully cleared and mined and crisscrossed with barbed wire, and if any Victor Charlie was dumb enough to take a shot at us, we'd

169

have his bony little ass in a sling. We had artillery concentrations preregistered around the perimeter, and bunkers with M-60 machine guns every two or three hundred meters along the line, and during the daylight hours, I would venture to guess that our perimeter line was about as safe a place as you could find in Vietnam.

I was halfway to the captain when a 105 round *karrrumped!* into the jungle on the far side of the wire. I ducked, as usual, but kept walking. We were either registering additional defensive concentrations around the Green Line or keeping the tree line clear of Charlie.

When I joined the group, the captain was still on the horn. Denny Wilson looked exhausted, but he didn't have to go with us this trip. Jim Kelly—nicknamed "Lurch" because he stood six-foot-four-inches tall and had a broad forehead like Frankenstein's monster—and First Sergeant Miller were talking together quietly. Gordy Grove, who'd recovered from Albany, was stretched out on his back, his hands clasped behind his head, his eyes blissfully closed. Jack Hibbard, our mortarman, was staring morosely over the wire. And Sergeant Eschbach, his bleary eyes bloodshot as usual, was smoking a cigarette, and I wondered fleetingly if his canteen was really filled with vodka and orange juice, as everyone suspected, or just plain water. Still, there wasn't a better field man in the battalion.

I nodded to Lurch, who smiled, and the first sergeant, who growled a "Sir."

"Chopper's on the way," the captain said.

Gordo sat bolt upright, his eyes wide open now, his hands clutching his rifle. Sergeant Eschbach took one more drag on his cigarette and flicked it into the boulders behind us. I watched it arc high in the air, bounce off a rock, scatter sparks down its side, then land, still smoking, in the dirt.

"Where's Hank?" I asked. Hank Dunn, our FO. He usually traveled with us wherever we went, especially on a leaders' recon.

"Up there," Joel said, pointing to a lone chopper circling overhead. "Registering perimeter fire."

Author at An Khe Pass, with Highway 19 in the background, dropping eastward to Qui Nhon and the South China Sea.

Author (left) with Captain Moore of MAC-V Advisory Team 51 in Vi Thanh, August 1965.

Sergeant First Class Hunter, senior NCO, Advisory Team 51.

Staff Sergeant Jones with Ha Si #1 and Ha Si #2 (foreground) and driver.

Typical lead company advisory team—Sergeant First Class Hunter (left rear), author (right), and ARVN RTOs in their tiger-stripe helmets—just prior to a "paddy walk" in Bac Lieu Province, August 1965.

Officers of Alpha Company, 2/7, before the Ia Drang. From left: 2d Lts. Jack Hibbard, Bill Sisson, and Mike Mantegna, Capt. Joel E. Sugdinis (CO), 1st Lt. Larry Gwin (XO), and 2d Lt. David "Pat" Payne.

1st Sgt. Frank Miller, making like a tree and sporting a rare smile before an operation.

2d Lts. Gordy Grove (left) and Jim Kelly on the newly cleared Green Line.

PFC Tom Costello (left), the author's radio telephone operator (RTO), with Sp4. Dennis Wilson, at An Khe base.

Sp4. Larry Sargent, Capt. Sugdinis's RTO, in "elephant grass."

Sp4. Dennis Wilson, Alpha 2/7's RTO/clerk, in the "bush." The "squawk box" on the back of his radio enabled all those nearby to hear incoming transmissions.

Bell UH1-D "Hueys" on the Golf Course at An Khe (Camp Radcliff). (Photo courtesy of Pat Payne)

Chinook "ladder training" on the Green Line in early 1966. (Photo courtesy of Pat Payne)

2d Lt. David "Pat" Payne, platoon leader of A 2/7, on the Green Line. He later became the recon platoon leader and, after that, XO of C 2/7.

Lt. Col. Robert MacDade presenting awards to 2d Lt. William Sisson and S.Sgt. Rother A. Temple (left), who later became platoon sergeant of Alpha's 3d Platoon.

1st Lt. Donald C. Cornett, XO of C 2/7, killed at LZ Albany in the Ia Drang. He received a Silver Star (posthumously) for his heroism during the battle.

2d Lt. Hank Dunn, A 2/7's artillery forward observer (FO) during the Ia Drang campaign.

A Huey approaching LZ Xray early in the morning of November 15, 1965. Smoke from air strikes on the Chu Pong Massif indicate the LZ is under attack. (Photo courtesy of Mike Alford)

2d Lt. Gordy Grove prior to boarding a C-123 bound for Bong Son in January 1966. The next flight out was a fatal one.

Lt. Col. Robert MacDade and interpreter interrogate captured PAVN soldiers twenty minutes before the ambush at LZ Albany. Captain Sugdinis is standing in the background. (Photo courtesy of Hank Dunn)

Captain Sugdinis and author at Pleiku just after returning from the Ia Drang. (Photo courtesy of Peter Cadigan)

Maj. Frank Henry, battalion executive officer, called in tactical air support to save the battalion at LZ Albany.

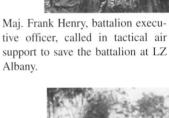

Capt. Jim Spires, battalion S-3, kept his cool during the fighting at LZ Albany.

Capt. William "Doc" Shucart, battalion surgeon, treated the wounded at the rear of the column at Albany. Late in his tour, he broke his back in a chopper crash but survived to practice neurosurgery in Boston. He was truly loved by the men of the battalion.

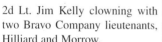

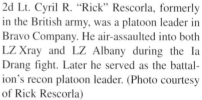

2d Lt. Jim Kelly clowning with two Bravo Company lieutenants, Hilliard and Morrow.

2d Lt. Cyril R. "Rick" Rescorla, formerly in the British army, was a platoon leader in Bravo Company. He air-assaulted into both LZ Xray and LZ Albany during the Ia Drang fight. Later he served as the battalion's recon platoon leader. (Photo courtesy of Rick Rescorla)

Capt. John "Skip" Fesmire (left), CO of C, 2/7, with his then XO, Pat Payne, after the Ia Drang battles. (Photo courtesy of Pat Payne)

Captain Cherry exhorting the troops after commandeering several cases of Grade A, Prime frozen beefsteaks for the company. Sp4. Willi Green (facing the camera) is charbroiling them with help from Sergeant Kimura.

SFC Winston "Cabbie" Carbonneau slicing the steaks with help from PFC Dave Robbins.

Inside the 2/7 officers club, constructed by the battalion's lieutenants, with Jack Hibbard facing the camera. (Photo courtesy of Pat Payne)

Sgt. Jim Hibbitts's mortar squad. From left, back row: Specialists Fourth Class Montgomery and Donnie Allred (wounded at LZ Xray) and Sergeant Hibbitts. Front row: Privates First Class Prigin, Gosha, and Formosa. (Photo courtesy of Dale Nelson)

Capt. Daniel Davison, CO of A 2/7, took the company into Bong Son for the fight at Thanh Son 2. He later contracted typhus but recovered to resume command.

Jack Hibbard, XO of B 2/7, at Thanh Son 2 with PAVN dead splayed in the foreground. (Photo courtesy of Jack Hibbard)

2d Lt. Marty Hammer, leader of A 2/7's 2d Platoon when he was wounded three times at Thanh Son 2 but continued the assault against an entrenched NVA battalion. He received the Distinguished Service Cross, personally awarded by President Johnson, for his actions that day. (Photo courtesy of Marty Hammer)

Three lieutenants. From left: 1st Lt. George Polli, mortar platoon leader, grew into his job; 2d Lt. Dick Hogarth, killed in action at Thanh Son 2; and 2d Lt. Bruce Morrison, A 2/7's artillery FO for several hot months in 1966. (Photo courtesy of Marty Hammer)

Battalion color guard passes in review during an awards ceremony. Rick Rescorla and Joel Sugdinis are in the front row nearest the camera. (Photo courtesy of Mike Alford)

As if to prove the point, another 105 round *karrrumped!* into the far tree line, a hundred yards away. I ducked again, involuntarily. We all did. I looked up, past the wire, and saw a thin gray wisp of smoke drifting lazily from the jungle.

I glanced at Lurch. He was fine. So was the first sergeant. It's funny how you got used to it—the artillery rounds crashing around you. If you'd been in country a while, you didn't think about it much. Only the new guys were embarrassed when they flinched. After a while, they got used to it, too. Sometimes, though, when a round went off nearby, you might glance at a friend, and you'd both know, deep inside, that it was getting a little too close, and you'd shake your head, or crack a joke, or say something stupid, just to let the fear out. But you never said anything about it—the fear, that is—especially to a new guy. They were edgy enough as it was, and they'd get used to it without your saying anything. They'd get used to it all, sooner or later—the headaches, the dry mouth, the shakes at night, the wondering when your turn was coming that you stifled every minute of every day, just so you could handle another mission.

"You'd think they could wait for us to get off the goddamn perimeter," Jack Hibbard said. He wasn't smiling, either.

Suddenly a lone Huey came thundering around the hill crest to our right, heading in our direction, about a hundred feet off the ground.

"That's ours," the captain said.

"Taxi!" Gordy shouted as he scrambled to his feet. Good old Gordo. Always groping for a laugh. God knows, we needed one.

As the Huey roared in and flared its nose for a landing, Joel started jogging toward the ship. I turned, flashed a thumbs-up at the first sergeant, and followed.

The Huey landed heading due north, back up the line from where I'd come. The pilot and copilot were talking to each other. The crew chief was sitting in his jump seat behind the cargo bay, his face deadpan, his door gun pointing downward into the dust.

We scrambled aboard and settled in on the Huey's studded

floor—Gordo, Joel, and Eschbach up front, with their backs to the cockpit; Hibbard, me, and Lurch in back, facing forward. We'd boarded choppers hundreds of times, or what seemed like hundreds of times, and this was just a reconnaissance flight, so we were wisecracking and joking with each other, not worried about much of anything. As the chopper's turbine picked up torque, and the bird began to rise, I glanced out the open bay. Denny Wilson and the first sergeant were already striding back to battalion. Another day, another dollar.

I turned back and glanced at my compatriots, feeling the cool air whoosh through the bay as the chopper lifted off and gathered speed. I always liked liftoffs, rising from the ground in a great whirling roar, the chopper's engine throbbing with the strain. As we rose above the treetops, I looked out the door again, at our base camp falling away beneath us, and beyond it, the division's giant helipad, the Golf Course. A dozen Chinooks—big cargo ships—were nestled in the grass like sleeping hippos. Two long rows of unmanned Hueys sat waiting for the word to crank up. And farther away, on the repair line, a gaggle of sweaty mechanics labored over a row of busted aircraft, patching them up so they could fly us into battle once again.

We gained altitude slowly, heading north to clear the wire and pick up speed. I don't know how far we'd gone, or how high we'd climbed, when the ship made a gentle 180-degree turn to the right, a "lazy 180," and headed back along the wire from where we'd come. As we roared past the road from the perimeter back to battalion, I could see Wilson and the first sergeant far below us. They stopped for a moment and waved.

Kabooom!

Something bounced us high in the air. The chopper veered wildly to the right, then back to the left, and we began shaking and shimmering and losing altitude fast, and right away I knew something awful had happened. The ship was careening so crazily I had to grab hold of the cargo-bay pole in back of Lurch. He'd grabbed it, too.

The ship began to buck like a machine gone awry, and we were dropping even faster. The turbine seemed to be screaming in agony, not at all the way it normally sounded, and I suddenly realized we were going to crash.

I looked at Joel. His eyes were wide with shock and disbelief. Everyone was wild-eyed, frozen in their seats, but nobody said a word. God knows what was going on in their minds, because I don't remember anything that was going on in mine, except a kaleidoscope of confusion and fear, and a sudden rush of sadness that *this* was the way it was going to end for us after everything we'd been through. I still couldn't believe how badly the chopper was careening in the sky, its turbines shrieking and the ground racing up at us. There was no way in hell we were going to walk away from this one. We were goners.

Joel swiveled around toward the cockpit. I could see the pilot struggling with the controls. His back and neck were rigid. The ship began to rattle and shake and groan so hard I was sure it was going to break up in the air, and the ground was coming up fast. I could see the rolls of triple concertina wire, and the barbed-wire stakes, and the same rocky outcrop where Sergeant Eschbach had flicked his cigarette. We were dropping fast. Much too fast.

Joel turned back to us. "Lock arms!" he screamed. "We're going down!"

We tried, but the chopper kept bucking and shaking, with its turbine screeching, and the mainframe groaning as if it were being ripped apart, and Gordo started screaming something I couldn't understand, and I started praying we wouldn't explode on impact, and the ground was rushing up at us so fast you just had to grit your teeth and hold on tight. And then we hit, and the nose dipped, hurling Lurch and me into Joel. And then we were all trying desperately to untangle ourselves from each other, and clawing our way out of the ship before it blew, and scrambling out the door as fast as we could, yelling *"Go! Go! Go!"* and *"Move! Move! Move!"* and I was out and sprinting as fast as I could to get as far away from it as I could before it blew, and everyone was yelling "Move out!" or "Jesus Christ!" or "Son of a bitch!", but now that I think about it, I doubt if anyone was yelling anything understandable because we all had the same simple thought on our minds, and that was to get the hell away from that ship before it exploded so we wouldn't be broiled alive or end up with a back full of burning shrapnel, and then, all of a sudden, through the gagging dry-mouthed fear, the mind-numbing terror, and the chaos of it all, I suddenly knew I was safe, that the chopper wouldn't blow, and that even if it did, everyone had gotten off okay, and was out of danger. So I stopped, leaned over, and with my hands on my knees, started gasping for air. Then I looked back and saw the pilot and copilot, casual as could be, getting slowly out of the ship, calmly shaking their heads, and the crew chief, his face still deadpan, checking out the cargo bay as if nothing had happened.

The Huey was a shambles. It looked like a dragonfly with a broken leg and a busted wing. Both landing struts had crumpled on impact, and the main rotor blade was listing at its side. The Plexiglas windshield was shattered, too. What a mess!

My heart was still pounding, but I was beginning to catch my breath. Everyone around me started chattering like a bunch of wild monkeys, talking and swearing, hooting and hollering, shaking each other's hand and asking what had happened. I looked up, and there was the first sergeant, bless his soul, bounding down the slope like a giant gazelle, heading right toward us, with poor Denny Wilson close behind him, loping along as fast as he could with the radio on his back, its antenna jiggling crazily over his head.

Then I heard the captain asking if everybody was okay.

Miraculously, we were—all of us—just a little scared—scared shitless, actually—and wondering what had happened.

"Jesus, sir," the first sergeant said, shaking his head in disbelief. He was puffing like an asthmatic rhinoceros. "I'll be a son of a bitch if a 105 round didn't go off right underneath you. You looked like a Ping-Pong ball on a gusher. I thought for sure you'd bought it!"

"A 105 round!" Jack Hibbard said, incredulous. "What the goddamn fucking hell is the goddamn fucking artillery registering fire for while we're taking off from the goddamn fucking perimeter?"

Good question. And our own FO was the man calling the shots.

"They figured we'd cleared the zone," Sergeant Eschbach said. He had a wry, almost sheepish grin on his face when he said it. Then he shook his head and spit a huge wad of tobacco juice on the ground. Where he'd found the chaw, I couldn't say—maybe where he got his vodka—but if anyone could figure out what had happened, Sergeant Eschbach was the man. "We did a 180-degree turn, didn't we?"

He was right. We'd done just that. We'd taken off, flown half a mile, done a big U-turn, and headed right back over the spot we'd just left. And our own FO, a man we knew and respected, had called for another round. Once the artillery had fired it, they couldn't call it back.

I looked at the crumpled chopper. The concussion of the artillery round had broken its rotor blade, or bent the shaft, or screwed up the turbine, or something, and we hadn't gained enough altitude to autorotate to the ground. Without the pilot holding on to the controls the way he had, we would have flipped over, crashed, and burned.

I was suddenly conscious of the captain again. He was walking toward us. His face was pale, his eyes grim. He'd gone back to the chopper and talked briefly to the pilot, and after he'd learned what had happened, he didn't want to think about it anymore. He did have something to say, though.

"Another Huey's on the way," he said, looking each of us in the eye. "It'll be here in ten minutes."

That's what he said. I remember it clear as day.

I remember something else about that day, too—my hands starting to shake as I tried to light a cigarette. They shook for the next six months, and deep inside, I'm still shaking.

Chapter 15

―――――

Signs of Strain

The most extreme experience a human being can go through is being a combat infantryman.
　　　　　　　　　—STEVEN E. AMBROSE,
　　　　　　　　　D Day: June 6, 1944

The next day, Joel cracked. I don't use the term lightly, but it's true, and I'd venture to say that everyone who saw him out there would agree with me.

Except for the extreme heat, the mission after our chopper crash was an easy one-day affair, a simple search-and-destroy operation within artillery range of the base camp. We flew out, landed on a cold LZ, walked a while, found an abandoned village, and called battalion. They told us to torch it. We burned all the hootches and headed back.

It was terribly hot and no one had enjoyed leveling the village, but no bad guys had been there, and nothing of any significance had happened—nothing to indicate any threat to us, anyway. But just before the helicopters arrived to take us home, Joel started acting strange.

Our extraction was to be in two waves. As usual, Joel would go with the first flight, and I would close in behind. Suddenly, he changed his mind. He wanted me to fly out first. For some reason, he was sure that a large enemy force was getting close. He started fidgeting. Then his face flushed, and his eyes began to dart around wildly.

At first, I thought he was dehydrated, maybe suffering from heat exhaustion. It was, after all, very hot, and we hadn't had much water that day. But it was worse than that. Jim Kelly, our 1st Platoon leader, was there, and the headquarters group, and we all knew that something was wrong with the captain. We urged him to sit down and relax, but he ignored us. He was sure we were about to be attacked. Then he started to babble.

"You go out first, Larry. I'll bring the men back. You gotta get out of here. They're coming. I know it. They're getting close."

I tried to calm him down, but he wasn't listening. To him, the enemy was closing in. I asked a medic to check him out, but Joel would have nothing to do with that. He started whimpering, almost blubbering, about how I should take the first flight out. He'd bring the rest in behind me.

"You get out of here, Larry, take the first wave in. I'll get the rest out. I'll take care of them. I'll get them out . . ."

He was waving his hands in the air, even staggered a bit, and then he started to whine. The desperation in his eyes was almost frightening.

Jim Kelly looked at me, clearly concerned.

"Okay, I'll go," I said to Joel, knowing Jim would bring the Old Man in. "Keep an eye on him," I said to Jim, as the first wave of choppers arrived.

Jim nodded, and I ran for the ships.

Twenty minutes later, the rest of the company closed in behind us without incident. When I saw Joel again, striding off the perimeter where he'd landed, his composure had returned. He seemed jovial, almost happy. When I asked him how he was feeling, he acted as if nothing untoward had happened.

But it had, and it had scared the shit out of me. The men were as much my responsibility as his, and if he lost it during a firefight, we'd all be in a pickle.

I didn't know what to do, but I had to do something. Reporting the incident to MacDade was out of the question. First, I respected Joel too much for that—certainly more than MacDade—and second, it would have been an unforgivable breach of loyalty, like stabbing him in the back after all he'd done for us. But I had to do something. His mental balance seemed to be dangling by a thread.

I went to Doc Shucart, the battalion surgeon. He knew us both well, had been with us at Albany, and I respected his judgment. I told him what I'd seen that day, gushed out my

concern, and asked him if there was something he could do.
He didn't think there was, but assured me that he'd keep an
eye on Joel and that he'd do whatever he could. I left the doc's
tent somewhat relieved, and that was the end of the matter.

Several nights later, Alpha Company was the battalion's
reaction force. We'd been on alert before, and nothing usually
came of it, so I'd spent the evening at the officers club writing
letters and BS-ing with my fellow lieutenants and then had
retired early. The night was calm, and I dozed off quickly.

Around midnight, Captain Sugdinis woke me out of a deep
sleep.

"Get up, Larry," he said. "Get up. We've got a mission."
There was urgency in his voice.

I slowly roused myself, and sat up, rubbing my face.

"We're going out tonight, in an hour, on a company air assault five klicks northwest of here."

Oh, shit, not again, I thought.

"Division thinks a PAVN division is heading for the base
camp, and we're going out to set up a trip-wire defensive
line."

Holy Mother of God, I thought. A division?

"I'm giving a briefing in fifteen minutes. Are you up?"

"I'm up," I said, reaching for my boots. "What kind of lift?"

"A full company assault. The ships are coming in at 0100
hours. We'll fly out, set up, stay the night, and walk back in at
dawn."

"The troops up?"

"Affirmative. The first sergeant is passing out ammo."

"Jesus," I said. "A PAVN division?"

"That's what they think. We're going to be the trip wire."

"Right," I said, swallowing my fear. "I'll see you in fifteen
minutes."

The Old Man left the tent, leaving me sweating and shaking
as I dressed. What if they *were* really coming? We wouldn't
stand a chance. We wouldn't last fifteen minutes before they
walked right over us. Christ! What the hell could we do?

I pulled on my fatigues, laced up my boots, grabbed my

weapon and gear, and reported to the Old Man's tent (he had his own by then), as alert as I'd been all month and scared as hell. It could be a massacre. It could make Albany look like a picnic. I was already beginning to shake.

Everyone was grim as they entered the Old Man's tent, and we listened intently as he issued his op order.

We were going in with only three platoons. The mortars would stay back and provide us cover from the base camp. Order of assault was 1st, 2d, and 3d platoons. The captain would be on the first lift and direct the platoons into position after we landed. I was to close up on him from the last ship. We'd set up trip flares and claymores—no digging, absolute silence—find some cover, and wait.

"If they come," he said, "we hit them with a mad minute. A green flare will signal cease fire. Then we'll fall back a hundred meters, keeping on line as best we can. When you've reached that hundred meters, simply turn around and wait again. We'll do that again and again until we have our backs to the base camp wire if we have to. Any questions?"

"What about artillery?" Kelly asked.

"Hank will be with me," the captain replied. "He's got registrations already marked. There's a lot of help inside the perimeter. ARA is there, too, if we need them."

"Any special gear?" Gordo asked.

"Yes. Each platoon will bring extra claymores. Six. First and 3d platoons will take the starlight scopes. Designate a good man to carry them," he said, glancing at Kelly and Eschbach. "Anything else?"

No one moved.

"Okay, that's it. Meet me on the Green Line in twenty minutes. I'll be on the access road. Good luck."

And with that, we were on our way.

All I had to do was check with the first sergeant to find out how many men were in each platoon, assign them to their lift ships, and go. I would do that when they reported to the Green Line. But I was having trouble functioning. My gear had never weighed so much. It was just a matter of getting up to the Green Line and waiting for the ships. I knew that, but I was still having trouble moving.

The first sergeant had already finished passing out the ammo by the time I got to the Conexes. He'd cleaned out our claymore allotment and all the grenades and trip flares.

"They're all distributed, sir," he said, calmly. "We're all set."

"Got a headcount?"

"Yes, sir. Twenty-eight in 1st Platoon. Thirty-five in 2d. Thirty-two in 3d. Plus ten in Headquarters."

One hundred five men in all, heading out into the pitch black night to fend off a PAVN Division. I was trying not to think about it, waiting alone out there, eyes and ears keyed to the night, praying I wouldn't see the ghostly forms of PAVN regulars moving silently toward the base camp.

"Right, Top. One hundred five in all. Thanks. See you up there."

There wasn't anything else to say. We'd load up and go where they sent us, we'd do the best we could. But Jesus Christ, what did they think 105 men could do to stop a division! It was suicide. That's what it was. We were expendable, just like a trip wire.

Somehow, I made it to the Green Line and told the platoon sergeants what ships to board. It was all SOP, nothing new but for the darkness. We'd never gone in at night before.

Waiting in the cold night air, I was having trouble staying calm. The Old Man had lost it, had had a breakdown, just two days before, and if he lost it again, we'd be in deep shit. But he seemed to be holding up fine, greeting the men of each platoon as they came up on line, encouraging the platoon leaders with last-minute instructions, and being seen clearly in control. Thank God he was, because I was getting the shakes. I tried to light a cigarette, but my hand was shaking so bad that I couldn't hold the Zippo steady. Somehow, I got one lit, and was finishing it as the drone of revving Hueys began to rumble from the Golf Course.

Minutes later, in they came—eighteen ships this time. Six men to a ship. They came in in platoon Vs and waited for us to board, their rotors whirling as we double-timed to our assigned birds. I was on the lead ship of the last V, hopped aboard, and started praying. Make it a quiet LZ. Make it a quiet LZ.

We flew directly to our destination. No farting around, no false drops, no artillery prep, no nothing. We were supposed to get in fast, set up, and wait. As my ship flared its nose for the landing, the first sergeant, Costello, Gosey (my new RTO), and two men from the 3d Platoon exited into the dark whirling night, into some waist-high grass, and waited on one knee while the entire flight lifted off and disappeared into the dark on its way back to the Golf Course.

When the choppers had cleared the LZ and the drone of their engines had faded, I was struck by the sudden silence, and the darkness, and the fact that I could see the eerie forms of our troops moving quietly into position. I moved along the direction of our flight until I could make out Joel's form, marked by his RTOs and Hank Dunn's RTO. Joel was single-handedly guiding the platoons into position.

"That's it," I whispered to him, indicating that the company was all closed up.

"Good," he said. "Our line runs from there—" he pointed, and I could actually see a sort of light grassy line forming our line of defense, "to there"—he pointed to a clump of trees behind us and to the right. "I'm setting up with the 2d Platoon," he said. "Find a place with the first sergeant and settle in with the 3d Herd." I think Joel was smiling as he said this. I'm not sure. But he was calm and confident—fully in control.

"Right," I whispered. "We'll be over there." I had seen a fallen log behind us, and was pointing to it, checking behind me to try to see the base camp. Though I couldn't make out anything, I knew it was there and where it was. After I joined the first sergeant, we found a place behind the log. Costello and Gosey shared a spot ten meters to our right. There was someone on our left, too, but I didn't know who it was. After a few moments of staring into the darkness and determining the most likely line of approach just in front of us, I turned to the first sergeant and told him I'd place the claymore I was carrying to our front.

"Right, sir," he whispered.

Now laying out a claymore is no big thing, but with the prospect of a PAVN division coming out of the jungle to our front, I wanted to maximize its efficiency. The claymore, I mean. As I headed out through the high grass into the darkness, I could see the silent forms of men on my right and left, about twenty yards on either side, working in the night. They were doing the same thing I was, setting up their first line of defense, a line of trip flares and claymores that would pinpoint and then decimate whoever triggered them. I found a place that would provide a maximum killing zone, then set up the claymore, attaching its detonator and slowly moving back to my position, stringing out the detonating wire bit by bit. Back behind the log, I attached it to the triggering mechanism, pointed it out to the first sergeant, and settled in.

All this time we hadn't said a word to each other, except in whispers, and we kept silent for the next six hours, waiting stoically behind our fallen-log cover, trying not to move, trying to stay awake, and praying that nothing would come. But if you've never sat alone at night, staring through the waist-high grass to your front at the outline of a dark tree line ahead of you, a tree line that might be hiding the approach of six thousand hard-core PAVN regulars, you'll never know how you start imagining things, and they don't let you relax. I sat there, leaning forward against the log, listening and waiting and listening some more.

Night sounds in the highlands are unique. Crickets, cicadas, geckos, all forms of tree frogs, and the steady, incessant, never-changing drone of a million buzzing insects can lull you into somnambulance, can numb your sense of hearing and smell and sight until you start seeing things in the night. I sat there, occasionally looking over at the first sergeant, nodding at him, seeing the whites of his eyes, and knowing that there was not a man in the company I felt more secure with than good old 1st Sgt. Frank Miller, U.S. Army, a strong, tough, quiet man who cared about his troops, but took no guff. And at Albany, I'd seen him cool as a cucumber, doing just what was necessary to survive. We'd been literally back-to-back at Albany, had flown into a score of different LZs together, hot and cold, and had spent the last three months in the field, sharing our food and our jokes and our fear. The first sergeant sat there like a stone, his eyes scanning the far tree line, where the bad guys would come from, ready to do his job, ready to die with his company, all for the glory of the Cav.

We sat and stared and listened and waited and thought. What if they come? What if they come from another direction? What if they come up behind us? You can't worry about that. You just gotta react to what happens. You just gotta stay awake. Keep your eyes open, and your mouth shut, and your ears attuned to any change in the night sounds. The longer we stayed there, the better our night vision, and I could almost convince myself that I could see the far tree line, could see if any figures came out of it, or came toward us, or walked by. And we sat alone, in the dark night, waiting.

I think I dozed off. The first sergeant did once, too. I could hear the beginning of a snore and shook his shoulder. He nodded in response and rubbed his face. But when I dozed off, he let me sleep. At least I think he did. Maybe he was sleeping, too.

Whatever, I think I dozed off. And when I woke up, staring into the night, it seemed to be clearing in the east, to our right rear, the sky lightening, and my fear with it. As the dawn came, I could see our long line of troopers, quietly waiting in the grass.

"Net call, net call, this is Braveboy Six." I heard Joel's voice on the radio. When the platoon leaders had responded in turn, he told us it was over. We could move. And after picking up our claymores, we could proceed back to the base camp, order of movement the same as we came in. And I began to breathe normally again.

Thus ended that long scary night, a night of truth and fear and waiting for Death to come. It's faded now, but I remember it still, how expendable we were, and how lucky. I often wonder what would have happened if division had been right. How many of us would have made it back to the base camp?

Not many.

Chapter 16

The Crash

*Let us cross over the river, and
rest under the shade of the trees.*
—THOMAS "STONEWALL"
JACKSON (*last words*)

Late in January, we found ourselves preparing for another operation, grandly code-named Masher before President Johnson ordered it to be renamed White Wing for public relations reasons. It was going to be the biggest operation we'd undertaken to date, and the battalion was abuzz with anticipation. For some of us, the tension was palpable.

We'd be going to a place called Bong Son, northeast of An Khe, in Binh Dinh Province, and we'd be working not only with the U.S. Marines, who would be coming down from the north, but also with the Korean Tiger Division that had recently assumed tactical responsibility for the lowlands east of An Khe Pass.

What I remember about that week was the number of strap hangers who suddenly materialized around our base camp. Reporters, for one, were familiarizing themselves with our people, mostly the brass, and it was strange and exciting to have nationally renowned journalists like Bob Poos and Henri Huet hanging out with us at the O-club. We'd made a name for ourselves, I guess, primarily because of the fighting west of Pleiku, and the reporters could smell another story coming. The second group of visitors were teams of officers from the Korean Tiger Division designated to work with and observe each line unit down to company level. Alpha Company had a cadre of five Koreans who were going to travel with us, and they arrived a few days before we departed to get accustomed to our ways, and faces. I must have been partially responsible for making them feel comfortable, but all I can really remember about them now was their smell. Kimchi. They ate kimchi, a kind of fermented cabbage, and it stunk worse than any food I had smelled before. Whenever the Koreans came to visit us, either in our HQ tent or our company area, we could literally smell them coming.

On January 24, 1966, we learned that we'd be trucked the next morning to the An Khe airstrip, where I'd landed back in September, then shuttled up to Bong Son by air force C-123s. From Bong Son, we would chopper into the bush and look for Charlie.

The next morning was hot and dry, and I remember watching as the men of our company boarded the three C-123s assigned to ferry us up to Bong Son. I said good-bye to Joel as he headed out on the first ship with Jim Kelly and the 1st Platoon, and I took a picture of Gordy Grove just before he led his 2d Platoon onto the second aircraft.

Shortly after the third ship took off, we heard that it had crashed. I didn't hear any explosion, but somehow the word spread that it had gone down. We may have been able to see black smoke rising from behind the mountains north of An Khe, but I'm not sure. I do remember a sense of disbelief as I was summoned to battalion HQ—just a jeep with a long-range radio on it by the airstrip—and told by Captain Johnson, our adjutant, that the plane that had gone down was the third C-123 that had been carrying our people, that it had, indeed, crashed and burned on the far side of the mountain, and that repeated explosions from the mortar rounds on board were making it impossible for rescuers to approach the aircraft.

I can't describe how I felt when I heard that horrible news. I knew who'd been on that plane—our entire 3d Platoon and a squad from our Mortar Platoon—but I couldn't believe they were all suddenly gone, dead, crashed into a mountain and obliterated. The bottom seemed to drop out.

"Captain Sugdinis is on the line for you," the adjutant said, handing me the handset of the long-range radio on the jeep.

"This is Braveboy Five. Over," I said.

Joel's voice was distant, but clear. He was at Bong Son. He confirmed that the plane with our 3d Platoon had gone down. Then he proceeded to tell me what we were going to do about it. He said that the rest of the Mortar Platoon was to continue to Bong Son without the mortar tube or any related gear or ammunition. He'd organize them into a provisional rifle platoon when they arrived. Second, he instructed me to stay behind and attend to the airplane crash, to identify the bodies and pack up the personal effects of the men who'd gone down.

"After you've done that," Joel said, "take your R & R and rejoin us in the field."

I rogered his instructions, wished him luck, and signed off.

The rest of our mortar people took off on the next lift, leaving their tube, base plate, tripod, and ammo on the airstrip. Tom Costello and I arranged for the gear's transportation back to base camp and returned there to await further instructions. I learned that the crash site was still unapproachable due to secondary explosions of the mortar ammunition on board, but that we would get a jeep the following morning to drive to An Khe Pass and visit the site (which was being secured by another battalion of the Cav).

It was early the next morning when three of us from Alpha Company drove down Highway 19 to the An Khe Pass, continued beyond the crest to where an MP was stationed, parked the jeep on the side of the road, and proceeded along a freshly beaten path to the crash site. Costello and a PFC named Doc Dockery, an old-timer of twenty-two who knew most of the 3d Platoon, were with me. When we emerged from the shadows, we saw the wreckage.

The C-123 had suddenly lost power after takeoff, hit the crest of a ridge, cartwheeled down the far slope, and exploded. The tumbling aircraft had cut a huge swath down the mountainside, narrow at its peak, wide at its base. Fire had turned the jungle brown. Bits of aluminum and chunks of twisted steel littered the ground like confetti. The only recognizable vestiges of the aircraft were its wheel housings. The tires hadn't burned. One rested halfway up the slope. The other was wedged between two tree trunks, sheared off waist-high, as if some giant hand had snapped them like match-sticks. Men from the graves registration unit, the oft-maligned GRU, poked listlessly through the wreckage. Though steeled for scenes of carnage, we were spared them. Just an empty helmet lying upside down in the brush.

"We've pretty much cleaned up everything, sir," said the sergeant from the GRU. "The remains are back at An Khe for ID. There wasn't much left."

That his task had been horrendous was clear.

"They never knew what hit 'em, sir," he said.

GRU called the next day. They needed someone to identify the bodies. Tom, Doc, and I drove over there after dark.

Their compound consisted of two tents, one big, one small. A lopsided sign stenciled 7TH GRU dangled above the small tent's entrance. A silver-gray, square-bodied truck was parked nearby. Its refrigeration unit hummed above its cab. "Reefer trucks," we called them. They kept the corpses cool.

We parked. A grizzled old sergeant emerged from the tent. He'd been waiting.

"We've been working two days straight on this one, sir," he said, pointing us in the direction of the big tent. "The ones we've pieced together are in there."

"Let's get this over with," I said.

The sergeant led us into the larger tent, holding its front flap open for us as we entered. Eight stretchers on waist-high supports filled the interior. Two Coleman lanterns hissed from the tent's center pole. They cast an eerie glow on the scene. Dark rubber body bags were laid out on each stretcher. Some of them looked empty.

"You set for this?" the sergeant asked, dropping the tent flap behind him. We nodded. He shuffled to the nearest stretcher. "We've had to do some reconstruction work, you'll see, so I'll just expose the heads."

The lanterns sputtered. The light dimmed. The reefer truck hummed outside. I smelled the stench of death.

"If you'll just stand right here," the sergeant said, lining us up alongside the first stretcher. Gently, almost reverently, his grimy fingers worked the body bag's zipper, tugging at it, then drawing it slowly downward to expose a head.

Sergeant Kim, I think.

He rested in the cowl of his body bag, his swarthy forehead crowned with a jet-black crew cut. His ears, neck, and shoulders were intact, but his face was gone. Just a black gaping maw staring upward.

"That's Sergeant Kim, I think," Doc said, tentatively, as if by identifying the obscenity before us he would seal Kim's fate.

"I think you're right," I heard myself say. Costello concurred with a nod.

A deep, sick, empty rage welled up in me as the GRU man shepherded us to the next stretcher. What wonders of his handiwork would we be subjected to next? This bag was basically empty. Again, the expert fingers plied the zipper. Paralyzed, I couldn't look away.

The GRU man spread the bag around a pasty white face, almost unblemished, round and flat, like a pie, its eyes shut, its lips gray, its dirty blond hair matted against its forehead. I didn't know this one at all. A total stranger.

"All the bones in this man's face have been broken," the sergeant said. His hands cupped the round face. His grimy fingers probed the cheekbones, pushing them gently together. The face narrowed slightly.

"Oh, my God," Tom whispered. "It's Sergeant Boren."

And it was.

None of the others we looked at were recognizable.

We'd lost another forty-two of our men—the entire 3d Platoon, Sergeant Eschbach among them, and their new lieutenant, who'd replaced the injured Willy Z. He'd been with us less than two weeks. The crash was more than tragic, though. It was horribly ironic. The 3d Platoon had been airlifted out of Xray with Colonel Moore's battalion and had missed the ambush at Albany. Now it had been wiped out by the plane crash.

The proud rifle company that Joel and I had taken responsibility for three months ago had been ravaged. Three of our four platoons and a third of the Mortar Platoon had been killed in combat or perished in the plane crash. I, for one, was devastated.

Somehow, though, we carried on.

Chapter 17

The Long Walk

The rifleman fights without promise of either reward or relief. Behind every river there's another hill—and behind that hill, another river. After weeks or months in the line only a wound can offer him the comfort of safety, shelter, and a bed. Those who are left to fight, fight on, evading death but knowing that with each day of evasion they have exhausted one more chance for survival. Sooner or later, unless victory comes, this chase must end on the litter or in the grave.

—GENERAL OMAR N. BRADLEY

After attending to the personal effects of the men who'd died in the plane crash, I was ready for a break, and it came in the form of a five-day R & R (rest and recuperation) in Hong Kong, where, during my stay at the President Hotel, I spent $596.95. That's what my hotel bill read. God knows what else I spent stumbling around the crowded streets and dingy alleys of Kowloon trying to forget the prior week. Long story short, I got back to An Khe on February 4, 1966, the day I turned twenty-four.

The next morning, I flew up to LZ Dog, where Alpha Company was licking its wounds after another two-day fight at LZ 4. We had lost seven more men killed in action on January 29 and 30, mostly from Gordy Grove's platoon, but I was relieved to hear that Captain Sugdinis had done a superb job holding things together. Alpha Company had been trying to help Charlie Company extricate itself from an untenable situation, and the fighting had been intense. Though we'd suffered more casualties, the spirits of the troops were extremely high, and the men I'd welcomed to Alpha Company the previous week, the men who'd been diverted from the 82d's 3d Brigade to make up for the losses we'd suffered in the plane crash, seemed proud that they'd already been in their first firefight and survived.

What I remember clearly about returning to the company was how happy I was to be back with friends, to be back in the fold, to be back with the best group of men I'd ever been with.

And I was just in time for another operation. We were heading out the next day to a place called the Crow's Foot.

Alpha Company had been given the dubious honor of being the blocking force in the operation—a brigade-size air assault into the Crow's Foot, southwest of Bong Son, an area previously untouched by ARVN and rumored to be a hotbed of Viet Cong activity. Joel had inherited the Recon Platoon, commanded now by 2d Lt. Cyril B. "Rick" Rescorla, formerly of Bravo Company, who had already distinguished himself in two fights—one in the Happy Valley and the other at Xray—and had flown in with Myron Diduryk to save us at Albany. Rick had replaced Pat Payne, who'd been promoted to the XO's slot in Charlie Company. With the Recon Platoon attached, Alpha Company was almost up to snuff, manpowerwise.

Our mission in the coming operation was to set up a company-size ambush along one of the escape routes from the Crow's Foot, a valley with talonlike exits through the mountains to the west. We would be going in alone, under strict radio silence, and would be on our own for three days, at least. No big deal, unless we ran into a nest of PAVN. The prospect of another Ia Drang fiasco weighed heavily on my mind that night, as it must have for most of the old-timers, but I did manage to get a few hours of zzzs and recover from my drunken nights in Hong Kong. By dawn the next day, I was ready.

We boarded the ships around noon, fully loaded for bear, with three days of C rations dangling from our harnesses. Everyone had been briefed. We'd be dropped off on a high mountain plateau, five klicks and two ridgelines from our ambush site, with orders to cover the remaining distance in the remaining hours of daylight, and to set up an ambush before the oncoming assault the following morning. There would be no radio transmissions back to battalion unless absolutely necessary, no air cover, no other assistance of any kind, no nothing. It was going to be very lonely out there in the boondocks, behind enemy lines, behind a supposed VC headquarters and whatever other PAVN units might be in the Crow's Foot, but that was our job, and we wanted to kill more PAVN, so off we went.

It was a beautiful afternoon, a bit hot, but we were used to that, and the initial part of our flight was peaceful and at a high altitude, so we didn't have to worry about enemy rounds coming up through the floor of our choppers. The flight was quite long, though, and we'd started off without map coverage of our flight path, so when it came time to land, neither Joel, in the lead ship, nor I, eighteen birds behind him, had any idea whether the helicopters had dropped us in the right place. I didn't like that aspect of the operation at all, but sometimes you have to trust to luck, and the competence of the other members of your team, so I didn't let myself worry about it until we were well on our way. I did think about it, however, when our flight began to wind through the valleys and around the ridgelines, and actually descended toward a razor-backed ridge and then veered away. As we approached the ridge, I could see American troops in soft hats and olive drab uniforms waving us off, or waving to us, perhaps, but the flight path of the chopper formation was so confusing that even if I'd had a map of the area, I wouldn't have been able to follow our progress. Not from the air in a careening ship.

I didn't call Joel because of the radio silence directive, but I received a transmission from him. Costello tapped me on the shoulder and handed the handset to me.

"Braveboy Five," I answered.

"This is Six. A few false landings for deception," he said, explaining vaguely why we were careening through the maze of peaks and valleys in that foreboding mountain range.

"Roger," I acknowledged, but the strain in Joel's voice unnerved me. So much for comforting clarifications.

After flying around some more, we ended up heading in for another landing, and this time the crew chief let us know by hand-and-arm signals that we were to disembark on this pass, so we did. I jumped off the ship and hit the ground running, surprised by the height of the tall grass (about five feet), but eager to get the hell off the ridgeline, exposed as it was to possible grazing fire. When I reached the tree line on the north slope of the ridge, I stopped to catch my breath and count noses. We were all there.

The company had gone in with four platoons, the 1st, with Jim Kelly in command, the 2d, with Gordy Grove, the provisional 3d Platoon, with a brand-spanking-new second lieutenant named Hogarth who'd just joined us, and Rescorla's bunch, the best forty men in the battalion, well disciplined, well drilled, and wary, I'm sure, of being attached to a regular line company. But Rescorla would do a good job, and he, in turn, must have known that Joel and I were two of the best (most experienced, anyway) company-grade officers in the outfit, so he didn't have any complaints. I hoped. All in all, we numbered about a hundred men, heavily armed, well provisioned, and ready.

Most of us, by that time, had seen combat. Even the new men who had come into the unit after the plane crash had seen action at LZ 4. All but our new lieutenant. Most of Rescorla's Recon Platoon were Ia Drang veterans, as were Joel and I, so we were mentally prepared for the worst, but ready to do the job. If it had been otherwise, we wouldn't have been sent so far behind the VC lines. At least, I'd like to think that.

Right off the bat we had problems. After clearing the landing zone and taking inventory, the 2d Platoon reported one man with a broken ankle. He'd busted it landing and hadn't been able to get back onto his chopper before it flew out. So, now we had a man who couldn't walk. I remember his face as clearly now as if it were yesterday, but his name eludes me. I'll call him Riley. The word we got from Grove was that even though Riley had broken his ankle, he'd make it to the ambush site. Christ almighty, I thought. What a way to start.

On the good side, we'd landed without opposition, the afternoon was absolutely clear, and from our position we could see the first of the two ridgelines we had to cross. It was on the other side of a small ravine, and looked fairly close. We soon learned otherwise.

Joel gave the word to move out, and we headed silently down the mountainside, platoons in column. It wasn't long before the descent was so steep that we had to grab hold of the trees to stop our fall, and our progress slowed to a crawl, actually a slow controlled fall down the mountainside as we scratched and clawed and hung on for dear life every inch. By the time we'd reached the streambed at the bottom of the ravine, the sun seemed to have set behind the ridges to our west. It was close to four o'clock, and we still had two ridgelines to cross.

The first was very steep, and our progress was as slow going up as it had been disastrous going down. But with sixty to seventy pounds of gear, ammo, and provisions on our backs, not to mention the radiomen with their extra batteries, we were fighting gravity all the way up that goddamn mountain, yet no one said anything, nobody bellyached, nobody complained that I recall, and nobody fell behind.

About halfway up the ridge the column stopped. I made my way forward and saw Joel conferring with Jim Kelly.

"Brown and Herrera have malaria," Joel informed me as I approached. Brown and Herrera were two of Jim's people, good men, suddenly rendered helpless by a mosquito. I looked at Jim. There was nothing we could do or say.

"Have someone carry their gear," Joel said. "And have someone stay with them." Good advice. Men suffering a malaria attack become delirious on their feet, and unless someone watches them, they can wander off into the jungle unattended, collapse, and die. Jim nodded, shrugged his shoulders at me, and returned to his men. A few minutes later, we resumed our march.

Up, up, up that goddamned hill we trekked, pulling ourselves from vine to vine, sapling to sapling, slipping and falling, pushing and shoving, scraping our knees and elbows as we clawed our way up that endless fucking slope. I don't recall how long it actually took us to reach the top, but when we got there, the sun was nowhere to be seen. Dusk was descending silently and fast. With less than an hour of daylight ahead of us, we had another ridgeline to go. We weren't going to be able to make it, that was clear.

Checking our location on the map, and our proposed route on the ground, Joel and I decided to go as far as we could that evening, circle the wagons wherever we ended up, and make the rest of the trip the following morning. If we were lucky, we'd be able to set up something before the battalion came roaring into the valley to our east, chasing the supposed hordes of fleeing enemy up the valley we were supposed to block. Only time would tell.

Joel passed the word to speed it up, and as we headed down the ridgeline, I wondered how far we'd go before having to dig in and wait. Perhaps we wouldn't dig in at all. The thought made me nervous. (I was always nervous in the field.) Then I saw Riley staggering down the trail, or the slick muddy path his predecessors had tramped down before him. I couldn't believe that the man was still on his feet, stumbling along grim-faced, completely blanched, using his M-16 as a crutch (or more like a brake), stifling what must have been incredible pain. I whispered some words of encouragement as he staggered by me, but he didn't respond. Nor did he waver. I wondered fleetingly how the two malaria cases were doing, and noted that we'd soon be decimated at a loss rate of three men an hour. If you're delirious, it's hard to fight.

The second stream we crossed was a raging torrent. The trouble with raging torrents is you can't hear anything but the roar of the stream and, so deafened, you hope and pray that you can get over it without being ambushed. We crossed it quickly and professionally, if I say so myself, with the help of a very large tree trunk that had fallen over the stream.

We were heading up the other side, leaving the distant rumble of the streambed behind us, when I began to hear Joel on the radio, calling for Rescorla's platoon to close up the rear. I didn't know why he was doing this, seeing as how he couldn't have known where the trailing platoon was, but he was. I was also surprised by the curt responses of my British compatriot, who answered that his men were moving just as he had ordered.

And then things got hairy.

The captain was getting angry on the radio. I could hear him halfway down the column on my squawk box.

"Four-six, this is Six," the captain said. He sounded tired. We all were. We'd been humping those fucking mountains since we'd landed, and the day had been a steambath. "I want you to close up on Three-six's people, and I want you to do it now."

I could hear the strain in his voice. He'd been at this game for four months, since well before Albany, and the stress had taken its toll. It was late, too, and getting dark, and he didn't want our column all spread out.

Neither did I. That's why I was standing just off the trail, encouraging each man as he struggled by, step by slippery step. "Dark's coming," I'd say. "Close it up."

You see, in daylight, you keep at least five, maybe ten yards apart, depending on the terrain and visibility. Visual contact is important. But dispersion is, too. You don't want to be bunched up when a mine goes off, or you get hit with a burst of machine-gun fire, or a mortar shell drops nearby. Keeping spread out makes sense. But as it gets dark, you have to close up the column so it doesn't get strung out and break. You can't lose sight of the man in front of you or you'll end up wandering off in the wrong direction, taking everyone else behind you. And if it's pitch-black, so dark you can't see your hand in front of your face, you have to grab hold of the web gear of the guy in front of you. Sometimes, that's the only way to move.

So, that evening, on that mountainside, Joel and I were

putting out the word to close it up. But Joel was also in a rush to reach the top of the ridge we were on, and to set up the ambush on the other side, so the guys in back had to hurry. That was hard, too, because the trail was steep and slippery with everyone's footprints, and we were all beat to hell. We'd been humping, as I said, all afternoon, nonstop except to fill our canteens, and it was ninety-nine degrees out, at least.

The radio crackled, again. "Four-six, this is Six. I want your people to speed it up."

Then, instead of the usual "Roger, wilco" (I understand and will comply), this is what I heard.

"Six, this is Four-six," Rick responded. "They're my people all right, and I'll bloody well move them the way I want. Out."

Oooooweeee! That was telling it like it was. The Old Man didn't respond. I couldn't see him 'cause he was a couple of hundred meters up the trail, but I could feel him seething inside. He didn't get mad very often, but when he did, watch out!

Then I saw Rescorla, and all I can say is that I'm glad he was on our side. Jesus, he looked mean. He saw me, too, and we were friends, but his mind was like a steel trap, tense and ready to spring, and he walked right by me as if I weren't there. He was walking slowly, watching where he put his feet. His people followed him like ghosts, gliding by me silently with their camouflaged faces, soft hats, eyes scanning the trees, weapons at the ready. Had it been dark, I doubt I would have heard them. It was eerie.

Our people were good, and we could move as well as anyone, but Rick's people, they were Recon. They patrolled all the time, usually in small groups, alone and far from help. If they got caught out in the bush all alone, they could say *sayonara*. That evening, on that trail, I saw a look in Rick's eyes that I'll never forget.

Enough said. We continued up that steep, heavily-vegetated slope, using whatever we could grab to climb up the hill, and wondering when our hearts were going to burst with the strain. By the time we reached the top of that second ridge, it was just about completely dark.

Joel called a halt.

We circled the wagons on the military crest of the ridge, which means that we headed down the far side to a relatively flat area, formed a tight perimeter, and dropped to the ground in place. The word was whispered from mouth to mouth. Rest in place. No smoking. No digging. Absolute silence. Luckily, being the executive officer, I didn't have to worry about tying in fields of fire, or making sure each man knew who was on his right and on his left, so I just lay out my rubber poncho, put my head on my helmet, took a long swig of water, and fell asleep.

A short burst from an M-16 woke me up. It was pitch-black. I listened further, but nothing else happened. Nothing else disturbed the night. I checked my watch. It was 0320. Exhausted, I dozed off again.

It was dawn when I woke up. My head was splitting from dehydration. I shifted to my right, then my left. Nobody was moving. I lay there for several minutes, enjoying the quiet, the cold dampness of the ground, the fact that I was still alive. Then I heard someone stirring near Joel's position, twenty yards away. Joel and Larry Sargent, his radioman, were heating up some water, so I joined them.

"Did you hear the burst last night?" Joel asked.

"Yes, sir. What was it?"

"You remember Cruller?"

Cruller was a clerk, an odd-looking redhead, almost albino, who had volunteered to leave his desk job at division headquarters to come out with the infantry—the grunts in the bush, the guys who did the fighting, the men who saw the action. This was his first time out in the field, his maiden voyage, so to speak, his shakedown cruise.

I nodded.

"He got up last night to take a leak," Joel said. "Didn't tell anyone. Johnson heard the noise and let him have it—a quick burst through the chest. Cruller's dead."

"Jesus," I said, thinking it was getting so that we lost 'em before we got to know 'em. I'd seen Cruller and had been struck by his strange appearance and his willingness to come out with us and see action. But what a terrible way to go—so sad, so quick, so ironic.

"What are we going to do with him?" I asked.

"Bring him with us," Joel said.

I nodded, returned to my poncho, and started to heat up some water. Another corpse to drag around. That's what I thought. I was heartsick, too, but I didn't know it at the time.

After breakfast, we headed down that ridgeline once again. We had time, we thought, to make it to our ambush site, but we'd be strapped for time to set it up properly. The good news was the terrain had changed. The descent was not as steep, and the undergrowth had opened up so you could see a few meters to your right and left. Joel changed our formation from a column of platoons to two up, one back, and we continued down the slope. Unlike before, I could see men from the 3d Platoon on my left, and men from the 2d Platoon on my right. Kelly and Rescorla's people were trailing. The ground was covered with moss and decaying leaves instead of grass, and the slope was much gentler than it had been the day before. It was still early, too. The heat hadn't reached its peak. Down the ridge we went, wending our way as quietly as we could, which was very quiet, nobody saying a word, everyone keyed up and alert. Our HQ group was in the middle of the two lead platoons and making decent progress, though slow.

About a hundred meters from the bottom of the ridge, although we couldn't see the ravine yet, the column suddenly stopped. Things got eerily quiet. Then suddenly, out of the blue, we heard several bursts of M-16 fire from the ravine. Joel and I glanced at each other, wondering what the hell was happening, and after a long pregnant silence, he got on the horn and asked.

Dick Hogarth, our new platoon leader, informed us that his point squad had just killed two Victor Charlies and captured a third. His men had reached the stream, surveyed it for a few minutes, and been surprised by three VC diddly-bopping down the trail alongside the stream. The point's response had been deadly. By the time Joel and I had made our way to the front of the column, Gordy Grove's people had already crossed the stream and put security out. Dick Hogarth's platoon sergeant, another new man, an E-7 named Winston "Cabbie" Carbonneau, whom I didn't know, was carefully searching the bodies of the men they had killed. They were splayed on the trail, dead as smelt, and the third guy, wearing a gray shirt, khaki trousers, and a belt with an NVA buckle, had already been bound, blindfolded, and gagged. He looked like a little kid, but he'd been armed, and the 3d Platoon guys were proudly brandishing the AK-47s they'd just lifted from the dead.

Joel was quick to appreciate that we were sitting on a trail by a streambed and had a ways to go yet, so he ordered Grove to assume the point and continue the march. The prisoner, still bound and blindfolded, was put in the custody of Sergeant Carbonneau and the 3d Platoon, and we started off again, crossing the stream platoons in column again because of the terrain. We had one more ridge to climb and we'd be there.

We continued up that hillside, in good tactical formation considering its steepness, and I remember pausing about halfway up the hill, turning around, and watching the rest of the company move quietly past me. I then turned and took up the rear of the column for a few hundred meters. The vegetation had thinned out, and you could see about a hundred yards to either side, and the prospect of reaching our ambush site in time gave us hope. As my two RTOs, the first sergeant, and I continued up the hill, I looked back once more to check our rear. Something struck me as odd as I looked back down the hillside to my left. There was something dark and unnatural down there, but it was so far down the hillside that no one else had seen or even noticed it. Or if they had, they hadn't said anything.

I called Joel on the radio.

"Six, this is Five. Hold the column up for a minute, will you? There's something back here I want to check out."

"Roger, Five. Will do."

The company held up for a break. I started down the slope, heading toward the unnaturally dark undergrowth with the first sergeant and my two RTOs. The closer we got to that dark mass on the hillside, the clearer it became. It was a hootch of some kind, hidden under the jungle canopy but visible from the ground.

"Six, this is Five. I see a hootch down there. We're going to check it out."

"Roger, Five."

My heart was pounding and my mouth dry as we slowly moved toward the hootch. Silently, stealthily, we approached it, weapons ready. There was no one there, fortunately, so I made my way around to the doorway, on the downhill side of the slope, and stuck my head inside.

The hootch was filled with weapons! I could see two recoilless rifles, two tripod-mounted machine guns, several types of small arms, crates of ammunition, boxes of grenades, and lots of other stuff. Bingo! We'd hit the jackpot!

"Six, this is Five, over."

"This is Six, over."

"This is Five. We've struck it rich down here. It's a weapons cache, two recoilless rifles, lots of crates, some machine guns, the works."

My heart was beating so fast I thought I could hear it. What a bonanza!

"This is Six," Joel said. "Hold in place, I'm coming down. Four-six, form a perimeter around Five's position."

Rescorla acknowledged that, and we began to circle the wagons once again, short of our ambush site, but certainly worth the diversion.

I rummaged quickly through the material in the hootch, found a VC flag in a canvas pouch, and stuffed the flag under my shirt. I'd be damned if I wasn't going to claim something from this find. And the entire company had walked right by it! They must have been thinking about where we were going, and they'd totally missed the biggest weapons cache I'd ever seen.

Joel broke radio silence to advise battalion of the contents of the hootch, and our mission was changed on the spot. We were ordered to prepare a small landing zone for a bird to extract the captured weapons and equipment. A Chinook with a hook would drop a sling to us, we'd fill it up with the contents of the hootch, and the Chinook would haul it away.

During the next several hours, then, we lugged the contents of that hootch up to the landing zone—just a narrow opening in the jungle canopy on a flat part of the ridge—and the Chinook managed to winch it all out. It took three loads, three trips back and forth, and on the final lift, we placed that poor little NVA prisoner, still blindfolded and bound, onto the last remnants of the cache, covered him with a tarpaulin, and gave the signal for the Chinook to lift off. As it did, with its rotors whirling and its down draft pounding us, I watched the sling lift off the ground and rise slowly out of sight through the treetops, and wondered what that poor little NVA was thinking. He must have been shitting in his pants.

By noon, we'd accomplished that task. We were then told to continue down the ridgeline to an LZ and be prepared for another mission. When we reached that LZ, we were finally able to call for medevac, which came in and picked up Riley, still suffering stoically with his broken ankle, Brown and Herrera, the two malaria cases just barely hanging on, and the lifeless body of PFC James D. Cruller, killed in the Kim Song Valley of the Republic of South Vietnam on February 12, 1966.

The good news was how well our new platoon leader and all of our new men had performed. We were feeling pretty good when we rejoined the battalion and spent the next few days at a firebase near a river where the men could get a swim.

We were also regaled by the rest of the battalion as to how successful their air assault had been into the Crow's Foot. Pat Payne told me that when Charlie Company flew into the valley, he'd seen a platoon of VC simply drop their weapons and run. I was beginning to think that airmobility was a good way to catch the bad guys with their pants down. It was one of the few times we did.

BOOK FOUR

Bitter Fruit

Chapter 18

Take That Hill, Lieutenant!

What the fuck? Over.
—Unattributed

Soon after we returned from the Crow's Foot, Captain Sugdinis was "promoted upstairs" to the assistant S-3's slot at brigade. I learned that when I ran into him showing his replacement around the base camp. It was midday—hot, bright, and sunny. I was walking down the road to battalion HQ, with the dry rice paddy on my left, when I saw Joel and a new, i.e., unfamiliar, captain walking toward me. I flashed them a salute, and Joel stopped me with a big smile on his face and enthusiastically introduced me to his replacement, my new company commander, and told me that he would be signing over the property books that afternoon. The new captain's name was Cherry, Captain Cherry, and he looked a lot older than Joel, had apparently just come in from Korea, definitely needed a haircut, and was as cordial as a jar of cold piss.

I was slightly taken aback, welcomed him aboard, saluted again, and walked away with my head spinning.

So, I thought, Joel had made it through his tour with us, had been promoted upstairs, and would be leaving before the day was out. I was happy for him. Really happy for him. He'd been a great company commander. He'd made it, and he deserved the best. But with the passing of any commander, you can't help but wonder how his replacement is going to work out, and it's unnerving. I had no idea whether Captain Cherry was a good man, whether he was competent, reasonable, or fair, whether he was a brave man, or a man who cared about his troops. Only time would tell.

205

* * *

That very night, Viet Cong sappers surprised and overran the small signal corps outpost on the top of Hong Kong Mountain overlooking the Golf Course. Alpha Company happened to be the brigade's reaction force (again), and Captain Cherry was ordered to detach a platoon to brigade for a night air assault onto the top of Hong Kong Mountain. Wittingly or not, I never found out, he chose the 3d Platoon, the platoon with our least experienced officer, Lt. Dick Hogarth, in command. I didn't learn about this until well after midnight, however, and long after Dick Hogarth and his men had taken off for their perilous night assault.

Captain Cherry woke me up around two A.M., told me what he had done, and said he wanted the rest of the company formed up and ready to move at 0500. We would be going up the mountain on foot to relieve the 3d Platoon. It took a while for all of this to sink in, and all I remember him saying to me as he walked out of my tent was, "I'll be at the officers club."

I got dressed, walked down to the orderly room and conferred with First Sergeant Miller as to what he knew, what he'd done, who was awake, when to wake up the company, etc., etc., and then headed down to the battalion TOC to see what I could learn about how Dick Hogarth's people were doing.

Walking down there, I could see lights flashing on and around the top of Hong Kong, but nothing else. It could have been Hueys landing, but I wasn't sure. All I knew was that of all the platoons to be sent up there, Dick Hogarth's had the least experienced platoon leader, and all I could think of was how horrific it must have been to be ordered to make a night air assault onto the top of a mountain peak that had just been overrun by Viet Cong sappers.

I learned from the TOC that Dick's people had landed okay and didn't seem to be in any kind of serious trouble, but that the signal corps detachment had been badly mauled. The VC had caught them by surprise, overrun them, blown the radio towers, and disappeared into the night.

* * *

At 0500, Alpha Company minus the 3d Platoon was formed up, ready, and resting in place when Captain Cherry appeared out of the darkness and advised me that I was to take the company up the mountain, that he would be flying around overhead in Lieutenant Colonel MacDade's C & C ship "directing the operation."

Well, I'll be damned, I thought.

I asked him the usual questions—about a jump-off spot, a line of departure, what friendly units were in the area, what kind of artillery support we would have, radio communication, frequencies, etc., etc., information that I had to know if I was the commander on the ground—and he seemed put off, almost impatient, with my questions. I had the distinct impression that he was testing us, subjecting the company to some kind of "let's see what you're made of " kind of test. Well, if he was, no big deal. We'd been doing that sort of thing for five months and were damn good at it, that's for sure, so if that's what he was doing, so be it. But I also had this horrible sinking feeling that things were going to be different for the officers and men of good old Alpha Company. Here was a CO who would send his men up a mountain and into a possible firefight while he was circling around overhead in a safe C & C ship. He must have thought he was a colonel!

The last thing he said as he strode off toward battalion was, "I'll see you on the mountain."

"Okay, Gordy," I said. "Lead us out. Use the road. I'll be right behind you. Jim, you follow. Jack, when we get to the jump-off spot, set up your tube inside the wire and support us from there.

"When we've got clearance, we'll pass through the wire in a file, cross the LD (line of departure), then form a column of platoons, 2d leading, followed by 1st. We'll decide on the route when we get there. As soon as we're through the wire, spread out and keep good dispersion. And for Christ's sakes, look out for an ambush. That's it."

"Gotcha," Gordy said and turned to Sergeant Caple. "Pick 'em up, Sergeant. Let's go!"

I could feel the electricity spreading through the company, cigarettes tossed, ground into the dirt, muffled clicks and clunks as weapons were checked and hoisted to the ready, grunts and groans as people rose slowly, stiffly, to their feet. A collective hush settled over us as we swung into action like a big deadly uncoiling serpent and started humping down the oil-soaked interior road, boots crunching on the pebbled surface, sounding ominous and strange in the dark, occasional wisecracks breaking like sparks from the column, whispered shouts of "keep it down" from nervous team leaders, then a collective sigh of resignation and acceptance as our ninety-plus men moved smartly toward the line of departure for a company-size assault on Hong Kong Mountain.

I'd never paid much attention to good old Hong Kong Mountain before. It was just there, a massive, hulking, jungle-covered four-thousand-foot hill dominating the base camp, too big for the division to encircle. So it had just loomed there, outside the perimeter. At one point, I'm not sure when, exactly, someone had painted a huge 1st Cavalry patch on top of the mountain, on the side facing the base camp. It had been an awesome job of artistry. How they'd done it I had no idea. But they had, and it looked great. Unfortunately, whoever had been up there the previous night had let their guard down, and now we were going up there to save their asses, or assist them in whatever way we could. Too bad we were too late. Whatever, as we began our march along the division base camp's interior road to the far side of the perimeter, I studied that piece of terrain harder than any other hillside I'd ever seen, and the closer we got to it, the bigger and more foreboding it looked.

Dawn broke about halfway there.

Moving on the road was a cinch, so I quickly joined Gordy Grove who was leading the column with his RTO beside him. Gordy seemed happy, almost eager, certainly steadfast. As we walked toward the mountain, we looked for the best way up. We wanted an easy approach—no one wants to be struggling up the side of a mountain when Charlie opens up—and we could see what appeared to be a fairly gentle ridgeline running west to east, i.e., right to left, from the bottom of the mountain to the top. But that's where Charlie would expect us, on that ridgeline. As we got closer, I could see another ridgeline directly ahead, but it looked like it reached only two thirds of the way up before disappearing into the mountain's dark crown of vegetation. It was steeper and less inviting than the obvious approach, but it would get us up there faster, so we decided to try it.

A jeep came up behind us as we walked. Joel Sugdinis was in it.

"Well, well," he said, as the jeep slowed to our pace. "You guys are moving pretty fast."

"How come we never had a road when you were the CO?" Gordy asked.

"We're just making it easier for you—now that you're on your own," Joel said. Then his jaw set, and he got down to business. "There's a road guard from the 2d of the 5th waiting up ahead. He'll flag you down and guide you through the wire. The unit on line is expecting you, so there won't be any problems coordinating with them. You can pass right through the wire and start your climb."

"Thanks," I said, not breaking stride.

"I'll check on the guides now and make sure they're there," Joel said, waving the driver on. "Good luck," he said as he sped away.

Good old Joel, I thought. At least someone was doing his job.

There was, indeed, a team of guides to lead us from the road to the jump-off spot, and we passed through the wire and crossed the LD without incident, silently slipping past the last roll of concertina and spreading out in the waist-high grass that grew at the base of the mountain. We had three hundred yards of open ground to cross before we ran into the thick stuff. Grove's platoon had preceded me through the wire. When I got to it, it was being held open for us by three men with M-16s slung over their shoulders, obviously not grunts, probably the "night riders" from the support units inside the perimeter, the HQ REMFs who came from their air-conditioned tents to man the Green Line at night. I nodded to them as I walked by. God, was I proud to be a grunt!

Gordy Grove was there waiting for me, watching his men spread out expertly as soon as they hit the grass. We stood together for a moment and watched. For some reason, Gordy seemed happy, almost ebullient. Maybe he was just proud of his platoon. I certainly was. Wherever the new CO might be—we hadn't heard from him since he'd disappeared into the darkness—we could do the job just fine. The thought made me feel good—better than feeling scared, which I was. Gordy suddenly turned to me, flashed his infectious, gap-toothed grin, and said, "If he wants us to take this hill, we'll take this goddamn hill." Then he strode off after his men.

"Just don't rush it," I said as he headed out into the open field.

He waved acknowledgment without looking back.

An hour later, we'd made it about a third of the way up the hill. It was getting very hot, and the slope was steep, and the undergrowth was surprisingly thick. Not enough to give us shade, though, and we were beginning to feel the sun's brutal, relentless heat. I called a halt, ordered Kelly's people to move through Grove's people and assume the point, and followed them as they plodded through the 2d Platoon's well-dispersed formation. When the 1st Platoon was ready, I gave them the green light, and we continued our march up that hill.

Captain Cherry's unfamiliar voice came over the radio. "Braveboy Five, this is Braveboy Six. Over," he called. I couldn't for the life of me hear any choppers overhead.

"This is Braveboy Five. Over," I answered.

"This is Six," he said. "What is your progress? Over."

"This is Braveboy Five. Estimate one-third of the distance covered. Over." I was trying to be as cryptic as I could.

"Why are you moving so slowly?" he asked. His voice had a guttural sound to it, and I could feel his impatience. Everyone near the squawk box could, too, and that didn't help things.

"This is Braveboy Five. The terrain is steep. Over." That was all I said, and he signed off.

We continued slowly upward. The terrain got steadily worse. Everyone was using both hands, now, to pull themselves up certain particularly steep sections of the route, and that's always scary because you want your M-16 in your hands, not slung over your shoulder, when the firing starts. But we were helping each other out, keeping security teams alert when the going got steep, and we continued steadily, if not swiftly, up the slope. By 0900, everyone was soaked, exhausted, and getting frustrated by the steepness and difficulty of the climb, but we continued grimly up that hill. We were more than halfway up when the radio sputtered again.

"Braveboy Five, this is Braveboy Six. Over."

"This is Five. Over."

"This is Six. Situation report. Over."

"This is Five. Progress steady but slow. We're about two-thirds of the way up, I'd guess. Over."

"This is Six," he said. "That's entirely too slow. I want you to move faster!"

Well that's just jim dandy, I thought. That's perfect. The son of a bitch is up there in his air-conditioned chopper, with the world at his feet, and we're down here, sweating our balls off, clawing our way up this goddamn mountain in the blazing hot sun, with God knows how many Victor Charlies still around, and he wants us to hurry up. Why doesn't he come down here and join us?

"This is Five. Roger that. Over," I said, knowing that none of us would move one centimeter per hour faster than we were already moving. If he wasn't willing to hump with us, I certainly wasn't going to kill myself for him. And I certainly wasn't going to get the men around me killed because of his impatience.

He signed off abruptly, and we continued up the hill. Slowly but steadily. About half an hour later, Jim Kelly's voice came over the squawk box. He sounded excited. I answered.

"This is One-six," he said. "We just grabbed us one Victor Charlie. He's got a weapon. There's a dead one here, too. We dug him out of a cave. The live one is slightly wounded. What'll we do with them, over?"

"This is Five," I said. "That's beautiful! Good work. But keep your eyes peeled. I'll ask upstairs."

I called the captain for instructions. He had not been monitoring the radio. When he came onto the net, this is what he said.

"This is Six. Where the hell are you? Why aren't you at the top?"

"This is Five," I responded. "We've just dug two Victor Charlies out of a cave about three-quarters of the way up. One's dead, the other wounded. No other contact yet. Request instructions. Over."

That would shut him up, I thought.

After a moment or two, he came back on the line. "This is Six. Bring them with you. Over."

He'd obviously never dragged a dead man up a mountain. We were having enough trouble as it was.

"This is Five. Over. I suggest we leave the dead one as is, or pick him up on the way back down. It's steep as hell down here."

"This is Six," I heard. "Just bring the live one, then, and be sure to search the area thoroughly."

What the fuck did he think we were doing?!

"Wilco," I said, as calmly as I could. I asked Kelly if he'd monitored that transmission. He had, so we started back up the hill.

After another hour or so, we reached the top of the mountain. Approaching the crest, I looked up, and there was Captain Cherry, standing on the hillside watching as Kelly's point squad clambered over the last steep rock outcropping and radioed me that they'd made it to the top. Cherry was wearing the same brand-new soft cap and jungle fatigues and jungle boots I'd seen the day before. He was smoking a cigar, too, and looked the goddamned picture of a Saigon commando if I'd ever seen one. He was pleased, though. That was clear. His new command had accomplished its mission without mishap, had taken a prisoner, to boot, and now he knew what we could do.

I was relieved as hell to reach the top, to reach it without running into an ambush, and I was delighted to see Dick Hogarth's smiling face as I scrambled up the last steep stretch to level ground.

I walked to the captain and reported. "Long climb," was all I said. I was exhausted, out of breath, my heart pounding so hard I wasn't sure he'd heard me.

He nodded, took the cigar out of his mouth, and said something.

I'm not sure what it was, but I didn't care. I felt good. We'd done what we'd been asked to do, and done it well.

I turned to Dick Hogarth. "A little pucker-factor last night, eh, Richard?" I said, reaching out to shake his hand.

"All in a night's work," he said, smiling broadly. "We had the easy part. You guys had to walk."

I was beginning to like this guy. He had a real spark to him. Balls, too. That was good.

"How bad was it?" I asked.

"Awful," he said. "Come on. I'll show you around."

We excused ourselves from the captain and took a walk around the place. As we checked the outpost, or what was left of it, it was clear that we could have lost Dick Hogarth and the men he'd been with last night. We'd dodged another bullet.

Except for our people, no one else was there. The place was deserted. Choppers had come in at first light, while we'd been humping to the jump-off spot, and taken out the wounded, the dead, and the handful of survivors. They'd been signal corps troops, not grunts, and they'd made the cardinal mistake of letting their guard down, slacking off in their vigilance, and what I saw told me a grim tale. A Quonset hut ringed with sandbags had been totally blown apart. Its sides and roof just twisted metal now. A junk pile. Two radio antennae, tall, steep, triangular ones maybe fifty feet high, lay bent and broken on the ground. Only one sandbagged bunker remained intact. It had provided the shaken survivors with just enough shelter to make a last-ditch stand.

"Look at this," Dick said, walking to the foxholes ringing the perimeter and pointing into the underbrush on the other side of the barbed wire.

A dozen or more empty beer cans told the story. They were scattered near a hole that had been blown in the wire, the entryway through which Death had charged. Someone on guard had been boozing, and it was his last party. The VC had come through that hole in the wire, grabbed the man's M-60, and turned it on the compound. And that was all she wrote.

"They said it happened all at once." Dick was shaking his head as he spoke. "The VC mustered there," he pointed to a heavy clump of brush and small trees fifty meters from the overrun machine-gun post. "They must have come in real quiet, caught 'em napping, and walked right in. They blasted the place for ten minutes, blew the radio shack, knocked the towers down, then disappeared. It was all over when we landed." He was gazing around at the carnage and wasn't smiling. He'd had a long night.

"How you doing?" I asked.

"Fine," he said. "Better than those guys." He was nodding at the empty foxholes around the place.

I could feel the anger welling up inside me. Who the hell had been up here? A bunch of dummies? The whole set up stank. The place hadn't been cleared of brush. No fields of fire. Nothing. The machine-gun position was in hand-grenade range. How could anyone up here be so fucking stupid? Signal corps types, I guess. No brains at all. No combat experience, anyway. And the beer! Jesus! What the hell did they think they were on? Some kind of a picnic? I felt the anger growing and tried to stifle it, suppress it, keep it from showing. After all, they were only signal types, not grunts. They didn't know any better. But they should have had more protection. At least dug in a little smarter. I turned away in disgust, thinking what a shame it was that they'd been killed so fast, and so easily.

Captain Cherry reappeared from the other side of the outpost and came over to us. "As soon as my chopper comes in,

Gwin, you can lead the company back down," he said. "I'll take the prisoner with me and deliver him to interrogation."

"Yes, sir," I said, thinking fuck you, you son of a bitch. "I'd like to give the men a few more minutes to rest."

"Of course," he said, nodding.

"It's almost noon, too, sir," I said. "Is there a chance someone might fly us up some lunch?"

"Hold on," he said. "I'll ask."

He used my radio to call battalion. I didn't hear what he said because he was out of earshot, but when he came back, he was smiling.

"A Chinook will be arriving shortly to ferry you back down."

"Oh, good," I said. "Maybe they'll get a hot lunch after all."

"They will," he said, and that was that.

His C & C ship flew in a few minutes later and picked him up. I could see Colonel MacDade in it, too. Half an hour later, a Chinook flew in and ferried the rest of us off the mountain.

We left it as it was. Empty. Another outfit was going to reestablish the radio tower and signal outpost that afternoon.

When we returned to base camp, we got a hot lunch and the afternoon off. Captain Cherry resumed what turned out to be his usual place at the poker table in the officers club, and we waited for orders. The next day, a company from the 2d Brigade swept the mountain, combed its caves, and cleaned up the mess on top, making it a defensible position from a grunt's perspective, and suitable for another signal corps power station.

Sometime after that, the division's perimeter was expanded to include Hong Kong Mountain, and its peak was never overrun again.

Chapter 19

Rescorla's Game

He would have a good weekend. He would make love to a beautiful woman and throw a football with his son and pound down a cold Genessee and see the leaves— everything he'd dreamed of in Vietnam. He was alive, and to forget that, to live as if this world were something other than a paradise, would be to dishonor the memory of his friends.
—STEWART O'NAN,
The Names of the Dead

When I think of Rick Rescorla, I think of the twinkle in his eye—half joyful, half crazed, like a wild Cornish hawk. He was, after all, a Brit. When he was working, though, or out in the bush, that crazed irreverent twinkle disappeared—snuffed out like a candle in a strong wind and replaced by a cold steely glint that could sear right through you like the icy stare of death. When Rick looked that way, he was ready for a kill.

I'd first seen that glint at LZ Albany. He had just jumped ten feet from a hovering helicopter, killed three enemy soldiers on the ground, and maneuvered with his men into our last-ditch perimeter. The next time I saw that glint was during that long painful trek over the mountains west of the Crow's Foot, and it had scared the hell out of me.

But the way I want to remember Rick is that night in the O-club, when he showed us how to beer walk—an exercise in absurdity that captured the hearts and minds of the battalion's younger officers and made for untold hours of chaos, oblivion, and joy. It was mid-February, I think, after Bong Son—after Captain Cherry had joined us.

The O-club was up. We'd built it ourselves: poured-concrete floor, wood-slat walls, screened windows, corrugated roof. It had a makeshift bar in one corner, a few pieces of bamboo furniture we'd scrounged up in An Khe, a generator-powered refrigerator, and lights! The place was safe, too. It rested in a defilade. All hell could break loose on the Green Line, and we could still sip our beers in peace. All we needed was a stereo and some women.

I remember that night quite distinctly. Eight or nine of us were there—lieutenants mostly, platoon leaders, artillery FOs, rifle company XOs—guys who humped the bush. It was late, too—long after chow. We must have been on a stand-down. We had one every now and then—a night off to shower, or drink, or sleep, or catch up on all those unstarted projects. I'd been in the club a while, drinking beer and horsing around, as we all were, when in walked Rick Rescorla.

"Ahah!" he chortled, that twinkle in his eye, seeing a bunch of us sitting there, ripe for a challenge.

I'd never appreciated the man's subtle joy for sport. I knew his reputation, that he'd served in the British army, that he'd signed up with ours "because it was the only one that had a war on," that he'd been wounded lightly once and already recommended for two Silver Stars—one for the Ia Drang and one for Happy Valley. I also knew that he was, with a few of us anyway, delightful company. His favorite expression, an accusation, really, was that some of our field-grade officers (colonels and majors) "saw things through the rosey red hue." He was, without question, one of the best officers in the battalion, and the toughest, bar none. He was older, too. From our youthful vantage point, he'd reached the ancient age of twenty-eight.

After the usual banter, for he was good at that (and a raconteur of sorts, if I remember correctly), he sensed a lull in the evening's revelry and issued his challenge.

"All right! All right!" he said, standing up, fortified now with a beer. "Let's see how coordinated you chaps really are. Let's see if the strength you profess matches the bullshit I'm sure you're full of."

He said this loud enough for everyone to hear it, and his jaw jutted out with such mock ferocity that he simultaneously captured the attention and piqued the competitive ire of everyone present. That was when I saw the first inkling of the greatest twinkle in any man's eye I've ever seen.

"I'll need two beers," he said. "Untapped." He made a tentative move toward the bar, then stopped, knowing intuitively that a younger man, a contender, perhaps, would get the beers for him. Sure enough, a muscle-bound second lieutenant named Morrow, a new guy from Brooklyn, responded, and Rick found himself with two fresh cans in his hands—a Schlitz and a Carlings Black Label. He looked them over disdainfully, inspecting them, really, then held them up for everyone to see. Like a barker at a fair, he'd bagged us.

He turned and strode briskly to the far wall. Swinging back to face us, he backed up against the wooden siding, banging the Corfam heels of his jungle boots against the framework. We clustered around him.

"Give me some room!" he barked, waving his arms in front of him in a breaststroking motion, and we backed off a bit.

I saw Joel Sugdinis coming through the O-club door then. He saw us, stopped, and smiled. He didn't go for a drink. He just stood there, watching.

"Now," Rick said. "You place your heels against the wall, like this"—he tapped them one at a time against the wall—"and you hold your beers like this"—he raised his arms and held them straight out, one beer in each hand, the tops of the cans pressed flat against his palms, the bottoms pointing outward so that each can was simply an extension of his hand and arm. He flexed his wrists up and down so all could see.

"You then reach down, extending your arms as you go, and walk on your hands, using the beer cans to keep you from touching the floor. You walk out as far as you can go, leaving one of the cans on the floor—as far away from the wall as you can leave it. Then, using the other as a crutch, you work yourself back to a standing position without any part of your body touching the floor."

He then demonstrated, bending over quickly, keeping his knees stiff and walking several steps comfortably on his beer-can-extended hands. He stretched himself out with three or four more quick "steps" until he was in a push-up position, reached out effortlessly, and placed the can of Carlings an arm's length to his front. He then placed his free hand back on the hand holding the Schlitz, and with a series of quick, short backward thrusts, righted himself again without any part of his body touching the floor. When he'd straightened up, he raised his arms triumphantly and said, "Voila!"

The twinkle in his eyes was starting to glow.

"Who wants to try it?" he said.

Morrow, the guy from Brooklyn, was quick to accept the challenge, but to our surprise, he couldn't right himself after depositing his can several inches beyond Rick's Black Label beer can. Gordy Grove tried it next and failed as well, landing hard on his shoulder in dismay. Dick Hogarth tried it, too, losing his balance while teetering on his steel-encased pedestal. (In those days of yesteryear, beer cans were made of steel.) Jim Kelly then took up the challenge, and being six-feet-four-inches tall, and built like coiled steel, managed to surpass all the previously disqualified attempts, stretching out and pushing his red-white-and-blue can of Pabst Blue Ribbon a good ten inches past Rescorla's mark.

"Yeah!" someone growled.

"Right, Jim!" another cheered.

"Atta go, Lurch!" I heard myself say.

But Jim wasn't finished yet. We all waited, holding our breaths, while he assumed his two-handed recovery position and balanced for a tension-packed moment on his single remaining can. He concentrated. His jaw set. He grimaced. And with one prodigious effort he thrust himself backward six inches, the bottom of his beer can scraping loudly against the cement as he did so. He steadied himself, grimaced again, and repeated his backward thrust, gaining another foot or so.

Then, with growing confidence, he thrust himself backward two or three more times and stood up with a look of surprise on his face, surprise at how difficult that apparently simple task had really been.

The place went crazy for a while. Cheers, guffaws, and laughter filled the air as people pounded his back and swamped him with congratulations. Then everyone quieted down. Matching Lurch's effort appeared totally out of the question for Rick. He was, after all, only six feet tall, and it looked as if he'd extended himself as far as he could on his demonstration run.

But Rescorla was ready. He picked his own beers this time: Budweisers. He stepped back to the starting line and calmly surveyed the crowd. We were hungry for the cocky Brit's humiliation, and the room went deathly still. Rick was smiling, though—not at us, but to himself—as if humming some inner mantra and concentrating on an extension of himself beyond the limits of human endeavor. Then he dropped again, took five quick steps on his beer-can hands to the point where his body was virtually parallel to the floor, slipped his Budweiser six inches past Kelly's can of Pabst and, after a single tension-packed moment teetering on his precarious, steel-encased pedestal, pushed himself back to a standing position to the utter amazement of everyone in the room.

After a few seconds of stunned silence, the place went absolutely berserk, with people jumping up and down, screaming and yelling, cheering and laughing, pounding Rick on the back, and clambering all over themselves to get at the beer supply. For a few happy moments, the O-club turned into bedlam. All of its members but me. For I had seen the look in Rick's eyes when he'd risen from the challenge just met. It showed such sublime pleasure, such pure delight, such unabashed joy, such glee, such incredible inner discipline, that it all began to make sense when later, after most of us had tried, and failed, and tried again to match his mark, he quietly retired from the contest and became a spectator.

I never saw him try it again. He'd had his fun. He'd shared his game. And he'd conned us one and all.

"Beer walking," as we later called it, became the battalion's junior officers' favorite pastime, with Jim "Lurch" Kelly ultimately attaining the much-coveted "Battalion Beer Walking Championship" and holding on to it tenaciously, challenge after challenge. The hours we spent after that memorable night, watching grown men teetering precariously on beer cans, straining to return to standing positions, bellowing in rage when they slipped, or collapsed, or a knee touched the floor, or a beer can crumpled beneath them, cursing at themselves in disgust, or glaring at the blisters rising from their already calloused and sometimes bleeding palms, all those mindless hours of chaos helped us forget where we were, why we were there, what we were doing, and being asked to do. They were wonderful, crazy, carefree hours, and they helped us purge our pain.

Rick Rescorla gave us that, and for that, I want to thank him. Thanks, Rick.

Chapter 20

Compliments of the General Staff

Thanks, Pop, but today's kids don't
want money, they want leadership.
—Cartoon caption in
The New Yorker

One thing grunts begrudged the REMFs was good hot food. We subsisted primarily on C rations, or, if lucky, slightly more dignified B rations, cooked in the battalion mess area and served to us on steel mess trays, generally hot chow to be enjoyed with our buddies while sitting on the wooden picnic-style tables that eventually graced the mess hall. Every now and then, like Thanksgiving or Christmas, we'd be served the full-course, fresh-food specialties, meals diligently prepared and lovingly served by the small army of mess sergeants sweating under the clucking leer of our battalion mess sergeant. He was a man everyone in the battalion grew to appreciate, and I regret to this day that I never walked over to him and thanked him for all his hard work and efforts. But, as I said, we grunts usually subsisted on C rations.

Now it came to pass that Alpha Company returned to man the defensive positions guarding the top of An Khe Pass, duty which we generally considered as almost rest and recreation compared to humping the bush, and there, under our uncommunicative, almost surly new captain, we sat and vegetated for roughly two weeks. Bruce Morrison, a brand new artillery forward observer, joined us, and it was good to have a new man in the fold.

We sent out listless patrols during the day, and half-hearted ambushes at night, but otherwise we rested and recuperated—standard operating procedure for duty at An Khe Pass. Luckily, the month of March was a quiet one. We needed it.

One day, however, we had a good laugh, and, thanks to the captain, a special treat. It happened, sort of, like this.

Our command post was a heavily sandbagged, two-compartment bunker that dominated the military crest of An Khe Pass. You could walk out the bunker's narrow entrance, take ten steps forward, and see the entire valley vista open up at your feet, the hairpin turns of Highway 19 curving up the mountainside like stepping-stones cut in the dark green roadside jungle. The view always reminded me of pictures I'd seen of the Burma Road in World War II. Agent Orange hadn't made its insidious presence felt, yet, although it was being sprayed along the highways farther east up the coast (and, I learned later, at our base camp!). The black macadam road crested twenty meters to our left, where it flattened out and continued westward, past an abandoned artillery position, to An Khe and Camp Radcliff. Along the tarmac artery chugged the lifeline of the Cav, not a pipeline, but hundreds and hundreds of trucks—big ones, deuce-and-a-halfs, cattle cars, and, on that particular day, a fairly sizable, albeit well-spread-out, convoy of ponderously slow-moving refrigerator vans.

We were sitting around shirtless in the morning sun, jaw-boning about something or other, with Gordy Grove, Sergeant Wittlesey, a great young E-5 with a handlebar mustache who was one of Grove's squad leaders, and the CP group, minus First Sergeant Miller, who'd come down with malaria and was resting back at base camp. The refrigerator trucks began rumbling by us every five or ten minutes, and maybe ten had passed before Sp4. Willie Green, a happy-go-lucky black RTO with a gold star inlaid in his left front tooth, asked, "What's in them freezer trucks, anyway?"

"Ice," said Sergeant Rodriguez.

"Ice?" Green exclaimed. "You gotta be shittin' me, man. No ice in them trucks. Eve'body back in the Big Circle (base camp) got re-frig-er-a-tors—I seen them fat cats up at div. They's all sittin' 'round clinking their fuckin' ice cubes in them fancy-dancy cups. They don't got no need for ice."

We pondered over his question some more.

"Beer, man. Beer," said Denny Wilson. Larry Sargent grunted in accord.

Nobody challenged Wilson, so he elaborated. "You 'magine what a case of hot beer would do bouncin' up and down on this road in this hundred-degree heat? Explode man, one big gusher! Gotta carry beer when it's cold. Only way," he said, knowingly.

I was beginning to think that, too.

"I don't think so," said our new FO, captivated by the highly intellectual level of our conversation. "You can shake a beer can all day in the hottest weather around, and it won't blow up until you open it."

Costello and Grove agreed with him.

"Meat," grunted Sergeant Carbonneau, who was our field first sergeant that day. Everybody turned to him. "Only one thing them big freezer trucks haul in here," he said in his Vermonter accent. "Perishable food, and that means steak."

"You sure about that?" asked Sergeant Wittlesey.

"I did two years in quartermasters in Korea. Yeah. I'm sure. I bet those mothers is filled with cartons of hard-frozen, prime, grade-A, number-one beef—on its way to the general's mess."

We sat there thinking about it for a few quiet minutes.

Another big refrigerator truck rumbled by us then, straining mightily in first gear as it reached the level section of the tarmac, then picked up speed and roared away, delivering fresh frozen steaks to the bigwig fat cats sitting in the air-conditioned comfort of their rear-echelon palisade.

Captain Cherry, who'd been standing up, smoking, and listening to our conjecture with an expression that evolved from amused contempt to bemused interest and then to a hitherto unsurpassed jaw-jutting resolve, suddenly spoke.

"Lieutenant Grove, I want a squad of your best men here on the double, no gear necessary, ready for a procurement mission of the highest priority."

Everyone was startled, not sure what was going on in the captain's mind, but Grove jumped up and punched Wittlesey in the shoulder. "Your squad, Wit! Go get 'em." The young E-5's jaw set. He stood up quickly, took five steps away from the bunker, and yelled for his people.

Captain Cherry winked at me and said, "The men can use a little fresh beef, don't you think?"

"Yes, sir. They sure can." I somehow knew what he was up to, but wasn't sure how he'd do it. Pictures of what happened next bring a smile to my heart.

"You people stay where you are," Cherry commanded, pointing to all of us except Grove. "Now, Gordo, you and I are going to flag the next van down. Your men will hide in that ditch, and while I'm talking to the driver, they'll raid the truck. Get enough for everyone, then close the truck back up. We'll call it a donation." Cherry was actually smiling when he said this, not with his mouth—not a broad friendly man-to-man grin like you'd see on the face of a friend—but in his eyes. It was the first, and one of the only times, I felt he had a sense of humor.

We watched the scene unfolding like a play. Everyone was getting excited, and Bruce Morrison had this Cheshire cat grin on his face that made me want to burst out laughing. Sergeant Wittlesey's squad arrived intact, seven men including himself, and Gordy guided them into position. The gleam of the chase changed their listless expressions into beacons of anticipation, and we settled down in the hot sun for the target vehicle to make its appearance. We didn't have to wait long.

The straining engine of a big refrigerator van broke the midday silence.

The driver of the big eight-by-eight trailer hit the brakes as soon as he saw Captain Cherry and Gordy Grove flagging him down, and the meat wagon ground to a halt conveniently within earshot of the half dozen or so of us lounging around the front of our HQ bunker, watching as casually as we could. The driver wasn't alone. A second head popped up from the passenger's side. He must have been catching a few zzz's, or checking something under the dashboard. Captain Cherry and Gordy Grove made such a drama of waving the truck to a halt, that they thoroughly distracted the driver, who failed to see Wittlesey's men break quickly from their conceal- ment and duck behind the rear of the truck. They had already opened its back door when the vehicle lumbered to a stop.

We were trying to be casual, but listened intently.

"Possible ambush up ahead," Cherry's voice was deep- throated and authoritative if not downright imperious. "My people are checking it out now."

He'd picked a good line. Who'd proceed with that threat ahead?

"Lieutenant," Cherry turned to Grove. "Check with 3d Platoon on the radio and give me a signal when the area's been cleared."

Grove sprang into action like a cat. "Yes, sir!" he yelled, jogging to where Wilson was trying out his most casual lounging act near the bunker. Gordy grabbed the handset and made like he was transmitting, but he was watching the progress of Wittlesey's team. They had entered the trailer, and we could see C ration–size cartons flying out of the truck, caught by one of four "stackers" standing directly behind the vehicle. The cache was already waist-high and four cartons deep. The truck idled there, its big diesel engine rumbling and rattling away, the refrigerator generator unit on top of the cab whirring loudly, masking the grunts and groans of Wittlesey's raiding party.

Cherry seemed to strut around the cab, saying something gruffly to the two men up front, gesticulating up the road with his cigarette like it was a pointer. He could have been de- scribing the company's positions. He could have been waxing eloquent about his days on the big trucks. He could have been briefing General Westmoreland. Whatever he was saying, the stacks of purloined cartons grew to be chest-high, and Wittlesey signaled enough. As the two tossers inside the truck jumped back down to the hard-top and shut the door stealthily behind them, Grove yelled to the captain, "All clear ahead, sir!" Cherry then returned the driver's salute and stood there calmly as the truck started up again, straining to regain its forward motion, moving reluctantly from its cloud of gray-black diesel smoke. Wittlesey's men stood bunched together on the road, shielding their cache from the rearview mirror of the truck, and everyone seemed to give its teamsters a final wave as the truck disappeared from sight.

The whole exercise had taken less than three minutes.

"It's steak, sir!" Wittlesey yelled for all of us to hear. "Prime, grade-A, frozen-solid steer beef, fresh from the good ole US of A!" Then he let out this great war whoop of joy, and the men around him began to lug the cartons off the road and into the ditch. Everyone was laughing, cheering, congratulating themselves, and patting themselves on the back about the beauty of it all. It was a scene unmatched in my memories of "good times in country." And that day, for the first time in country that I can remember, we ate steaks. Sergeant Carbonneau and Sp4. Willie Green grilled them over a hot-coal fire, and every man in the company had two—compliments of Wittlesey's Raiders—and nothing has ever tasted quite as delicious as those stolen grade-A beefsteaks.

"Compliments of the general staff," was all the captain said to us as he walked back from the road. And for a fleeting second, I thought he might be okay.

Dream on, Lieutenant. Dream on.

Shortly after we returned from the An Khe Pass, Gordy Grove was "promoted" to the XO slot in Delta Company, a break he richly deserved. A newly arrived lieutenant named Marty Hammer, whom I'd known in the 82d Airborne, joined us to fill Gordy's shoes. Marty was a veteran of the 82d's deployment to the Dominican Republic, and I was delighted he'd been assigned to us. It didn't take him long to get his feet wet.

Chapter 21

In the Dust of Plei Me

*Life as a crapshoot is epitomized
by war.*

—THOMAS TAYLOR,
Lightning in the Storm

In late March of '66, we found ourselves laagering at Plei Me, preparing to stick our noses into the Ia Drang Valley once again. Until our assault into that ghost-ridden place, however, we kept ourselves busy by digging in around the Plei Me Special Forces Camp, the one that had come under siege the prior October, when everything had started for the Cav. When Captain Cherry took us into Plei Me, though, only 30 of our company's original 146 men were still with us. And we were anxious. At least I was.

We'd flown in that afternoon and were setting up a battalion-size defensive perimeter for the night. The next morning, we would fly back into the Ia Drang Valley to search for the 325th PAVN Division, our earlier nemesis. But that afternoon, in the hot dry sun, we were able to relax—as much as we ever could in the field—write some letters home, and bag some rays.

The Plei Me Special Forces Compound sat atop a small gently sloping hill in the middle of a valley. From where we were set up, all I could see was the section of the camp immediately to our rear (within a hundred meters or so), with its rows of staked barbed wire, crude wooden watchtowers, red-dirt berms, and trenches. I couldn't see too much of it, being surrounded by berms and all, but you could hear the Vietnamese in the compound, with their chickens clucking and their pigs squealing and their women jabbering.

Security around the place was pretty lax. Helicopters flew in and out sporadically, kicking up great swirling clouds of red dust, and jeeps occasionally barreled in and out of the compound's gate. I vaguely recall a jeep. Battalion must have brought it in because we never had one in the field. I do recall the jeep, though, because I was able to sit in it and write a letter home. I remember the letter because I wrote it on the back of a C ration box, like a postcard, and it was all smudged with ochre splotches when I mailed it. I also remember it because when I wrote it, I thought it was going to be my last letter home. Anyway, the jeep was there, and I was able to sit in it, keeping comfortably off the ground. Total luxury.

The troops were farther out, along the perimeter, in a ragged line of foxholes dug on the lower slope of the hill—not a great place to be if PAVN decided to make another run at the compound—but nobody was really worried about that because the whole battalion was there, and Charlie never attacked when we had all our troops massed. But I was still concerned about going into the valley the next morning, and maybe that's why I recall what happened so vividly.

As was my custom, I started digging my foxhole soon after we'd arrived. (All the Ia Drang Valley vets dug their holes as soon as they could.) We had set up our defensive positions and tied in with our sister units, and as soon as the company CP had been selected by Captain Cherry, on the upper slope looking down into the valley, I began to dig. For some reason (I think it was the jeep), the CO and the first sergeant and the RTOs in our headquarters hadn't begun to dig yet. The captain never dug, of course. He hardly ever did anything, really, but that's not the point of this story. Nor had Brucey-Goosey Morrison, our new and untested artillery forward observer, who, with his own RTO, was also happily ensconced in the jeep, bullshitting about something or other. I, on the other hand, old worrywart that I was, began to dig.

Now a foxhole isn't a very complicated affair. Depending on how much time you have to dig it, it can range from a "fighting hole," something long and shallow to lie in, to a "spider hole" (which our redoubtable foe had perfected) in which to hide, and snipe from, unseen. Our usual choice, the good old all-American foxhole, was usually three feet wide, five feet long, and six feet deep (or is it the other way around?), with a seat cut away at the bottom, on which you could stand if the rain was heavy, or doze if you had a buddy with you on alert. And sometimes, if you dug it deep enough, you could sink way down in it and light a cigarette (yes, a cigarette, nothing else)—something you'd never do at night unless you were deep in the sacred recesses of a well-dug hole.

Fifty yards to the east of us, along the contour of the slope, our mortarmen were setting up their tube. We carried only one because it was heavy. The ammunition alone weighed eight pounds a round, and with the tube twenty-five, and the base plate and bipod another thirty pounds each, and the ammo bearers lugging four rounds apiece, you could manage only one tube. And to do that was a chore. Why we did it at all I'll never know. But we did. We carried that goddamn mortar tube around with us for ten months, and never once used it to any real advantage. (The Cav finally dropped the idea of a mortar platoon, reorganizing it, instead, into a straight infantry platoon of forty-six men, with rifles, grenade launchers, and machine guns, but back in early '66, we still carried our mortar with us, in case we needed immediate, close-in support.)

A mortar is like a big steel stovepipe, but heavier. When set up to fire, its closed end rests on a round steel base plate, and the tube is supported by a bipod. To fire a mortar, all the gunner has to do is lay it in (aim it), fix a small powder charge to the bottom of the round (which looks like a small bomb, with fins), and drop the round down the stovepipe, fin first. The round slides down the tube. The gunpowder charge attached to the round's fin explodes against the firing pin at the bottom of the tube, forcing the round back out, arcing it high in the air toward its target. A very simple weapon really. Simple to operate, simple in design, simple to fire, and almost foolproof. I say again, almost.

The primary problem with mortars was their weight, but the higher-ups didn't have to lug them around, and didn't appreciate what a pain in the ass that could be. What they did know about mortars was their killing range. They were, indeed, a highly effective casualty producer. An 81-millimeter HE (high explosive) round has a killing radius of approximately twenty-five meters. That means, anyone standing within twenty-five yards of its point of detonation would be rendered instantaneously dead on arrival. And its shrapnel flies all over the place, like an unguided missile. Those little shards of steel can kill you just as dead as the big bang can—more than fifty yards from the point of detonation.

All of this is very technical information, if not downright dull, but it's necessary if you're going to appreciate this tale.

So, as I was saying, that afternoon was hot and dry and dusty, and we were lollygagging around the jeep at Plei Me, joking and smoking and getting ready for the next day's operation. I'd finished my foxhole, a nice deep, six-foot hole in the soft red chalky dirt, and our mortar platoon was getting ready to register defensive fires for the night. I looked over at them and watched Specialist Fourth Class Formosa and Sgt. (E-5) Jim Hibbits, both of them Ia Drang Valley veterans, carefully extracting mortar rounds from their long, black, cylindrical cardboard containers.

We were all looking forward to seeing the mortar team in action. We rarely had that chance. Captain Cherry had finagled battalion's permission to fire a dozen rounds as target practice, and the mortar guys were looking forward to playing with their much-maligned, oft-hated, never-really-appreciated, and hardly-ever-fired-in-anger overweight instrument of death.

"Fire mission!" Sergeant Hibbitts yelled as the mortar boys began their game. Five men scrambled to their appointed places around the gun, and the fire direction center (FDC) began to calculate the setting of the tube and the charge necessary for the round to reach its target. After a few seconds, FDC called out the charge, and the elevation, and the squad hopped to again. Formosa reached over and took the properly prepared round from Brooks, the assistant gunner, then swung back and held the round suspended over the open end of the tube.

"Fire!" yelled Sergeant Hibbitts, and Formosa let go of the round.

You could hear it sliding down the tube, sort of a dull metallic rattling, and then a loud *whonk!*, as the charge exploded and the round was sent on its way.

"There it is!" one of the RTOs exclaimed, pointing in the air. I looked up, and by God, you could really see it, that deadly mortar round, just a black speck, arcing high in the sky out of sight.

The target, we knew, was a small stand of trees on the far slope of the high ground on the other side of the valley, about a thousand meters away, and we counted to ourselves, waiting for the round to drop.

A small gray puff and then a cloud of brown dust rose from the earth about fifty yards short of the trees, followed almost immediately by a loud *kaarrrruuummp!* that shook the ground and echoed through the valley. We had really smacked the landscape with that one.

I heard some minor adjustments being called out from the FDC, and the usual scurrying around the gun tube, and Sergeant Hibbitts gave the second command to fire. Formosa dropped the round down the tube, and the deadly process was repeated. This time the round landed right in the middle of the trees.

Nice shot, I thought.

"Fire for effect!" Sergeant Hibbitts yelled, meaning Formosa would drop three more rounds down the tube, one right after the other, sending a three-round salvo on its way toward the target and ultimately wiping out that nice little clump of trees.

I watched as he dropped the first round down the tube, swiveled to his right, grabbed the second round from Brooks, then swiveled back to the tube. *Whonk!* went the first round out the tube, and Formosa dropped the second round down the tube. Then he swiveled to his right again, grabbed the third round from Brooks, and swiveled back . . .

As his hand with the third round swung back toward the tube, the second round fired. *Whonk!* Simultaneously, I saw the third round, knocked suddenly from Formosa's grasp, fall harmlessly to the ground. He grabbed his left hand and began a crazy little dance around the gun pit, shaking his hands up and down, his face contorted with pain. I then looked up and saw that the second round, deflected from its intended path by Formosa's overeager hand, was arcing almost straight up in the air, directly overhead (instead of heading off toward the clump of trees across the valley). As it hovered at the top of its arc, I realized, too late perhaps, that it was going to come right back down where we were standing.

I heard someone scream *"Misfire!,"* and everyone scrambled for cover.

No big deal, I thought. I had *my* foxhole. But as I turned to jump into it, so did everyone else in our headquarters, and before I had made even a tentative lunge for it, there, into my carefully dug foxhole, dove the captain, his RTOs, and Bruce Morrison—all 230 pounds of him. Their legs looked like worms in a can.

The mortar round was still high in the air, but coming down.

Struck by the sudden inevitability of my imminent demise, I opted for stoicism in the face of disaster, and, instead of screaming hysterically at those assholes in my foxhole, and thereby "losing it" in front of the men, I dove unceremoniously to the ground, buried my face in the dirt, and started praying. Yes, I admit it. I can say categorically and without equivocation that for the next few breathless seconds, I prayed as ardently and as fervently as I've ever prayed in my life. I prayed to God, and to Jesus, and to Mary, and to all the Saints in Heaven, that that goddamn fucking mortar round wouldn't land right on top of us and blow us all to shit.

Kaaarrrruuuummmmppp! I heard, and a tremor shook the ground. I looked up to see where the round had landed, and what damage it had done.

Luckily, it had dropped harmlessly to our south, about fifty yards away, and nobody was hurt, except Formosa. He'd almost lost a finger, severed by the second round as it had blasted out of the tube. Poor Formosa. But it could have been worse. The round could have exploded on contact with his hand—although that's unlikely, because each round has a safety pin in it that doesn't eject until the round has traveled fifty meters into the air—or it could have taken off his head. Anyway, after what he'd been through, the loss of a finger wasn't much. In fact, it was a quick ticket home, and you couldn't get much luckier than that. So Formosa learned a lesson, but he'd also make it home, so nobody felt too bad for him.

As for me, I was furious. After yelling and screaming at our headquarters group about using my foxhole when they should have had their own holes dug, I finally calmed down. The RTOs, who knew me well enough to know I was joking, just laughed. I laughed, too, eventually. But when Captain Cherry, our new CO, looked up at me from my carefully dug foxhole and said, "Tough shit, Lieutenant. RHIP," I knew we were heading for trouble.

RHIP—rank has its privileges. Somehow, I didn't find that very funny.

The day after Formosa almost had his finger sliced off, we flew back into the Ia Drang Valley to look for PAVN. The day was crystal clear and hot, and the terrain we were searching was flat, but mostly forest—the same kind that had surrounded us at Xray and Albany. I remember we assaulted an LZ in the morning, walked all day through a forest, were extracted late that afternoon, and flew back to Plei Me. I remember two other incidents, as well.

One was funny. We had been trekking through the forest for about an hour, the company in a column of platoons, searching for whatever signs of PAVN we could find, and we were being as quiet as we possibly could. Unlike the movies, when a company is on the move in the jungle, you move as quietly as you can. If the enemy hears you coming, he can do one of two things. He can run away, which is what he usually did, or he can stand and fight, which is what he did at Albany. And not knowing how many bad guys are behind the next tree line, you tend to be as stealthy as you can. Silence is golden in the jungle. That doesn't mean that everything else around you is quiet, though, and sometimes it's unnerving.

We were in relatively open terrain, spread out well, and moving silently. The forest was thicker on our right, but not too bad. All you could hear except the usual jungle buzz was the occasional breaking of squelch on our radios, the short rush of static that precedes the receipt of a transmission. There were probably some birds in the trees, too, singing or calling to each other, whatever it is they do, and maybe even a monkey or two occasionally giving out a yowl, but that's about all we could hear. And that was fine with me, I assure you. If it was too quiet, you'd get the creeps. Too quiet meant someone else was around. Someone else was keeping the animals and the birds from sounding off. But that particular morning, everything seemed okay.

Suddenly I heard something crashing through the forest on our right. Everyone froze. Some of us dropped to one knee. All of us raised our weapons and waited. The crashing got louder, coming closer, and I was wondering what was making all that noise, when a deer, a big beautiful buck with an impressive spread of antlers, broke from the canebrake on our right and loped across the open ground within fifty meters of where I was kneeling. It disappeared into the woods and was gone. One of our flankers had scared it, I guess. It was truly a beautiful animal, but it scared the hell out of me, too!

Except for that deer, we didn't see or hear anything of significance for the rest of that day, and when we reached our designated pickup zone, Captain Cherry called battalion. A flight of eight Hueys was on its way.

Eight could take half our people, so Captain Cherry said he'd take the 1st Platoon and the Mortar Platoon with him on the first lift, and I'd bring the rest of the company in on the second lift. That was fine with me, but I was concerned because of what I remembered about Albany, and none of us knew who might be nearby. Just because we'd not heard or seen anything didn't mean a battalion of PAVN might not be just on the other side of the tree line.

One other slight concern. A flight of eight ships makes a lot of noise, and anyone within a thousand meters of our location would know where we were when the ships landed. If the bad guys heard them, and wanted to, they could investigate, and there would only be two platoons of good guys still on the ground. But that's the name of the game. Extract what you can with the resources at hand, and come back for the rest when you can.

The first flight came in, picked up Captain Cherry with half of our troops, and took off. That left me, with Marty Hammer's 2d Platoon, on one side of the pickup zone, and Dick Hogarth's people on the other side, about a hundred yards away. After the first lift had gone, an eerie silence settled over our little corner of the world. Our normal practice, our SOP, was to wait quietly in place, keeping security out until the ships returned, then fall back to the LZ and hop on board. I was resting in the grass near a small tree with the men of 2d Platoon spread out around me and keeping their eyes peeled, when I looked across the LZ and saw several men in Dick Hogarth's platoon lollygagging around a big fallen tree in the open, grabbing ass, horsing around, and certainly not lying low.

Those stupid fucking jerks! Something in me exploded. I raised my M-16, took aim at a spot about halfway up the trunk of a big tree in the center of their position, and fired a single round. It cracked over their heads, sending them diving for cover. You should have seen them dive for the ground! It would have been funny if it hadn't been so serious. After my rifle shot shattered the quiet and echoed through the valley, telling anyone who hadn't heard the helicopters exactly where we were, an even eerier silence fell around us. Everyone waited to find out what had happened—those who hadn't seen me fire that shot, anyway.

Hogarth's voice came over the radio, reporting an incoming round.

"That was me," I said. "Now keep your goddamn heads down and your eyes peeled until we're out of here. Out!"

And that was it. About ten minutes later, the second flight thundered into the LZ and picked us up. I was mighty glad to see them, too, and to see the rest of our men boarding them as they landed. When it was clear that all our people were aboard, I gave the crew chief a thumbs-up, and the flight lifted off as one, cleared the treetops, and headed back to Plei Me.

I looked back one more time to check the LZ, to see where we'd been, to see if I could see any bad guys converging on our position, but there weren't any. Then I happened to glance down at my M-16, and saw that a round had jammed in the chamber. I had fired one shot, and my weapon had jammed, and I was so uptight, so wound up, so concerned about keeping our people alert until we were extracted, that I hadn't even noticed that my M-16's chamber was open, with a bright brass cartridge jammed inside, while we waited for that flight to pick us up. If I'd needed to fire at anything, if I'd raised my M-16 to my shoulder and pulled the trigger, nothing would have happened.

"Jesus Christ," I said to myself, clearing the jammed round and loading another into the chamber. That was close. It was a reminder of how important it was to keep your weapon clean, test-fired, and checked again and again.

I don't think anyone in the chopper saw what I'd done, or what I did when I cleared the round, but I knew what had happened, and how deadly a mistake that would have been had I needed to fire that weapon again, and it scared me. It humbled me, too. I said a silent prayer of thanks as we lifted above the forest and made a beeline for the safety of Plei Me.

Chapter 22

Machine Gun Valley

In truth it is the irony of things, as they were in those days, that has forced me back on my tracks, as it has a habit of doing, whenever writing of what I then went through.
—ALFRED M. HALE,
Royal Flying Corps
(unpublished memoir)

Looking back on those days with Captain Cherry, I remember we didn't have many laughs. Those few we had were bittersweet. And once, I recall, Old Charlie had the last laugh on us.

'Twas early April '66. We were southwest of Pleiku, still searching for PAVN. We'd been out for a week, and, except for punji stakes, hadn't seen a trace of either Victor Charles or his redoubtable cousins from the north. I was stumbling along as well as anyone, tending our new FO. Morrison, you will remember, was his name—Bruce for short—and he was still carrying thirty extra pounds of Stateside lard. The temperature hovered near a hundred, and he was hurting. So was his RTO. Luckily, we were next to water, and though it looked like coffee regular, we could always get a drink.

We numbered a hundred strong that day, following the river south. Punji stakes lined its banks. Punjis were everywhere in that valley. Old Victor Charles, who didn't like us encroaching on his territory, had littered the fields with sharpened stakes of split bamboo. They weren't deadly, mind you, not to us, but a dung-tipped punji in the ankle or shin could ruin your day. It would take you out of action, too—not

238

as dramatically as a bullet, perhaps, but just as fast—so we kept our eyes peeled. Sergeant Buckley, from the 2d Platoon, had skewered his kneecap the previous day, and we'd had to fly him out. There weren't just new punjis in this valley, cleverly hidden in the grass, but old ones, too, from the war with the French. The old ones listed forlornly in untended cornfields or drooped beside footpaths long-since shunned by the locals. To them, a punji wound was fatal.

Bruce and I trailed the lead platoon—Kelly's people that day. They were stretched a little thin, from the riverbank on our left to a heavily forested ridgeline that loomed on our right like a giant sleeping lizard. The valley floor was dusty and overgrown with shriveled trees and clumps of waist-high scrub—clear terrain really. I mean, you didn't have to worry about a division of North Viets charging out of the woods and catching you with your pants down, so everyone was pretty lax, and tired because it was hot and close to four o'clock. It was quiet, too. You could hear the water flow.

We had stopped for a break near a short, fat tree standing squat in the middle of a clearing. People were filling canteens, or sitting around smoking, or bitching about the heat and the flies, or changing socks, or grabbing a quick constitutional to flush away the worms (worms were beginning to decimate the line companies), or just waiting for the word to move. I was jawboning with the new guy and into my second cigarette, when a goddamn machine gun opened up on us, real close, and twenty rounds popped right around us. Three little geysers of sand erupted between Morrison and me, and we dove for cover. There was a frozen moment of silence, and then everyone started yelling. Who was shooting? Was anyone hit? But after that first sudden burst, not a shot was fired. Not that minute anyway. After all, we were pros, and pros didn't shoot unless they knew who they were shooting at.

"There he goes!" Kelly shouted from our right front flank. "One Victor Charlie, heading for the hills."

That's when Mr. Morrison did his thing.

"Hamburger Six, this is Thunderclap Alpha." He was on

the radio, calling for help—the only kind he knew. "Fire mission. Over."

Gunships had been on station all day, flying high lazy circles in the graying sky. In seconds they were on their way, from the north, beyond the river, two Huey gunships thundering down the valley at eighty knots, with big square rocket pods, one on each side just above the landing strut. Bruce had them on his radio.

"Throw red smoke," he yelled. His eyes were blazing. His breath came in short quick puffs. I could hear the quiver in his voice and feel his anticipation. This was his first live-fire mission, and he was doing it by the book. He fumbled for his compass, raised it to his eye, and sighted in on the ridgeline. The grenade I popped was hissing in the sand, spewing a deep red roiling dust that gushed from its nozzle and billowed around us in a cloud of chalky pink.

"One Victor Charlie, maybe more, with automatic weapons, midway up the ridge. Azimuth two hundred eighty-five degrees from my smoke. Fire!" He said the words as clearly as if he'd been practicing them all night, and he said them only once.

Ppphhhssshhheeeeewwwwwwwww! Two 2.75-inch rockets screeched overhead and smacked into the hillside. I looked for the tiny white puffs. A wisp of smoke drifted from the jungle, halfway up the hill. The choppers were still behind us, on a steady approach, getting louder.

"That's it," Bruce said. "Fire for effect!"

From high and just behind us both ships let fly with a salvo. Thirty-six rockets wooshed overhead like hot rods at a drag strip, and the ridgeline erupted in an ear-piercing, gray-smoke, tree-splintering explosion, as if engineers had planted rows of TNT along the hillside and detonated them all at once. The earth seemed to scream from its wound, a long mournful howl that echoed down the valley as the gunships thundered past us on a beeline for the target. Jesus, what a show! They disappeared behind the ridgeline's crest, but you could hear them circling to the right, coming around for another pass.

We lay there, dumbfounded. The once-covered ridgeline was exposed to us now, as if some giant farmer had suddenly scythed it clean. Only shattered trees, smoking earth, and chunks of gray-black rock remained. Appreciative murmuring, the "oohs" and "aahs" and "holy shits" of awe, bubbled from the troops.

"That'll teach the fucker," Wilson said. I was speechless.

"What do you think?" Bruce asked. I shrugged and looked for the captain.

Cherry had dived behind a hummock twenty yards to our right and stayed there through it all. He raised his head slowly. His eyes were wide. His lips were moving, but nothing came out.

"Enough, don't you think?" Bruce said. His voice had calmed. It was lower, more assured than before he'd performed his magic. He'd reacted well, I thought, and if anyone had been anywhere near that ridgeline, they'd have one hell of a headache.

"Yes," Cherry said, wiping the sand from his mouth. "That should do it." He started to get up, then crouched again. "Kelly!" he bellowed. "Check your front. All the way to the ridge. Find out where he came from."

We all knew who *he* was. Brave little bastard, I thought.

Bruce called off the gunships with a thank-you, and they started back home to reload. During the next few minutes, we dusted ourselves off and counted heads. Incredibly, no one was hurt. That lone VC had heard us coming, hidden in the brush, waited for us to settle down, and then let fly with a full magazine before bugging out and hauling his bony little ass up the hillside. If Kelly hadn't seen him, he'd have gotten clean away. Maybe he had, but after what I'd seen, I had my doubts.

Kelly's people returned empty-handed, and we picked up to resume our march.

A low rumbling thunder started from farther down in the valley. Everyone stopped and listened. The rumble swelled to a roar. Choppers, I thought, craning my neck. There they were, Huey slicks this time, the kind that carry troops, flying up the valley in a V of four, about a thousand meters south. Friendlies. I relaxed.

Then they started shooting. The door gunners, all eight of them, were spraying the valley floor with machine-gun fire, peppering the riverbanks as effectively, if not spectacularly, as the gunships had blasted the ridgeline. And they were coming right at us.

"Call those idiots off!" Cherry screamed. That's what he should have been doing, but he just stood there with his hands on his hips and a scowl on his face, screaming, "Stop them, I said! Goddamn it! Right now. Call 'em off."

"Who *are* they?" Bruce asked.

"I don't know *who* they are," the captain yelled. His voice had risen an octave.

"I don't either," Bruce said. *"And they're not on my frequency."*

Cherry blanched. If they're not on your frequency, you can't talk to them.

"Oh, Jesus! Oh, shit!" I heard myself say. I looked around. Everyone froze in place. The Hueys kept coming up the valley with all guns blazing.

"Unidentified choppers," Bruce called on his radio. "This is Thunderclap Alpha. Friendlies on the riverbank. I say again. Friendlies on the riverbank. Cease fire. Cease fire!"

Everyone was diving for cover now, scattering as they had before, scrambling for whatever shelter they could find. I could hear the guys on our left jumping into the river. Cherry dodged behind the squat little tree and hid there, cringing. The Hueys were bearing down on us, three hundred yards and closing fast. We were going to get chopped up good.

"Get down, sir!" Wilson said, but I couldn't take my eyes off those choppers.

Then I started waving—my rifle in one hand and my helmet in the other. I waved them back and forth in big easy arcs as calmly and as slowly as I could. I was trying to stand so tall that nobody could miss me. Bruce was waving, too. They had to see us, to see we were grunts. If they didn't, *sayonara*.

A hundred feet in front of us the firing stopped, as abruptly as it had started, and the four slicks thundered overhead with their guns still smoking in the afternoon haze. The ships were full of grim-faced men—infantry like us. We waved, but not one of them so much as smiled back.

We never found out who they were. None of us had the presence of mind to notice markings on the choppers, and battalion didn't have a clue. The artillery people had only rocket ships up that day, and the higher-ups, well, they didn't seem to care. It's my guess those ships were 9th Cav scouts— a Blue Platoon, they would have called themselves—harbingers of death who flew with few restrictions. They were good, too, we'd heard, but crazy. Maybe they knew it was us all the time. I don't know.

I do know this: If the VC had been watching us, they'd have had the last laugh.

Chapter 23

The Water Hole Follies

It had seemed to Kabuo that his detachment from this world was somehow self-explanatory, that the judge, the jurors, and the people in the gallery would recognize the face of a war veteran who had forever sacrificed his tranquillity in order that they might have theirs.

—DAVID GUTERSON,
Snow Falling on Cedars

If you hadn't noticed by now, things were getting a little confused for me around this time in my tour. Captain Cherry's tenure was particularly troublesome because I didn't like him much, didn't understand him, couldn't fathom why he wouldn't communicate with us better, or why he did the things he did. I didn't trust him, either. But a rifle company XO isn't supposed to rock the boat, isn't supposed to do anything but his job, isn't supposed to be anything but loyal to his CO, so I basically kept my mouth shut and my anxieties to myself. But that didn't help alleviate the concern, the doubts, the mistrust, and the simmering anger I felt about how he was running the company.

He didn't seem to like us much, either. Any of us. He didn't have to, of course. That wasn't part of his job. But he did have to care about his men, and I didn't think he did. Not a whit.

Some of the memories I have about those weeks and months with Cherry are blurred, and the ones I've recounted so far involve a certain irony. That's how we remember things that happened over there. We remember the irony. Shooting ourselves out of the sky. Scaring ourselves half to death. Stealing steaks from our own general staff. And all the other odd, harebrained, crazy things we did when we weren't being scared out of our gourds, like beer walking.

One short take I'd like to mention is an incident I refer to as "the Water Hole Follies." But first things first.

Early in Cherry's tenure, Lieutenant Colonel MacDade was replaced by an aviator/infantry lieutenant colonel named Robert F. Litle, Jr., a tall friendly man with a wry sense of humor. Because we were so busy, though, out in the field and roaming around the Ia Drang Valley again, I don't remember the first time I met him, but I do remember hearing that Mac-Dade was gone, kaput, fini, *sayonara*, and that was fine with me. I'd seen MacDade at work. I'd seen his eyes bulging out and heard him yelling "Cease fire!" and "Withdraw!" during the debacle at Albany. I'd also heard he'd had some problems at LZ 4, too, though I can't say what, exactly, because I wasn't there. There had certainly been no love lost between Joel Sugdinis and MacDade, either, and that had been more than evident the last month Joel was our CO. He used to come back from battalion in a rage. Fit to be tied. It was awful. Long story short, when I heard that MacDade had been replaced, I felt relief.

So, we had a new battalion commander named Robert F. Litle, Jr.. He was an aviator as well as an infantryman and seemed to know what he was doing, and that alleviated any doubts we might have had about his competence and his ability to run the battalion. Major Henry, who'd really been the person who'd saved us at Albany and had always had our respect, stayed on, too, and that helped with the transition.

At any rate, when we went back into the Ia Drang Valley in March of '66, we had Jim Kelly, Marty Hammer, and Dick Hogarth as our rifle platoon leaders. Jack Hibbard may still have had the mortars. I'm not sure.

Soon after we'd had the bejesus scared out of us in Machine Gun Valley, we were picked up en masse and flown to a position way up in the mountains near the Cambodian border. I remember the LZ distinctly because it was one of the few places we stayed at for more than a night. Three, I think, we stayed there.

The LZ was high up in the mountains on a gently sloping hill covered with lush, green, waist-high grass and strewn with fallen trees and jagged stumps. Either a storm had blown the trees down, or someone had been doing some crude form of logging there. I also remember the LZ being surrounded by a deep, foreboding forest.

We came thundering into that LZ and set up shop on its eastern edge. From there, Captain Cherry sent out platoon-size patrols in a cloverleaf pattern, i.e., routes on a map that resembled a four-leaf clover—the division's new theory being that if we could cover enough terrain with these cloverleaf patterns, we would improve our chances of finding the bad guys, and then division could bring maximum hurt down on them. I'm not sure what division would do if a poor rifle company stumbled into a regiment of PAVN, but we'd have to cross that bridge when we came to it. I do remember having the sinking feeling, though, that if we ran into anything bigger than a battalion, we'd be hard-pressed to survive up there while division ran around getting us some help.

That's why we dug in so deeply. We spent that first afternoon setting up our company perimeter—digging deep three-man foxholes and cutting fields of fire. I distinctly remember a thick grove of bamboo nearby, and cutting enough down to make a crude sleeping platform—the only time I ever did that in the field. It was good I did, too, because I remember seeing at least two centipedes exploring the ground below me while I was there.

I hated the centipedes in Vietnam—more than the spiders, the snakes, and the leeches. The centipedes were the scariest insects we ran into over there. They were so big (six to eight inches long) and their venom so virulent, that, with only one bite, they could send a man to the aid station twitching spasmodically. During one of my first nights with the Cav—back in base camp when I was duty officer—a panicked young trooper came running into the TOC exclaiming that his buddy had just been bitten in the temple by a "foot-long centipede." He'd seen it crawling from underneath his buddy's head! I ran back with him to his pup tent. When we got there, his tent mate was going into what appeared to be an epileptic fit, and we had to hustle him off to the battalion aid station. It was a scary incident, and I promptly stomped on every centipede I saw after that (including the ones crawling under my bed). There were lots of them over there, though, and they were mean. I shudder every time I think of them.

And then there was the night, back at base camp, that we saw the spider . . .

Frozen in the cold beam of our headlights, it looked as big as my hand. Black it was, some kind of tarantula. It had stopped in the middle of the narrow dirt road, ten yards in front of our jeep when we were on our way back to our base camp. (We were returning from the division shower point after the first showers we'd had in a month.)

Denny Wilson was driving. He jammed on the brakes, and we skidded to a halt.

"It's harmless," Joel said. "Let's just see what it does."

"Those things are deadly," Gordy exclaimed. "Run the fucker over, squash it dead, right now."

"Holy shit! Will you look at the size of that son of a bitch!" said Kelly. "Let's get out of here!"

From my jump seat in back of the jeep, I stood up to get a better look.

Without warning, Wilson gunned the engine and popped the clutch, and the jeep shot forward into the night, heading straight for that unsuspecting arachnid, leaving me unceremoniously dumped on my ass in the choking swirling dust of that narrow dirt road. I watched the jeep's headlights race up that road through the darkness and heard the hoots and howls of my compatriots ring abrasively in my ear as the jeep roared off into the night.

Then I became suddenly and acutely aware that that spider,

no longer transfixed by the beam of our headlights, shared the very same tiny stretch of road upon which I sat. I pictured him in an attack mode, scuttling toward me as fast as he could, bent on some primitive revenge against the human whose friends had tried to run him down.

Now I've been known to rise quickly, but I've never jumped to my feet quite as fast as I did that night on that road in the dark with that spider. Nor have I ever sprinted through the woods after dark. But I did that night, as fast as my legs would carry me, and I'm lucky I didn't trip headlong over a stump and break my neck.

Finally clear of danger, I stopped, caught my breath, and resumed a more leisurely pace back on that road to our HQ. Reaching it, I saw Joel, Gordy, and Jim. They were standing in the light of a Coleman lantern and still laughing. They acknowledged my arrival with guffaws.

Wilson was still in the jeep, still sitting behind the wheel. "Sorry about that, sir," he said.

"No sweat," I said. I felt too stupid to say anything else.

Meanwhile, back in the mountains . . . On our third day at that makeshift base by the side of that mountaintop LZ, Captain Cherry sent two rifle platoons out on cloverleaf patrols, and the rest of us waited anxiously and listened to their progress over the radio. Dick Hogarth called in around midday and reported that he'd reached the checkpoint nearest the Cambodian border.

Captain Cherry asked him if he'd seen any signs.

"Negative," was the response.

"Keep going then," the captain said.

"Where to?" Dick asked.

"In the direction that you're headed," said the captain.

"I think we've crossed the line," Dick said.

"How can you tell that?" asked the captain.

"I can read a map," Dick said.

"Do you see any signs," repeated the captain.

"Negative," came the same response.

"Then keep on going," the captain said.

"Wilco, out," said Dick.

Half an hour later, I heard this conversation:

"Braveboy Six, this is Braveboy Three-six. Over," Hogarth called.

"This is Braveboy Six. Over," answered the captain.

"This is Three-six. We can see the signs now. You can't miss them. Over."

"What do they say?" asked the captain.

"New Jersey Turnpike, dead ahead," came the reply. "We're heading back now. Over."

The captain glanced at me and smiled. I smiled, too. Good for you, Dick, I'm thinking.

"Roger that," the captain said. "Permission granted. Out."

And that was our first (and last) Cambodian incursion, at least while I was there.

When Dick's bedraggled platoon traipsed back into our perimeter that afternoon, filthy, exhausted, and beat, I remember him telling the captain that they'd found a big water hole just south of our perimeter, about two hundred yards down the slope.

"How big is it?" the captain asked.

"Big," Dick said. "Huge. Like a swimming hole."

The next day, after the patrols had returned, the captain announced over the radio that the entire company was to pick itself up and proceed approximately two hundred meters south, that Lieutenant Hogarth would lead us to a water hole for a treat. The entire company picked up and headed down that hill and into the forest. And sure enough, about two hundred meters into it, we came upon a huge water hole. Dick was right. It was big. Big as a swimming pool. It was just there, too, surrounded by forest, a huge swimming hole in the middle of nowhere, close to the Cambodian border.

One side of the water hole was a sheer mud embankment, and a fallen tree formed a sort of diving platform from its bank. On the other end of the swimming hole there was a more gently sloping approach to the water, like the shallow end of a pool. The water was deep, dark, still, and clean. It was a miracle.

The captain ordered each of the platoons to set up a machine gun team for security, then told everyone that the water hole was open for swimming.

After a moment or two, with everyone sort of milling around nervously with their hands in their pockets, one of the more adventurous men of the company jumped out of his clothes and leaped into the water, and suddenly we forgot where we were. Almost everyone took a swim that afternoon. I certainly did, stripping bare-assed naked and sliding down the sloping bank into the water. It was clean and cool, deep enough to dive in, and absolutely wonderful.

Now picture, if you will, sixty or seventy men, bare-ass naked, each reverting to his most delirious childhood, cavorting around that swimming hole in the middle of the forest as if he'd nothing on his mind except to be the most daring and foolish guy in the company, laughing, joking, pushing, shoving, splashing, diving, jumping, and yelling. Water fights, of course, were common. Guys were jumping from the trunk of the tree that overhung the swimming hole. In a nutshell, people were having an absolute ball. I remember I was enjoying myself immensely when I looked up and saw the first sergeant talking to the captain, a look of grave concern on the first sergeant's face. Then the captain's face went pale. Suddenly he started yelling.

"Everyone out of the pool! Choppers are on the way. They're coming in to pick us up in fifteen minutes! Get back to the perimeter on the double and be ready to go!"

Now picture this: Sixty or seventy naked men suddenly scrambling out of the water and slithering up that muddy bank, heading for their gear.

I raced up that bank with everyone else and almost jumped into my clothes, pulling my fatigues on, then my socks, my boots, then lacing them up, buttoning my trousers and shirt and grabbing my weapon and slinging my harness over my shoulder, grabbing my helmet, and hotfooting it back up the hill. I'd never seen such a cluster-fuck as we were that afternoon, racing as fast as we could back up to that base camp, to break it down and fill in the holes and roll up our ponchos and stuff whatever gear we'd left there drying in the sun. Somehow we did it, though, got back to the camp and broke it down while I manifested the company and told the platoon sergeants who would get on which ships, then watched as we took our places around that LZ.

Just before the first flight came in, we got word that the ships could only take three men each. The heat, humidity, and altitude had something to do with reducing the lift capacity of a Huey. So my original manifest went out the window, and I had to inform the platoon sergeants that it had been changed, and what the new one was, and we still managed to get out of that LZ without mishap, and thundered off to someplace else.

Chapter 24

Ambush!

Wars never end for the warriors,
unless, of course, they're killed.
—PHILIP CAPUTO,
Means of Escape

Shortly after the water-hole follies, we found ourselves in the air again, weaving through the jungle-covered mountains of Kontum Province, along the Cambodian border. We were flying up a valley, following a river. Our LZ happened to be on that river. The farther we flew up that valley, the narrower it got, until it seemed just like a gorge. We could look out the chopper door on either side of us and see thick jungle undergrowth all around us, at eye level, clearly within rifle range. And we were going in in only four ships at a time!

When we reached our LZ, we had to jump from the ships while they hovered over the river. Luckily, it was shallow. Ankle-deep. After we'd off-loaded, we proceeded upriver about a hundred meters and set up a perimeter with Charlie Company, which had flown in behind us, on an island in the middle of the river.

Although heavily-jungled mountains rose steeply from the riverbanks on either side of us, we'd found a pretty good spot. The river was shallow and provided us with clear fields of fire for at least fifty meters all around the island. Charlie Company, which manned the upstream half of our island perimeter, was a damn good unit, too—disciplined, motivated, and hard. Captain Skip Fesmire still commanded it, and Pat Payne (former Alpha platoon leader and certainly one of the best lieutenants in the battalion) was his XO. Reconstituted

252

after its near annihilation at Albany, Charlie 2/7 had recaptured its old élan, and I was happy they were with us.

On the bad side, we couldn't dig in. The island, though big enough to hold two companies, wasn't high enough above the waterline to allow for foxholes. (We could dig them, but they'd just fill up.) Furthermore, the mountains around us rose so sharply, and the vegetation was so thick, that a regiment of PAVN could have been bivouaced just upstream, and we wouldn't have known it. Finally, the sound of water gurgling over the rocks in the riverbed, though soothing to some, made it hard to hear the sounds you needed to hear at night, like the chatter of approaching enemy soldiers, or the clink of steel on steel, or the telltale breaking of a branch, or the soft grunt of some intruder bumping his leg on a log.

Despite the shortcomings of the place, we were in relatively high cotton that night, with the stream flowing around us and the water cool and clear (a blessing in itself). As long as Victor Charlie wasn't hiding in force nearby, we'd be okay.

We'd landed, secured the island, coordinated our defenses with Charlie Company, and were just sitting around waiting for the word. When it came, we were told to stay put. Except for sending out ambush patrols that night, we were to stand pat and wait for further instructions.

Around 6:00 P.M., Captain Cherry came back from a meeting with Captain Fesmire and called the platoon leaders in. He ordered Marty Hammer to send out two ambush patrols that night—one on the west bank of the river about six hundred meters downstream and one on the east side of the river about four hundred meters up the slope. He wanted a reinforced squad at each site.

I was nonplused, as usual, by the lack of information Captain Cherry imparted. Joel Sugdinis had always given us as much information as he had, or as much as he thought we could handle. But Cherry was the opposite. He kept it mostly to himself—as if he thought too much information would confuse us—and that pissed me off.

At the end of the briefing, the captain turned to Marty and

said, "I'll brief the patrol leaders when they're ready to depart."

Marty said he wanted to go with the downstream patrol, and the captain didn't object.

I vaguely recall the patrol leaders' briefing. All the captain did was to show them on the map where he wanted them to go. I wasn't really listening, just watching where he pointed on the map. I wasn't that concerned because Hammer was in charge of one group, and the other group, with a squad leader named Buckley in charge, was just going across the river, almost within shouting distance. Our mortars could support them both, and we had artillery if we needed it.

I remember the patrols going out, though. They came through the company CP just as night settled over us, and I was able to wish Marty luck. I could also hear them coming up on the radio as they proceeded from checkpoint to checkpoint on the way to their ambush sites.

The night was lovely, I recall. The air cooled off quickly that high in the mountains, and the stars were out in force. The gentle gurgle of the river over the rocks gave us a sense of peace and tranquillity, even though we knew it was false.

I was sitting with Sergeant Carbonneau, our field first sergeant that trip, and Dick Hogarth, quietly jawboning before we hit the rack. We didn't have much of a command post—just the cover of some thick brush, I recall, and maybe a log or two to hide behind if something happened.

"Man, it's beautiful tonight," Dick said in the dark. He'd been with us two months, slightly longer than Captain Cherry. Dick was sitting with his back against a log, listening to the sitreps (situation reports) of the outgoing patrols, waiting for them to get settled in before he hit the hay.

The stars were lovely. With the sounds of the river over the rocks and the cool air of the mountains, I could put my head back and shut my eyes and almost forget where we were. Despite the mountains looming darkly over us, I was comfortable with our position. Charlie Company was behind us, and the river offered protection. As soon as the patrols settled in, I was through.

"*Psht. Psht.* Braveboy Base, this is Braveboy Two-six, reporting checkpoint Delta," came Marty Hammer's whisper through the speaker. Larry Sargent, the RTO on watch, pressed his squelch button twice to acknowledge the report. (That way, no sound would be transmitted to the patrol leader's radio except for two soft *psht*s signaling that we heard them and knew where they were.)

"That was mighty fast," Sergeant Carbonneau said in his wonderful downeast accent. Cabbie was doing double duty that night. He was acting as our field first sergeant as well as Hogarth's platoon sergeant.

"Sure was," Dick agreed.

I, too, was surprised at how fast Marty had moved his men into position, but I was glad he had. He'd had the longest distance to cover but had used the river as his route of approach to the ambush site, and that had eased the way. I also breathed a sigh of relief that PAVN hadn't set up an ambush on the river. I pictured Marty stealthily setting up his people, placing them in position for whatever kind of ambush he was setting up. They were in a saddle, I recall, about two hundred meters up from the river. Not a bad place to be, I guess, but certainly lonely, and no one knew what lay farther down the river. We were deep in PAVN country, after all.

Despite the slight breeze and the gurgling stream, I could still hear the mosquitoes buzzing around our heads. Thank God for bug juice, I thought.

Whump!

Brrrtttt! Brrrtttt!

Whump!

The firing came from behind us, up the eastern slope, where Buckley's patrol had gone. We sat helpless and frozen in place as the awful sounds of a brief but fierce firefight shattered the night. Then it stopped as abruptly as it started.

Seconds later, we heard the distraught voice of Sergeant Buckley over the squawk box.

"Braveboy Six, this is Braveboy Two-six-three. We've been hit! Maybe a squad. At least one automatic weapon. I got one elephant and two buffalo (one killed and two wounded), and we're pinned down! Over!"

Worse than his transmission, though, were the terrible sounds we could hear behind him on the radio—the confused cries of terrified men in the jungle at night, not knowing where the enemy was, or how many, or what they had with them—and the screams of the wounded, all from just three or four hundred meters away, deep in the thick, dark jungle across the river. I could hear them calling to each other in the distance—not on the radio this time—then another burst from an M-16 on automatic, then two more M-79 rounds, then something bigger. A claymore?

Captain Cherry appeared from out of nowhere and grabbed the handset. His face, though masked by the dark, was very grim. He looked at me but said nothing. "What's your location? Over!" he asked Buckley.

Though we could hear the firing and the screams in the dark, we didn't know exactly where they were. The terrible sounds of confusion—the shouts of panicked men and the god-awful screaming—continued to drift across the river. Then another burst, then three quick single shots, then silence.

"Six, this is Two-six," Marty Hammer's voice came quickly over the radio.

"This is Six," Cherry answered.

"This is Two-six. Request permission to proceed to that location."

"Negative," the captain barked. "Stay where you are."

"Braveboy Six, this is Two-six-three," Buckley said. "We're hit bad. I got four elephants now. They're above us. We can't get to them! I say again, four elephants! Please advise. Over."

Four dead! Jesus, half his squad! What the fuck was going on? (Luckily, he was wrong. He'd gotten his code words confused.)

"Two-six-three, this is Six. What's your location? Over."

Jesus Christ, Captain. You can hear 'em across the river!

A different and unfamiliar voice came over the battalion

radio then. "Braveboy Six, this is Champion Six." It was Captain Fesmire calling Cherry.

Larry Sargent handed the battalion handset to the captain. "Braveboy Six, this is Two-six-three." Buckley's voice again. "I say again, we're pinned down. Automatic weapons above us. We need help. We need illumination. We need medevac. We're pulling back. Pulling back. Do you roger?" Again, in the background, I could hear men yelling around him. You could hear the confusion and panic.

"Negative, Two-six-three. Stay put! Out!" Cherry barked this into the company handset, then answered Fesmire on the battalion net.

The gist of Fesmire's transmission was that someone had triggered one of his ambushes. After his people had popped their claymore, they'd heard Americans shouting back and forth to each other. He was afraid they were our people.

Cherry said he'd check, then called Sergeant Buckley and ordered him to cease fire and find out if they'd triggered a friendly ambush.

Marty Hammer came back on the line and asked for an update. (Marty wasn't on the battalion net, so he hadn't heard Fesmire's transmission.) I couldn't imagine how Marty felt, knowing that one of his squads had just been ambushed, that several of his men were down, and that there was nothing he could do about it. Not from his location, anyway.

Buckley called Hammer. "Two-six, this is Two-six-three. I got half my men down! We need medevac. Can you get us some help? Over."

Though the shouting in the background had ceased, it was clear that Buckley was in bad shape and needed help.

Cherry called him and told him to calm down, then told Hammer to stay off the net. Then he called Fesmire and asked if his people could make contact with our people. If they could, would they help bring our people down.

Fesmire said they could, and they would, but that one of his people had been killed, too.

Jesus, I was thinking. What the fuck had happened? How could Cherry have sent our men into Charlie Company's area of operations? That stupid fucking son of a bitch. Only a fucking idiot would be stupid enough to do something like that. And five or six KIAs? I was rip-shit.

Sergeant Buckley called again. He sounded totally drained.

"We've made contact with the other element up here," he said. "They're friendlies. We're coming down together. All of us. I got one KIA and four wounded. They got one KIA. We need medevac as soon as we get down. Over."

"Roger that, Two-six-three," Cherry responded, weakly.

I called Pat Payne. He'd already called for Dustoff (medevac). I told him we needed it for six. He said he knew that, that he'd see to it. I thanked him and signed off.

Then we waited, helpless and despondent, wondering what that squad must be going through, the terror of bringing their wounded down that jungle trail at night and the anguish of dragging their dead with them. We could only imagine the horror of that ambush—the shock, the terror, the chaos and confusion of it all.

Half an hour later, the medevac ship vectored into Charlie Company's position, landed in the shallows, and shut down. We continued waiting for the survivors of those two poor squads to stumble down that trail in the darkness. We could hear them by then, about a hundred yards out, and dispatched a squad to help them. When they finally appeared on the far bank of the river, several more men from Charlie Company crossed over and helped them back across the river. The Dustoff started up again, and I watched from our CP as our five casualties and the KIA from Charlie Company were loaded onto the ship.

After it lifted off and flew away in the darkness, I called Marty Hammer and told him that his people had been taken care of.

"Roger, Five," was all he could say.

I didn't talk to Sergeant Buckley. I couldn't. I didn't have the heart. I let Captain Cherry do that.

*   *   *

Early the next morning, Colonel Litle, the new battalion commander, flew into our perimeter in his C & C chopper to find out what had happened. By the time Marty Hammer's ambush patrol had closed back into our perimeter, the colonel, captains Fesmire and Cherry, the patrol leaders involved in the incident, and a squad from Charlie Company had crossed the river and headed up the mountainside to walk the ambush site.

We were trying to absorb what had happened. Marty was so angry when he got back that he couldn't talk. I was heartsick at the thought of losing five good men to one of our own ambushes. I was also seething inside, enraged at what the captain had done. He'd sent one of our ambush patrols into Charlie Company's area of operations. It was clearly his fault. Anyone with a pea brain knew it. It was gross incompetence at best, criminal negligence at worst.

Half an hour later, the vanguard of the colonel's reconnaissance party broke out of the jungle and started across the river. Then the colonel appeared with Captain Fesmire at his side. Cherry was walking behind them. As soon as they appeared, the C & C ship started up its engine, and by the time the colonel had crossed the river, it was warmed up and ready to go. I saw the three officers conferring one more time, then the colonel boarded his ship, and it took off.

Captain Cherry walked directly back to our command post. I was watching him as he came. When he got within earshot, he looked up, saw me, and called me over.

"I've just been shit-canned," he said to me. "As soon as we get back to An Khe, I'm relieved. The whole operation has been canceled, too. We're flying out of here in half an hour."

I tried to keep a straight face. I don't know what I said, if anything. But I was glad. I was happy. Happy and relieved. No, overjoyed, really, overjoyed at hearing that the worthless son of a bitch had been relieved. He'd been a worthless piece of shit since the day he'd joined us, and it was a miracle we hadn't lost more men. It would be over soon, I thought. Thank God.

"Will you inform the platoon leaders?" I asked.

"Yes, I guess I'll have to do that," he said. "Call them to the CP, will you?"

And with that, he walked past me to the CP, reached down and pulled a fresh cigar from his map case, lit it, and turned his back to us. He seemed to be staring at the mountains.

Fuck you, sir, was all I felt like saying.

By dusk the next day he was gone. History. A bad dream. And I had a brand-new company commander to worry about, a captain named Davison who looked a bit cherubic. I would have to help him along, help him familiarize himself with the company. But that was okay. Alpha was a battle-hardened group, hard core all the way, and he was lucky to get us. We were Alpha Company, 2d of the 7th, veterans of the Ia Drang, LZ 4, Bong Son, and the Crow's Foot. We knew what was happening and how to get things done. We were a good outfit with a damn good, experienced XO, two experienced platoon leaders, and a new one who'd done well that week. We'd suffered a rude shock, though, and learned a brutal lesson—you're only as good as your leaders.

Cherry was the worst CO I'd ever had. Thank God he was gone.

Thirty years later, I learned a terrible truth. I learned it from Sgt. Winston "Cabbie" Carbonneau when we got together for a brief reunion in Vermont in 1995. Cabbie reminded me that he had left Alpha Company in late April of '66. He'd contracted malaria and had been sent home to recover. Then he'd gone back to Vietnam and served with the 196th Infantry of the Americal Division near My Lai for a year. (He wasn't involved in the massacre, thank God.) After the war, Cabbie was Stateside, waiting in some airport terminal to catch a flight, when he saw, to his astonishment, Captain Cherry sitting nearby. But he wasn't a captain any longer. He was an E-6! He'd been riffed, demoted as part of the army's reduction in force program.

So be it.

BOOK FIVE

Retribution

Chapter 25

Bong Son II

War is the province of danger, and
therefore courage above all things
is the first quality of a warrior.
  —GENERAL KARL
   VON CLAUSEWITZ

Of all my company commanders, I should remember Captain Davison the best. He was the youngest, most thoughtful, and the last of the three I worked with. But I can hardly remember what he looked like. Relatively small when stacked up against the likes of Jim Kelly (six four), First Sergeant Miller (six three), and me (six two), so I'd guess he was in the five-ten category. I recall a recalcitrant forelock of brown hair and an innocent, almost cherubic, face. In fact, he looked barely old enough to shave, incredibly young. Maybe that's why I don't remember him that well. But he did have a quiet competence about him, an intensity with which he addressed his new responsibilities, and that reassured me as I got to know him better. I should remember him more clearly—he was involved in, and partially responsible for, two of the toughest moral crises I faced in Vietnam—but I don't.

Another officer joined us after Captain Cherry was shit-canned—a first lieutenant named George Polli. He succeeded Jack Hibbard as our Mortar Platoon leader. Jack had left us to fill the XO's slot in Bravo Company. (Another graduate, so to speak, of Alpha Company becoming an XO.) Polli was a big, brash, overweight guy, and he had a big mouth.

Captain Davison, Polli, and I got to know each other only superficially during the last week of April while the company was assigned to road security and perimeter watches and the other brigades were out searching for PAVN. Jim Kelly and I spent most of our free time with Rick Rescorla, Pat Payne, and the other old timers, drinking too much beer, keeping Lurch's battalion beer walking championship title intact, and trying, perhaps without knowing it, to keep our distance from the new generation of "young" lieutenants.

The battalion commander, Lt. Col. Robert F. Litle, Jr., appeared to be a competent and compassionate CO. As an aviator, he knew his airmobility tactics. After air assaults into various targets around the base camp, he would call us in and critique us, continually pushing for greater proficiency and effectiveness. He and Major Henry complemented each other nicely. Another new man, a captain named Ramon A. "Tony" Nadal, came over from the 1st Battalion to be our new S-3. I didn't know him at all, but he'd been the CO of Alpha 1/7 at Xray, and he'd certainly earned his stripes. I can't remember where Captain Spires went, but he'd been a good S-3. Myron Diduryk was now the S-4, and Mike Kalla had taken command of Bravo Company. Other than those changes, we'd stayed pretty much the same.

Our morale improved, too, and with Dick Hogarth's lilting Irish-tenor voice leading us, the strains of Garry Owen filled the officers club with a new sense of pride, as high as it ever was, and things seemed to be on the upswing.

In early May, however, the good times ended, and we were shuttled up the coast to Bong Son again for Operation Davy Crockett—a brigade assault into northeastern Binh Dinh Province, long a VC bastion. Alpha Company went close to full field strength, roughly 120 men, with Kelly, Hammer, Hogarth, and Polli, the platoon leaders, Captain Davison, and myself. We didn't last at full strength very long.

I knew we'd run into something. Bong Son was VC country. It had been crawling with the bastards back in February, when Alpha Company had fought at LZ 4, and intelligence had confirmed the presence of North Vietnamese units in the area—the elusive 325th PAVN Division for one. Maj. Gen. John Norton, our new division commander, whom I'd remembered as the commanding general of the 82d Airborne Division back at Bragg, wanted to find them.

Yes, this was going to be a hot one. I could feel it. Something was gnawing at my stomach, too. (I didn't know it was worms.) Would the new CO keep his cool if we ran into something? How good was the new guy, Polli? Were we headed for another blood bath?

We flew into a mustering area north of Bong Son and camped in a secured airfield beside the choppers that would rev up in the early morning and carry us farther north. We rested, cleaned our weapons, ate hot Cs, and absorbed Captain Davison's operations order that night. He'd flown over the target that afternoon—a razor-back, rock-strewn ridge overlooking a village ten klicks north. After an artillery and tear-gas prep, we would assault the ridge, four ships at a time. A simple dawn air assault—routine but for the tear gas. Enemy units were suspected in the area, but Davison had seen nothing suspicious that afternoon.

I slept on my poncho on the hard dry ground near the airstrip. Despite the cool air and the quiet night, I slept badly.

Day One—May 4, 1966

I woke up dry-mouthed and stiff, my head aching from dehydration, and my sphincter felt like I'd been swilling beer all week. But I'd felt worse. At least the weather was good.

Captain Davison seemed steady. The veterans—Kelly, First Sergeant Miller, and our headquarters people—ate quietly together. George Polli cracked jokes all through breakfast. Bad ones. He was nervous, that was obvious, but so was everyone else. That was okay, I thought, as long as he came through in the clutch.

Two troopers from Marty Hammer's 2d Platoon hit sick call that morning, doubled over with worms. Worms had spread like wildfire through the battalion that week. The cure was worse then the malady, I'd heard. Whatever, that left us with 118 men on our field roster.

At 0630, we lifted off and headed north. The sun blazed as it rose from the South China Sea. We flew at eighty knots, a thousand feet up. After just a few minutes in the air, I could see the objective, the razor-back ridge running east-to-west and looming from the far end of a paddy-filled valley. The ridgeline looked bare—just rocks and brush. I couldn't see the village behind it.

"Gas masks on!" I yelled, reaching for my own, pulling it from the bulky canvas carrier strapped to my left leg. Holding my helmet between my knees, I slipped the black rubber gas mask over my head. Its supple cloying warmth engulfed me. I adjusted the straps, replaced my steel pot, then buckled my chin strap. I hated gas masks—they suffocated you and curtailed your vision by half—but if the LZ was smoking with CS (tear gas), we'd need the protection. The first sergeant, my two RTOs, and Solis, the new company medic, were ready. Larry Sargent was fumbling with his straps, but finally got settled. Looking like creatures from Mars, we all thumbed up, signaling we were ready.

Our choppers dropped fast, swooping in behind the gunships that had blasted the ridgeline. I leaned out the door and watched the first wave land. Troops were dropping from the Hueys as they hovered over the hilltop. They had to jump. There was no place to land!

"Gonna have to jump!" I yelled, my words muffled by the mask, the roar of the Huey's turbine, and the wind whipping through the bay. First Sergeant Miller's goggle-eyed visage nodded acknowledgment, and he spread the word. A hundred meters out, I felt the rotor blades change pitch as our ship flared its nose for the approach.

Boone (my new RTO), who'd been monitoring the radio, tapped me on the shoulder. "PAVN in the village!" he yelled.

Oh, Jesus, here we go again, I thought, looking back out the door at the hilltop coming at us fast now, exposed, rocky, and bright with sunlight. White tracer rounds caromed crazily into the air from behind the ridge. I heard a vague *whump* in the distance. Another hot LZ.

The ship continued steadily toward the ridge. I had my right foot on a landing strut, and was holding on to the cargo-bay pole with my right hand. The door gunners started pumping rounds down the hillside. As we hovered over the ridge, I jumped. Too soon.

Crashing into the rocks on my back, I was momentarily paralyzed with pain. I couldn't breathe. I looked up. The chopper's landing strut and underbelly were coming down slowly, inexorably, the strut across my chest. I'm gonna get crushed, I thought. Then the other men jumped, masked grotesques from outer space, crashing all around me, falling, grunting, and cursing. The chopper suddenly stopped its downward course, stabilized, lifted slowly, then dipped its nose and fell away, down the far hillside toward the village.

That was close, I thought, struggling painfully to get up.

I ripped my gas mask off. The air was acrid but breathable.

Short bursts of M-60 fire rattled from our left, down the ridge. Tracers were floating into the village. It was tiny, no more than fifteen thatched huts snuggled in hedgerows and clumps of palm trees, about three hundred yards below us. Alpha Company troops were already set up along the ridgeline. Some were pointing, others shouting encouragement, others shooting. The villagers had scattered and hid, but I saw two figures suddenly dart behind a hootch. Gray shirts and weapons—PAVN! We'd found PAVN again!

I turned and saw the first sergeant writhing on the ground, his hands clutching his ankle.

"Doc!" I yelled. Solis was calmly stuffing his gas mask into his gas mask carrier as if he were on a training exercise. "Come here and check out the first sergeant!"

"How bad is it, Top?" I asked.

"I don't know, sir," he said, his teeth clenched and his eyes glazed with pain. "I don't think I can walk."

"Shit!" I said. "You'll be okay. Grab the last ship out of here with the others. It's coming in now."

"Right, sir," he said. "Good luck."

"Yeah, thanks," I said, patting him on the shoulder. We'd need it. I turned away and headed down the ridgeline to report to Captain Davison. We'd lost five men during the landing, all injured from the jump: Stephens, Rice, and Ramey from the 1st Platoon; Seither from the 3d; and the first sergeant. The last ship in picked them up. When I told Captain Davison, he simply nodded. By then we were killing PAVN. Good, I thought. The more the merrier.

All I had to do for the next ten minutes was sit and watch the show. ARA gunships were on station, and 2d Lt. Jim Schlottman, our new artillery FO, was already pinpointing targets for them. Schlottman was talking to the pilots, Davison to his platoon leaders. It was a turkey shoot, and I could see everything.

Better test my weapon, I thought, looking for a target in the village. You could never be too sure.

"Two PAVN near the hootch by the palm trees," I yelled to Davison, aiming where I'd last seen the PAVN. "Follow my tracer!" I flicked my safety off and let fly with three rounds, single shots, into the palm trees. Funny, I thought, you couldn't see your tracers if you looked down the sights, but you could if you fired from the hip.

"Roger!" Davison shouted and turned back to Schlottman. I checked my M-16. No problems. I jogged the last ten yards to the captain's position behind a rock and watched Lieutenant Schlottman do his job.

Two rocket ships buzzed the ridgeline protectively. Two H-13 bubble ships swept around the ridgeline's eastern flank and *rattattat*ed at the village. Three armed PAVN suddenly sprinted from a hootch in the middle of the village and disappeared behind a tall hedgerow on the western edge of town. A quick burst of tracer fire chased them through a gap in the hedge.

"Did you see 'em?" Schlottman asked over the radio.

"Clear as day," came the disembodied voice from his speaker. One of the ARA Hueys almost U-turned in midair and let loose a salvo. The hedgerow on the western edge of town disintegrated into a billowing cloud of smoke, dust, and debris. Sharp explosions resounded through the valley. *Boom! Boom! Boom!*

Noisy bastards, I thought.

"Scratch one gook," I heard the pilot say. He said it without emotion. "There's two dead in the ditch, and one out in the field. That's all we can see right now." He sounded a bit disappointed.

This is the life, I thought. Sit up here, out of range, no incoming fire, and watch our Hueys pick off PAVN. Not bad. Not bad at all. I continued to watch and wait. The two H-13s made one more low pass over the village but drew no fire. Charlie's hunkered down, I said to myself, but he's not out. He's not that stupid. I was suddenly very glad I wasn't being hunted by the 1st Air Cav.

"Okay, that's it!" Captain Davison said. "Let's head out!"

Alpha Company picked itself up, dusted itself off, and began a slow, steady, careful descent down the westward slope of the ridgeline. The gunships headed back to their base for refueling. We were on our way again.

Our plan was simple enough—move southward, scouring the wood lines, until we ran into something. Bravo Company had landed ten miles south of us and was working its way north.

I appreciated the sudden quiet and the downhill march. When we reached the valley floor, we turned south, away from the village, leaving it smoking and deserted in the early morning sun. We didn't even stop to check it out. I looked at my watch. It was 0650.

We spread out in company column, platoons in column, with Kelly's 1st leading the way. Ten to fifteen yards between each man, good dispersion, good coverage, we plodded through the countryside under a blazing sun in a cloudless sky. Compared to the jungle of the highlands and the mountains of the Crow's Foot, this terrain was easy. Long, low ridgelines covered with sparse vegetation gave way to grass-covered slopes interspersed with expanses of lush green rice paddy. Too bad it was so hot.

We saw practically no one all that day. Just an occasional farmer, or a family sitting anxiously by their hootch. As the heat intensified, so did our fatigue, but slowly, steadily, we moved along the tree line, angling south and west, farther and farther into the heart of the province, the remote zone, farther and farther from help.

After supper that night, the worms really hit me. We'd found a good bivouac, easily defensible, with three sides facing out into a rice paddy. We dug in hastily and grabbed some chow. Then my stomach suddenly cramped up, and I searched for a private place to defecate. Even after all those months in the field, I still felt a sense of modesty about taking a crap, but that night there was no time to think about it. I had barely scooped a small shovel hole in the soft wet earth when I felt the rush coming. I had just enough time to drop my trousers and squat as the stuff came gushing out, unchecked. After the first discharge, my stomach cramped horribly, as if a hand was squeezing it. The spasms passed quickly, but they were just precursors of worse to come, and when they did, they almost knocked me over.

Worms all right. By then I was sure. Half the company had them in one form or another. And when they got bad, you couldn't function. You had to get treated. A week of drugs to kill the worms, and a week to recover from the drugs. We had a dozen or so men in the hospital already. Returnees described the treatment as the worst they'd ever had, but worms caused horrible pain. Christ, I thought, the last thing I needed was worms.

I finished my tawdry business, felt the stomach cramps subside, and returned, completely exhausted, to my poncho.

Night settled over us, the stars twinkling in a black onyx sky, the air cool again after a hot sweltering day. And despite the onset of worms, I slept soundly.

Day Two—May 5, 1966

We roused ourselves at dawn. I limited myself to ham and eggs and cocoa for breakfast that morning. Although stomach cramps gripped me as we moved out, I literally fought them off, and they passed. Then, fifteen minutes into the stifling heat of our march, we heard over the radio that Bravo

Company had made contact to the south, and I forgot about my worms.

We marched that day for hours—hours of stop-and-go slugging through waist-high rice shoots and shin-deep mud, hours of clambering over muck-covered paddy dikes and plodding up and down rolling lowlands, hours of listening for the other shoe to drop. At two o'clock, Dick Hogarth's platoon, then in the lead, reported a village dead ahead, inhabited, the first we'd seen that day.

Battalion ordered us to surround and search it. "All males are considered to be VC suspects," our radio advised us.

"What the hell does that mean?" Captain Davison asked.

"If they run, we blast 'em!" Polli sneered. I ignored him.

"Let's see what we find," I said. "The place might be crawling with VC, but with so many villagers there, I doubt it. SOP says we round 'em up and ship all the men back. Anyone of fighting age. Division loves to add up VC suspects. We'd better call in gunships, though. Just in case."

The captain called for ARA and ordered Hogarth's platoon to set up along the western edge of the village and cut off the exits. Hammer's platoon was to deploy along the southern and eastern edges and seal them off, too. Kelly was to stand by. Half an hour later, with gunships circling overhead, Kelly's people walked quietly into the village and started rounding everyone up—half a dozen men, farmers mostly, some in black pajamas, all of fighting age, and thirty or so women and children. They were herded into two distinct groups: one of tight-lipped, shifty-eyed men; one of wailing, terrified women and children.

I hated the wailing—hags and mothers mostly, hands clasped prayerlike at their breasts, bowing, pleading, and crying. None of us could understand what they were saying, of course, but we knew what they were afraid of.

It made me angry. Who the hell were we to march in and disrupt this hamlet—march in, tear it up looking for weapons, drag everyone out of their homes like Gestapo in the night, and send the men off somewhere to be interrogated? Maybe it was necessary. Maybe not. Who knew? If they got carted off, at least they wouldn't be sneaking up behind us if we ran into something.

"Slicks are on the way," Davison said. He didn't like it much either, I could see.

Minutes later, two Huey slicks swept in from the east and landed in the paddy next to the village. Kelly's men tried to coax the farmers onto the ships, but they refused. Then our troops got firm, grabbing the Viets by their arms and literally dragging them to the choppers. One crewman would pull them inside and push them down onto the floor while the other guarded them with his M-16.

"A nice friendly ride to division," I said to myself, wondering if the "VC suspects" would ever make it back to their homes.

After the Hueys flew away, we picked up and continued southward, leaving the village behind us. But the wailing of those poor, terrified women seemed to stay with me all day.

After passing through two more hamlets, deserted, we heard that Charlie Company had also made contact farther south and had taken casualties. Sporadic artillery fire rumbled ominously in the distance, confirming the news, 105s, I guessed, the *whump, kaboom, whump, whump* increasing steadily. Clouds were forming to our south, too. I wondered what had happened to Bravo Company.

By six o'clock the sky had clouded over. We found ourselves, totally exhausted, on the southern edge of a gently sloping promontory that jutted out into a wide expanse of lush, green paddy. Four thatched huts had been deserted on the high dry ground.

"We'll hold up here for the night," Davison said. "Looks like we'll have some shelter," he added, pointing to the huts. They were well made, with thick thatched roofs and dry, hard-packed floors. "Let's take that one," the captain said. I could see a bamboo bed frame inside of it. A real hotel. Larry Sargent nodded, trooped over to the hut, and dropped to the ground, exhausted. The other RTOs joined him.

Numb with fatigue myself, I sat on a stump in the middle

of the promontory and lit up a cigarette. The thin strip of wood line across the paddies looked harmless. Quiet day, I thought. Some of the men around me began to dig, their shovels thumping into the dirt, their staccato punctuating the steadily increasing drone of mosquitoes. I was suddenly conscious of the relative quiet and wondered why the artillery had stopped. As if on cue, it started falling again, rumbling to our south. Somebody was catching it.

Suddenly the air exploded with the *pop! pop! pop!* of incoming fire—thirty rounds or so. Machine gun. I dove behind the stump and heard the loud *whack whack* of another burst. Dirt spurts kicked up around me. Shit! They had me in range! I jumped up, ran to the nearest hootch, and dove behind it, short of breath, my heart pounding, my mouth dry. I heard Kelly's M-60s open up, returning fire. Then Hammer's people with their automatic weapons, and the outgoing fire swelled in intensity.

We should have known the bastards were there! How fucking stupid can you be!! There could be hundreds!

I dodged over to the next hootch and crashed down next to Larry Sargent. He was crouched behind the hootch, listening to the radio, and shaking his head. Jim Kelly's voice broke into the net, reporting one killed and two wounded. Jim Schlottman was already calling in a fire mission. Marty Hammer came onto the net, too. He had another man, wounded.

I wondered who'd caught it this time, who we'd lost, when a 105 round crashed into the paddy, fifty yards short of the far tree line, and kicked up a spurt of muddy water. *Whump!*

"Add five zero, fire for effect," Schlottman said.

"On the way. Wait," came the response.

A series of six sharp *whacks!* resounded behind the wood line, and two thin gray wisps of smoke rose slowly above the treetops. That would shut 'em up.

I called for a medevac, and everyone started digging furiously. When the medevac appeared, however, coming in low over the rice paddy from the east, automatic-weapons fire erupted again from the far wood line. The chopper bobbed and weaved to a higher altitude. The pilot reported taking several hits and said he wouldn't come back until the LZ had cooled off.

We called for more artillery, and shortly thereafter the wood line resounded with another twelve rounds of howitzer fire, and then twelve more, and the commotion finally ceased. Marty Hammer came back on the radio. His wounded man had died—a squad leader named Rasmussen—another good man's life snuffed out.

"Roger, Two-six," was all I could say. "Dustoff's on the way. Throw smoke."

Seconds later, the medevac reappeared, flew in, and picked up our casualties—two dead now, two wounded. I hardly knew them.

Captain Davison called a briefing after dusk. We huddled in his headquarters hootch. Kelly was visibly angry. Hammer and Hogarth were grim. Polli, uncharacteristically, kept his mouth shut.

"There isn't anything we can do about what happened an hour ago," Davison said. "But we can tomorrow morning, and we're going to.

"Someone's over there. Hard core, most likely. Both Bravo and Charlie Companies have run into hard-core units south of here. We're all busy." He looked around and grimaced.

"At first light, we'll move out from here, staying behind that tree line"—he pointed out the door to a jagged line of vegetation on the southwest side of the village. "Using it as cover, we'll proceed to a small canal, cross it, and come on line for an assault on this village"—this time he pointed down to his map.

So that was it! Another village, due south, across the paddy.

"We'll form an assault line five hundred yards west of the objective: 1st Platoon on the right; 2d on the left; 3d, with me, in reserve. Weapons Platoon will provide support from here and follow us after the assault.

"Any questions?"

Nobody spoke, or moved.

"We'll have two things going for us," he said, straightening his back, resting his hands on his knees. "We'll have the tree line for cover, and as soon as the assault line is formed, Lieutenant Schlottman will call in a moving barrage. We'll follow it into the village."

"All right!" Hogarth exclaimed.

Jim Kelly glanced at me and shook his head. We'd never assaulted behind a moving barrage. In a nutshell, it was risky. If it went as planned, it would help. If it didn't, we'd lose people.

"The bad news," Davison added, "is that we're all by our lonesome on this one. Everyone's busy." He glanced around the circle. "Any questions?"

Again, nobody moved.

I wanted to ask one but didn't. "How many PAVN are over there—three with a machine gun, or three thousand?" We'd find out soon enough.

Day Three—May 6, 1966

Dry-mouthed, heads aching from lack of water and sleep, we started out again the next morning. I followed the 2d Platoon. We moved quickly, no one talking, each man wondering if he'd make it. Familiar backs kept pace steadily through the paddy muck and high grass, keeping good dispersion, keeping the line of trees to our left. We started west, then curved behind the wood line to the south and came to a small canal. About waist-deep, I recall. Silently we crossed it, one at a time, scrambled up over the dike, and began to form an assault line. The ground beyond the canal was sandy, sparsely covered with thick bushes and tall palms, and though we could see ourselves through the undergrowth, the village, our objective, was shielded from view. I could feel the tension building. Low curses, grumbling, angrily whispered orders filtered up and down the line as the NCOs aligned the troops for the assault, then stood there, deadpan, waiting for the word to move. Some men dropped to one knee. Others simply stood, waiting. About five minutes later, when he was sure the assault line was formed, the captain raised, then dropped his arm, and we all moved silently forward through the forest.

On cue, 105 and 81mm rounds began whooshing into the village, pounding the ground to our front. Round after round blasted everything in front of us. The noise and confusion were terrifying. I was concentrating on staying up with Hammer's platoon as it swept through billowing clouds of blinding cordite smoke and whirling dust. We began to pick up speed. I caught occasional glimpses of the men ahead of me, moving steadily behind the shifting artillery fire. I was aghast at its power and devastation. The ground shook. The noise was deafening. And through it all we walked—a long thin line of American troops—steadily, inexorably, just waiting for the enemy to open up.

We swept out of the tree line into the village, or what was left of it, and continued unopposed through the carnage and devastation. The 105s and 81s, their mission almost ended, lifted and shifted to the left, dropping six final rounds into the woods it had blasted the night before.

Dick Hogarth's 3d Platoon, trailing us, stopped at a clearing on our left. After a moment's hesitation, they spread out and started across. Christ, I thought. Wait! I watched as Hogarth charged across the open ground, firing from the hip as he went. They made it to the wood line, and disappeared into it, and the noise and confusion abated.

I stood by the edge of the village and looked around. It was a shambles. Smoking hootches, some still burning, most wrecked and smashed, formed a pathetic ragged circle in the shade of the shattered palm trees. I could see the silhouettes of Kelly's and Hammer's people on the far side moving almost casually to their left and right. Davison was somewhere up there, too. At first, I wondered where everyone else was, or if there had been anyone else at all. Then I heard the crying, and the sobs, and the wailing of shell-shocked civilians, and smelled the unmistakable stench of burning flesh.

"Two dead PAVN with AKs," I heard Hogarth's voice on the net. "That's all there is over here."

Well, that's something, I thought.

"Roger that. Regroup east of the village," Davison said. His voice sounded awful. I soon discovered why.

The real victims of our savage, unimpeded assault had been helpless, unarmed civilians. I saw three bodies, two women, one man, twisted and lifeless under the side of a smoldering hootch. About fifteen other villagers were wandering around dazed, mumbling incoherently, and close to shock. All of them were crying.

What a bloody fucking mess! What a stinking, god-awful, bloody, fucking mess! We had really done it this time!

But PAVN had been there. Hogarth had found two of them. There may have been others, too, the ones who'd killed our people last night. So, fuck these people, I thought. They should have known we'd come.

But why the hell had they stayed? Goddamn PAVN! That was the way they fought. Fire a few rounds and skedaddle. Let us chop up the civilians and get blamed. Goddamn them.

But try as I could, I couldn't tune out the wailing, the cries of anguish, and the stares of the shell-shocked kids.

They could have been our people—Boone, Kelly, Larry Sargent—lying there writhing with shrapnel in their guts. But they weren't.

A young boy, four or five years old, stood motionless near the door of a burning hootch. He stared at me as I walked by. His face expressionless. No tears. Nothing. He just stared. I'll never forget the look on his face.

Captain Davison stood in a clearing past the village. GIs were milling around, sitting around, or standing around dazed, silent, and depressed. Some were smoking, some eating, others stared listlessly across the paddy east of the village. Nobody was looking back from where we'd come.

"Medevac's on the way," Davison said to me, his face pale. "Get Solis and the other medics, and do what you can for the civilians. Then get the wounded ones out of here. All of them. We're staying. For a while at least."

I nodded to him and went to work. The medics had already set up their makeshift clinic near an undamaged hootch and were hard at it, feverishly bandaging the worst of the wounded.

I stood next to them and shouted *"Bac-si my! Bac-si my!"* (pronounced bach she me, meaning American doctor here) in my pathetic Vietnamese, as loudly as I could, over and over again. The dazed civilians ignored me. The medics kept working, as hard as they could. One of the wounded was a young girl, maybe twelve. Her leg had been blown off above the knee. She was burned, too, and going into shock. "American doctor here!" I called again, wanting to shout it so loud that all the world would hear me, wanting my voice to calm and soothe those poor battered villagers, to explain away the folly, the pain, the madness of the stupid fucking war.

Two old men, bowing and scraping, came out of a tunnel entrance twenty yards to my left, dusting themselves off as they kowtowed. They must have been village elders. Slowly, they began to gather the wounded villagers together and guide them to our crowded little clinic.

Jim Kelly appeared out of nowhere. "Four more PAVN over there," he said, deadpan, pointing to the southeastern edge of the village. "Blasted all to shit."

He suddenly grinned a grin I'd never seen before. It was almost ghoulish. "So were their AKs," he added. "Lots of blood trails, too. Heading south." Then he glanced at the wounded civilians, and his face went hard, like cement. "Could have been us," he said.

"This sucks," Larry Sargent said, spitting in the dirt. "I mean it really sucks!"

Captain Davison nodded in agreement.

Kelly, already heading back to his people, didn't hear him.

After the civilian casualties were flown out, we stayed near that village for an hour, eating, smoking, dozing, sometimes talking, all trying to forget. Davison and I and our RTOs had been resting as best we could in the shade of some tall palm trees, waiting for word from battalion, when a lone slick suddenly flew into the clearing to our east and landed in the paddy nearby. To our astonishment, a gaggle of reporters jumped out. Bent at the waist, cameras swinging from their necks, equipment bags bouncing at their sides, they jogged to the now-deserted village. Reaching the edge of it, they stopped and looked around in confusion.

"Oh, shit," the captain said. "What do we do with these people?"

The chopper cut its engine, and the rotors wound down slowly. I couldn't believe it was just sitting there, unprotected, in the rice paddy.

"Send 'em home," I said.

"Ask them for some women," Schlottman said.

Two of the reporters spotted us and headed our way. The others dispersed in all directions to find their own story. Captain Davison rose stiffly to his feet, dusted his trousers off, and met the reporters halfway. I sat there, chewing a blade of grass, and numbly watched them talk.

The two men questioned the captain and listened intently to his answers. Fifteen minutes later, one of them shouted something to his cohorts, and they hastily reappeared from the shadows and mustered at the chopper, milling around it until its engine started up again. Then they all got on board and flew away.

"What did they want?" I asked the captain when he returned.

"Same old thing," he said. "A story. They're hungry, those people, like sharks. They'll drive you nuts if you let them."

"What did you tell them?" I asked.

"That we'd had our little action for the day. That it was over." He sat there silently for a minute. "I told 'em to join up with one of the other companies. They're the ones with their hands full. If they stuck around with us, they'd miss their story."

Then he looked at me sheepishly. "I used to be a PIO guy myself," he said.

A public information officer? A fucking REMF publicity guy? Jesus Christ Almighty! I couldn't believe it.

"Well, I'll be damned," I said, and we went back to waiting.

It turned out that the captain was wrong about one thing. The thing about missing a story. He was just as wrong as he could be.

* * *

An hour after the journalists left, eighteen Huey slicks picked us up from a large rice paddy just south of the village, and we took off again in a great thundering roar, like Valkyries in giant dragonflies of death. The brigade had bagged a hard-core VC unit of unknown size and was pulling the drawstring tight, and we were going to be in on the action.

Heading south, our formation rose steadily to eight hundred feet, and the countryside opened up below us. Lush kelly-green rice paddies lay in rectangular patterns surrounded by irregular swaths of dark green vegetation and clumps of tall palm trees, and to the east, the gray-brown hills of the coastline's high ground appeared in the distant haze.

What a way to travel, I thought, clearing my mind for the coming assault, the cool air whipping through the cargo bay. We droned steadily south for five minutes, then angled west. In less than ten minutes, we'd covered the same distance we'd traveled on foot the last two days, but that leg of our journey was clean, quick, easy, and safe. We veered south again, and saw plumes of gray smoke rising from the valley floor about a thousand meters away.

"LZ coming up!" I shouted.

As we approached it, artillery and air strikes were pulverizing it, and clouds of smoke billowed from it. The sight reminded me, unnervingly, of LZ Xray in the Ia Drang, six months before.

We continued south, leaving that small patch of smoking jungle behind us, then began another slow 180-degree turn to the right, descending as we did, then straightened out and swooped into the LZ, a large open field about five hundred meters short of the action. There was a lot of commotion ahead of us, but no incoming. I leapt from the ship and sprinted to the shelter of a dirt berm surrounding a cemetery at the edge of the LZ. Dropping to the ground, I sat back and watched our troops come in behind me. The choppers lifted off in formation and swung away to the west. Beyond them, in the far tree line, I could see GIs. They looked like Charlie Company people, but were too far away to know for sure.

We'd assaulted heading north. At twelve o'clock—the far

end of the LZ—I could see a line of tall palm trees and a brown mass of some kind. Clouds of smoke obscured it, though, and the din was horrendous. A monster shoot-out was taking place on the other side of that tree line—not the staccato of small arms, but the steady rumbling thunder of artillery, occasionally punctuated by *whump*s of heavier stuff, bombs, most likely, and ARA gunships firing rockets.

I glanced back where we'd landed and saw Captain Davison walking nonchalantly toward us, talking calmly on his radio, its handset coil bouncing up and down like a rubber jump rope. Gosey was carrying his company radio now, and a new man named Russell from the 3d Platoon followed closely behind him with the battalion net. I didn't like seeing the Old Man walking so casually across that open field. He should have been jogging. At least staying low. He was either fearless or really dumb.

Behind the protection of our berm, he crouched down and called the platoon leaders in. They appeared quickly and gathered around us.

"We're moving forward to contact," the captain shouted over the din. "Two platoons on line. First Platoon on the left. Second on the right. Third behind them. Mortars set up here. Be prepared to give us fire when we need it."

Polli was out of breath, panting like a dog, his eyes bulging. "Got it," he said, nodding.

"Keep visual contact with Charlie Company on your left," the captain said to Kelly. "That's them over there." He pointed across the field. "We'll move out together. Stay on line and keep going until we run into something. Any questions?"

We shook our heads. Negative.

"All right. Let's go!" Captain Davison stood up then, casually reached over to Russell for his handset, and started walking forward toward the din. "This is Silent Slasher Six," I heard him say. "We're moving forward at this time." Then the noise drowned him out.

Moving to contact! I thought. Oh, shit. Here we go again.

* * *

The men are up now, on their feet, Kelly's people spread out in one long line in the open field, Captain Davison with them, moving forward toward the chaos ahead. I'm following Marty Hammer's people with my little XO team—my two RTOs, Solis the medic, an FO from the Delta Company mortars named Bercaw, and his RTO, Wickham. We are moving steadily and well, watching our spacing, keeping our eyes peeled. The ground is flat and dry and covered with ankle-high grass. Ahead, I can see the tall palm trees, evenly spaced, their trunks about ten yards apart. What's beyond them is obscured by an ominous gray-brown mass of some kind—vegetation, another berm, perhaps a trench line.

Salvo after salvo of artillery crunches into the jungle beyond it in a steady, urgent, pounding. It seems to beckon us. I see a bright flash in the sky—an A-1E Skyraider—diving then pulling up. A bomb drops from its underbelly and disappears into the jungle. *Karrumph!* A 250-pounder, I think, as it shakes the ground.

Pound 'em, baby. Pound 'em good. Kill 'em all.

Another A-1E begins its dive. Whoever's up ahead of us is getting clobbered.

The din gets louder and louder. The ground passes slowly beneath our feet. I can smell the cordite, and the burning forest.

We approach the tree line. I can see past it—a large open area, almost square, the ground worn bare, surrounded by a trench line and a waist-high berm. It looks like a parade ground. We continue steadily through the trees and cross the trench. It's well dug. Two roads breach it. I walk through one, glancing down the trench line as I do, and see the corpse of a PAVN soldier lying face down and twisted in the dirt. Clearly dead. He wears a khaki uniform and a combat harness, covered with dust. Just inside the wall, another PAVN lies faceup, on his back, splayed in the dirt, his arms stretched unnaturally over his head, his face burned black. Hard-core PAVN. No doubt about it. I'm getting nervous. Where are the rest of them?

As soon as we cross the trench, the firing ahead intensifies.

Rounds begin to crackle overhead. Not close, but definitely coming from the direction we're heading. Things are getting hairy. Beyond the trench line, the ground is worn down, a huge courtyard or parade ground of some kind. A big mound of hard-packed earth rises from the ground on our right. I can see another trench line on the far side of the parade ground, and beyond it, thick vegetation. Kelly's and Hammer's platoons walk steadily on line across the parade ground and drop into the far trench—Captain Davison with them. I hold up behind the big dirt mound—it's as big as a car—and watch Hogarth's people take up positions in the trench line to our right.

On our far left, across the courtyard, Charlie Company troops appear.

We hold up for a little while. The Skyraiders are still dive-bombing, and we feel the ground shake as their bombs hit. The firing has picked up significantly to our front, and rounds are beginning to *pop!* overhead. It's clear we're getting close. Our objective is still getting pounded, though, and the incoming fire is high and ineffective.

Suddenly, a gaggle of terrified civilians appears on our right, about ten of them, fleeing from the trench line. They are old, confused, and terrified and keep looking back over their shoulders as they come into the courtyard. A burst of fire breaks overhead, and we cringe behind the mound. The civilians freeze, not knowing where to turn. I run over, beckon to them, and guide them to our mound.

"Get down!" I yell, motioning for them to hug the ground. They huddle together like children. My team is hunkered down, too, and no one is smiling.

The firing continues unabated, and more artillery pounds the ground.

Suddenly, a lone Huey C & C (command and control) ship swings into view behind us, flies right in to the parade ground, and lands about thirty yards away. I can't believe it, flying in there by itself. The door slides open, and Col. Harold G. Moore, the new brigade CO, jumps out, followed by two radiomen and Major Dillon, the brigade S-3. I sprint over to them and report as calmly as I can.

"Where's your CO?" the colonel asks.

"In the trench line straight ahead, sir," I yell, pointing.

The colonel nods, turns, and walks calmly toward Davison's position, his RTOs following along behind him. Major Dillon stays and looks around, taking everything in. He's big, almost burly. I've never talked to him, but remember seeing him at LZ Xray. His gaze stops on the dead PAVN lying splayed in the dirt near the trench line.

"Is that man dead?" he asks me.

I stare at him in disbelief, then at the motionless, dust-covered corpse. I hadn't checked its pulse when I walked by it, so I raise my M-16, fire a round into its chest, then turn back to the major. "He's dead, sir," I respond.

The major gives me a dirty look but doesn't say anything, so I run back to my team behind the mound. Some of the civilians are staring at me. I stare back and they look away.

Minutes later, Colonel Moore returns to his ship, and it takes off. I watch it lift off slowly, hover about ten feet off the ground, turn 180 degrees, and fly off, barely clearing the tree line behind us.

For the next few minutes, we stay put, and things seem to quiet down. Colonel Moore has given Captain Davison orders to shift the company to the right and then continue forward to contact. The captain comes on the radio and orders everyone to move a hundred meters to the right and then stop. Charlie Company will keep the trap shut by filling in the trench as we move.

I watch with a mixture of pride and trepidation as we begin our shift to the right. The 3d Platoon clambers out of its trench line and disappears over the top of its berm. The 2d Platoon basically does a right face and moves down its trench line, its men scrambling out of it when they reach the corner. They, too, disappear out of sight. The 1st Platoon follows along behind them, but holds up still in the trench.

"Time to move it!" I yell. We have to cross the open ground and get to the trench line on our right to see what's happening. I jump up, sprint the distance, and land feet first in the trench. Larry Sargent and Boone crash in behind me, breathing hard. Solis and the FO team come next.

The trench line is empty, but wide and hard-packed with lots of use. I see a small entrance to a bunker of some kind—dark and foreboding. I think of dropping a grenade into it, then remember the civilians we killed that morning, and decide (foolishly, now that I think of it) not to.

While I'm scouring the trench, heavy firing breaks out to our left and front. Rounds are popping furiously overhead, but there's safety in the trench. We've run into something big—that's clear—and the radio quickly confirms it.

"Silent Slasher Six, this is Slasher Two-six. Over." Marty Hammer's voice comes over the net.

"This is Silent Slasher Six. Over." Captain Davison answers calmly.

"This is Slasher Two-six," Marty continues. "We're taking heavy fire from the front. I've got two elephants and three buffalo, over."

Two dead and three wounded! Jesus, that was fast.

"This is Slasher Six," Davison responds. "I roger that. Stay down. Out."

I stick my head up and examine the terrain beyond the trench line. All I can see ahead of us is more bare ground and a labyrinth of ditches. To our left, where the 2d Platoon disappeared, there's another row of palm trees, and beyond them, more dense growth and shadows. That's where the fire is coming from, where Hammer's people must be, but I can't see a single GI.

The firing swells again.

"Six, this is Two-six," Hammer says. His voice is strained. "We're pinned down here behind a hootch. I've got six buffalo now. Can't move."

Six wounded!

"I roger that," Davison acknowledges.

The firing picks up straight ahead of us now. Hogarth's people opening up, I think.

Suddenly a gray-shirted figure pops up thirty yards in front of us—a hatless PAVN soldier with a weapon—and sprints to the right. He dives into a ditch before I get a shot off.

"There goes one!" I yell, but he's disappeared. They're all over the place! I think, furious I couldn't get a shot off. What the hell is going on here? Christ, Captain, wake up! I'm getting scared.

"Keep your eyes open, gents," I say. "Solis, watch our rear."

Captain Davison calls Kelly and tells him to shift his people to the right, staying behind Two-six's position, to assume the right flank.

The right flank? Where's the 3d Platoon? I can't see the captain, or Hogarth's people, or any of Hammer's either, for that matter. Except for Jim Kelly's people on our left in their trench line, we're all alone.

"Roger," Jim says. "We're on the way."

The 1st Platoon breaks out of the trench and moves to their right in short rushes, staying behind Hammer's position. Twenty-six sweat-soaked, dust-covered, grim-faced men zigzagging across the ground in front of us. Kelly strides by, his six-four frame unmistakable, his RTO, Davida, tagging along behind him like a puppy.

"One of them just disappeared over there," I yell to Jim, pointing to where the PAVN disappeared.

Jim nods and sort of rolls his eyes. "Keep a look-see," he says to Davida. Then the two of them drop into one of the ditches in front of us, and I lose sight of them.

Sergeant Bercaw, the Delta mortar FO, asks if he can go help the captain. That makes sense to me, so I say yes. Bercaw and his RTO scramble out of our trench and head off after Kelly to find the captain.

Marty Hammer comes back on the radio. "This is Two-six," he says. "I've got two more buffalo." Two more wounded? He's getting clobbered! "They've got a couple of automatics in a hedgerow in front of us. I can't get to 'em from here. How about some help?"

I grab the radio. "Two-six, this is Five," I say. "We're coming up behind you."

"Roger, Five," he says. "Do you know where we are?"

"It ain't hard to guess," I say.

"Roger that, and thanks," he says. "Out."

I turn to my team, four men now. "Let's see what we can do."

We bob and weave through the curving trench line and forward over some mounds, keeping as low as we can. The firing seems to have leveled off. At the line of palm trees, I see another small clearing, twenty yards across, then more trees and a row of Spanish bayonet. Beyond them, I see six or seven hummocks—burial mounds. Past them, the undergrowth thickens. Try as I can, I can't see a hut. A burst of machine-gun fire snaps overhead. I sprint to the Spanish bayonet and dive behind it. The others follow, crashing down behind me on my right.

From out of the undergrowth ahead, Marty Hammer's figure, bent over at the waist, is zigzagging toward us. The firing is steady now, and all around us. Marty crashes down next to me, breathing hard. His left hand is wrapped in a bloody field bandage. His arm hangs limp.

"How ya doin'?" he asks.

"Fine," I say. "You okay?"

"Yeah, fine," he says. "No sweat. The bastards got us pinned down good, though." He reaches around, grabs his canteen with his good hand, and gulps a swallow. "We sure can use you," he says, stuffing his canteen back in its cover, then rolling over on his side, getting ready to move again.

"I'll go first," he says, "and wait for you on the other side."

"Okay," I say.

"You ready?" he asks.

I nod.

Suddenly he's up and running, dodging left and right through the grave mounds in the cemetery.

I'm up now, in a squatting position, watching him, getting ready to follow, when something explodes in front of me. I see the dirt kick up and feel something hot thrusting into the back of my thigh, knocking me ass over teakettle with palm fronds flashing overhead.

I know I've been shot, but I'm not sure from where.

"They're in the trees!" I yell, scrambling back behind the

Spanish bayonet. We're all up on our knees now, firing at the treetops. I let fly with several well-aimed bursts, spraying the tops of the palm trees around us until my magazine is empty. Then I fall back on my side and reload.

I'll be damned, I think. A Purple Heart.

There's no pain down there now; the back of my thigh is numb. I know something's inside me, but otherwise I'm fine.

"Are you hit, sir?" I hear Solis ask.

"Yeah," I say. "In the back of my leg. Stop the bleeding, will you?"

I fumble for my field dressing, pull it out of its carrier, and hand it to him. Then I lie there, feeling his hands rip the back of my trousers. He puts some pressure on the wound, then wraps the bandage around my thigh and pulls it tight.

"You've got a puncture there, sir," he says. "How's it feel?"

"Fine," I say, wondering why it doesn't hurt more.

Then I call Hammer.

"This is Two-six," he answers, almost immediately, his voice slurred.

"I won't be able to join you," I say.

"I don't believe it!" he says. He sounds drunk. "Did the same burst get you, too?"

"Yeah. How are you?"

"Fine," he says. "I'll be okay, but can you send up a medic and some ammo?"

I look at Solis. He nods.

"Affirmative," I say. "He'll be right up."

Solis takes what extra ammo we can spare, then jumps up and sprints across the clearing. We cover him, spraying the trees as he dodges past the burial mounds and disappears into the bushes on the far side of the clearing.

It's time for me to call Captain Davison.

Gosey answers. "This is Six-Alpha," he says. "Are you wounded?" he asks, breaking code.

"Affirmative," I say, "but nothing serious. Two-six is, too. What's going on over there?"

"Three-six is dead," he says. "And most of the Three-six element. They're out in the middle of a rice paddy."

Oh, God. Dick Hogarth dead? I can't believe it. Oh, Christ. What the fuck is happening to us? Hogarth and the 3d Platoon wiped out? Marty Hammer wounded and his platoon chopped up! Me with a bullet up my ass. It's Albany all over again!

"Who's with you?" I ask Gosey.

"Six and Six's group with Three-five and some others. We're pinned down here, though. Can't move."

At least the captain is still alive.

"I roger that, Six-Alpha. Hang in there. I'm going back for help."

The firing seems to ease off just a bit.

Captain Davison's voice comes over the radio. "Four-six, this is Six."

He's calling George Polli, and his voice is just as calm as it could be.

Polli acknowledges the call.

"This is Six. Bring your people forward," Davison says.

There's a long silence.

"This is Four-six," Polli says. "We are unable to move forward. Over."

"This is Six," Davison responds. "I say again. Bring your people up."

"This is Four-six," Polli answers. "The firing to our front is too heavy. We can not come forward at this time."

I can't believe it. The worthless bastard isn't going to help us out! I tear the handset out of Boone's hand. "Four-six, this is Five," I break in. "Get your fucking ass up here right now, goddamn it! Fast!"

"This is Four-six," Polli answers. "I cannot move forward at this time."

"This is Six," the captain breaks in. "Five, you stay out of this. I say again, Four-six. Move up. Bring your element forward. We need your help. As for you, Five, stay off the net. Get back to cover and call for resupply. The situation here will develop. Out."

The situation will develop? What the hell does he mean by that? Does battalion know what's going on?

I'm feeling frustrated, out of it, and scared. I know I should stay out of it—Polli is Davison's problem—but anyone listening to the radio knows what's happened. I want to grab that fat-assed, lily-livered, worthless son of a bitch by the throat and drag him up here—where the action is—but my leg is throbbing now, and I have to remain cool.

"Let's go get some help," I say, struggling to my feet. I put some weight on my leg, and it holds up okay. I won't win any races, but I can move. I begin limping back to the ditch we just left. My leg is stiff now, the pain beginning, but I can limp along just fine.

We make it to the ditch, then the trench line. We stumble back down it until we get to where we started. The big dirt mound is on our right. We limp across the parade ground to the berm, drop down behind it, and stretch out, safe at last. A squad of exhausted Charlie Company guys is lying there behind it, too, about twenty yards away. They look us over disinterestedly. The civilians have all gone.

The firing stops. The quiet, so strange after a shoot-out, is disconcerting. There's no traffic on the radio, either. It's eerie.

I radio Jim Brigham back at S-4, report our situation as best I can, and order more ammunition. I know medevac won't fly in until the situation stabilizes, but he tells me that, anyway.

Then, about half an hour later, a large formation of Hueys, twenty or so, thunders in and lands on the same LZ we used. Reinforcements! I can see them jumping from the choppers, moving toward us, and realize, quite suddenly, that we're going to make it out of here okay.

The rest of the afternoon passed in a gauzy haze. My RTOs and I stayed behind that berm, watching and waiting, listening and smoking, and wondering what would happen. We learned very little. The firefight continued on and off all afternoon, but it seemed behind us now, beyond our scope, somehow out of range. I lay there and chain-smoked as first

Charlie Company, then the reinforcements (who turned out to be Bravo Company), moved slowly, steadily through our position. Bravo Company managed to push the battalion's perimeter forward, past our forwardmost positions, past the dead PAVN we'd left in our wake, past most of our KIAs and wounded, and finally, around five o'clock, our tired and battered troops could take a breather.

Captain Davison called me at dusk. He told me to coordinate medevac with Sergeant Vannoy, Jim Kelly's platoon sergeant, who was taking over as field first sergeant. The captain also said that Pat Payne, Charlie Company's XO, would be responsible for securing a landing zone and calling in the Dustoffs after dark. For some reason, the captain had to stay put, but he instructed the platoon leaders to move their wounded back to my position and to wait there for further instructions.

As dusk fell, then, our wounded filtered back to our berm: Paulson and Dix from 1st Platoon, stumbling behind Sergeant Vannoy; Sergeant Howell and Griffin from 3d Platoon, staggering out of the shadows from the tree line just west of us, where the Old Man had been pinned down. Sergeant Howell had been shot in the face; Griffin in the arm. They were exhausted, filthy, and clearly haunted by the horrors of the day.

"Where are the others?" I asked.

"We're it, sir," Griffin said, shaking his head. "There must be ten guys still out there in the paddy. Can't get to 'em, sir. No way." He was swaying with exhaustion. "No way," he said, again.

It was almost dark when Marty Hammer and his people finally closed into our position. Marty had been wounded three times it turned out—in the left hand, the right arm, and later, in the shoulder—but he was still on his feet. Pain etched his face, and a morphine tag dangled from his shirt, but he was still standing. As he stumbled in, six more wounded hobbled behind him. They were dragging their weapons and gear. The rest of the 2d Platoon came in later, carrying their two KIAs. Sergeant Caple led them in. Good old Sergeant Caple! A

veteran of Xray and Albany, he'd survived another shoot-out.
I walked over to him, shook his hand, and smiled.

Marty Hammer was in bad shape, and I was getting there,
but Hammer refused to quit. I went over the field roster with
Sergeant Vannoy, then hobbled around from group to group
checking with the medics, who were still patching people up.
I toyed briefly with the idea of staying with the company that
night, but Solis checked my leg again and told me what I already knew. He said it would stiffen up during the night. I
realized, then, that I was going to fly out of there that night,
get away from it all, get some hot food, rest, and quiet. It was
almost over.

I called Captain Davison again and reported our situation.
"See you back home," I think he said.

I wondered if he would or not. I wondered how Jim Kelly
was doing, how Dick Hogarth had let himself and the others
get caught out in an open rice paddy, and I wondered, albeit
fleetingly, what had happened to that worthless fucking coward,
Polli. But he was the captain's problem. At least I thought so.
Then the first of the medevacs started coming in from the
south, its landing lights cutting a cone into the darkness, and
the first group of wounded guys was carried out to the ship. I
could see Pat Payne in the light, helping them get aboard.
Thank God he was there. I could rest. The red cross on the
medevac's door was somehow reassuring. It seemed to be a
message of mercy.

For the next hour or so, the medevacs came and went, one
ship at a time. I remember saying good-bye to Larry Sargent
and Boone, thanking Solis for a job well done, wishing sergeants Vannoy and Caple luck, then joining Marty Hammer,
who was standing patiently and alone in the dark, watching
the wounded depart. Marty and I stood there for a while
together, watching the Dustoffs do their work, flying in
carefully and waiting while the healthy men helped the
wounded men aboard, some working gingerly with the
wounded, others working less so with the dead. Except for
their comings and goings, the night was strangely quiet.

I suggested to Marty that he sit down, take a load off his

feet, but he declined, saying he didn't want to move. I saw a cigarette lighter flicker in the darkness, and heard the sudden rush of radio static from somewhere, and someone laughing. Then a rude burst of machine-gun fire erupted from somewhere inside the perimeter, and Marty and I both dropped to the ground like cement.

I knew he hadn't been hit. The rounds weren't even close.

Somebody shouted. A grenade exploded in the dark. There was more shouting, another burst of fire, then silence.

I was lying face down in the grass now, not really wanting to move, feeling very weak and tired, when I heard Marty's voice.

"Larry," he said. "Larry," he said again. "I don't think I can get up."

"Don't worry," I said. "You'll get up. We'll both get up. We'll make it. I assure you."

And then, as the last medevac began its slow, careful approach from the south, we struggled to our feet and hobbled painfully down to the pickup zone. It was finally our turn.

When the ship came in, its landing lights almost blinded me. I could hear Pat Payne yelling something to us about having a good trip. I thanked him, and we shook hands. His men were lifting bodies into the chopper, then two wounded, one with his head bandaged and another hit in the leg, and then it was our turn. Pat helped Marty onto the ship, and turned him over to one of the medics inside. I hopped on board and found a place on the floor, sitting with my legs out the door. I was sitting next to a dead guy. I couldn't recognize him. Someone squeezed my shoulder. It was one of the shipboard medics. He was asking me if I was okay. I flashed him a thumbs-up and grabbed the cargo-bay pole as the engine revved up.

Then we lifted into the air, away from the upturned faces of the men who had helped us on board, the men we were leaving behind, and we rose almost vertically into the cool, clean air, turned slowly to the south, and headed off into the pitch-black night to safety. I wondered what had happened inside the perimeter, who had fired that sudden burst, and then suddenly, I didn't care.

I was out of there.

Twenty minutes later, when we landed, two medics helped us off the ship and pointed us to a triage tent some twenty yards away up a hill. The tent was well lit, crowded with men, mostly wounded, some medics, and doctors, all busy.

"Can you make it up there okay, sir?" one of the medics asked me. I nodded, looking around for Marty.

He was being laid out on a stretcher. His eyes were closed. A medic was inserting an IV into his arm. I hobbled over to him, reached down, and patted his good shoulder. He opened his eyes. They were glazed with morphine, exhaustion, and pain.

"See you," I said.

He nodded. His mouth opened, then closed. He raised his one good hand and waved good-bye.

I straightened up, my leg very stiff, and hobbled painfully up the hill toward the light.

Chapter 26

A Touch of Heaven

To the muddy, greasy, foul infantryman, white sheets are the ultimate symbol of compensatory delight, safety, and comfort ... for soldiers whose business is killing the guiltless and unfortunate, white sheets become the all-time image of innocence.
—PAUL FUSSELL,
Doing Battle:
The Making of a Skeptic

I hobbled up to the triage tent. It was well lit, crowded, and bustling with activity—doctors in white, orderlies in green, all intently working on wounded men on stretchers. Two medics met me at the entrance. One read the tag that Doc Solis had fastened to my lapel. ("GSW [gunshot wound] left thigh.") The other gave me a shot of tetracycline in the buttocks. They checked the wound, asked me how I felt ("Okay, I guess"), pointed me in the direction of another tent about twenty yards away (the ambulatory ward, or awaiting-evacuation tent), and told me I'd be flown back to An Khe as soon as aircraft were available.

I asked if I could visit my battalion's rear HQ tent first.

"Yeah, sure," they said.

Hobbling away from the grimly chaotic but somehow hopeful bustle of the triage tent, I headed off into the darkness to find a familiar face. The first shadowy figure I ran into told me where the 2/7th HQ tent was and escorted me right to it.

I lifted the tent flap and stuck my head in. The battalion

295

sergeant major (CSM Bowen), Captain Johnson, and Mr. King, our senior warrant officer, were inside. Jim Brigham was out scrounging, and Major Henry was in the field with the colonel. It was fun to stick my head in, say "Garry Owen!" and see the looks on their faces. They were as glad to see me as I was to see them. They offered me a chair, sat me down, gave me a hot cup of coffee, and made me feel right at home. They knew about the fight. Radio reports had been coming in all afternoon. They knew how many killed and wounded we had, and who had flown in and out. We shot the breeze for a while, which cheered me up immensely, but then I had to get back to where I was supposed to be. But it was great to see those guys.

I hobbled back to the ambulatory ward, went inside, and joined about a dozen men all sitting quietly on benches—a grim crowd, but no one seriously wounded. I didn't know any of them.

We waited there for what seemed like hours. All I can remember about that tent was a small swarthy private sitting in the corner next to a redheaded guy, a spec four. The private appeared to be sleeping. He'd wake up, look around, and begin taking off his shirt. The redheaded guy would talk to him soothingly and help him get his shirt back on and rebuttoned. Then the little guy would fall asleep again. After a while, he'd wake up and start undressing again.

"What's wrong with him?" I asked, curious.

"Combat fatigue, sir," the spec four said, knowingly.

During the next hour or so, the same vignette repeated itself over and over again. The redheaded spec four was a true Samaritan.

Eventually, we were herded onto a three-quarter-ton truck, driven to an airfield (the old French one near LZ Dog, I think), led onto a Caribou, and flown back to An Khe. We arrived there well after midnight and had to wait around the airstrip for transportation to the MASH (the 2d Mobile Army Surgical Hospital, 43d Medical Group) at Camp Radcliff. That seemed to take forever. When we finally arrived at the

MASH, it must have been close to 2:00 A.M. Everyone was exhausted.

While the admitting people attended to the worst-off cases, I was given a blanket, pointed in the direction of an empty GP tent with its sides rolled up and lots of empty cots in it, and told that I'd get fixed up in the morning. That sounded good to me, so I limped downhill to the tent, stretched out on the first cot I came to, shut my eyes gratefully, and fell asleep.

I woke up several times that night. My leg was quite sore by then and throbbing terribly, but I was safe, and that's what mattered, so I'd pull the woolen blanket over me and go back to sleep.

The next morning, I remember being roused by one of the cheeriest, most upbeat men I ever met in Vietnam, an E-5 medic who'd come down to the tent to wake me up. He did so with a cheerful greeting, told me they were waiting for me up at admitting, pointed out where the latrine was, and said that all I had to do was make it up the hill and they'd take care of me. Then he left. I never saw him again but remember him with great affection.

I had to go to the bathroom something fierce, so I pushed myself up on one elbow and looked around. Except for me, the tent was empty. Up the hill I could see a headquarters area where we'd been admitted, and beyond it, some Quonset huts. There was activity up there, too, so I decided to get up.

When I pushed myself up to a sitting position, though, and swung my legs over the side of the cot and lowered them to the ground, I experienced one of the most agonizing waves of pain I've ever felt. It just rolled up from my wound, washed through my body, and exploded in my brain. I almost passed out. After that first horrific jolt, I just sat there, recovering slowly and steeling myself for the next effort. As painful as it was, I knew I could make it. I'd made it that far. Help was close at hand. Everything was going to be okay. Eventually, I managed to stand up, limp painfully to the latrine, and take a pee.

As soon as I walked through the portals of the admitting tent, I was treated like a king. After checking in, I was helped to a gurney and told to lie down. It felt wonderful to stretch out again. Another cheerful orderly wheeled me into an X-ray tent and took X rays of my left thigh.

"These are good, sir," he said, looking them over proudly.

He slipped them into a big manila envelope, handed it to me, and wheeled me back to the waiting room.

My next visitor was dressed in green surgical garb, introduced himself as Captain Someone-or-other, told me he was going to perform the surgery, glanced at the X rays, showed me where the bullet was (a nice undamaged 7.62mm round nestled next to my femur in the fleshy back part of my thigh), and told me how simple the surgery would be.

He asked if there was anything else he ought to know about, and I told him I thought I had worms.

"Oh, hell," he said, smiling. "No problem there. The antibiotics we'll be giving you will take care of them in no time. You don't have to worry about them."

I thanked him and he left.

The next person to come by was the anesthesiologist. He explained to me that I'd get a saddle block that would put me to sleep from the chest down. All I'd feel was a pinprick. After that, they'd do the surgery. I'd be awake the whole time.

After he left, the X-ray guy came back and escorted me to the operating room. All we had to do was walk through a couple of tent flaps and there it was—an operating room all right—clean as a whistle, all shiny and bright, with the operating table in the middle of an amphitheater of lights, surrounded by medical paraphernalia with dials and stainless-steel trays and clean white towels all around.

"Just take your clothes off and hop up on the table," he said. "Someone'll be here in a minute."

He left me standing there in the middle of the operating room, leaning against the operating table, suddenly feeling very alone, scared, and cold.

I stripped, stepped painfully out of my filthy, ripped, and bloody jungle fatigues, and left them lying there in a smelly heap on the floor. Again, very painfully, I managed to push myself backward up to a sitting position on the operating table, pull my legs up over the edge, then lie back comfortably and relax. While I was lying there on my back, stark naked, my legs comfortably spread, wondering what they were going to do next, I felt a slight breeze and then a chill. The place was air-conditioned!

Suddenly a woman's voice came wafting over my shoulder. "What's your serial number, Lieutenant?" she asked. Her voice was husky, pleasant, almost playful.

I looked behind me. She was a woman all right, a round-eyed American female, probably a nurse. She was dressed in fatigues, had short reddish brown hair, a pockmarked face, and a clipboard in her hand. She wasn't gawking—just filling out forms.

I gave her my serial number and the other bare essentials, not thinking twice about the fact that I was lying there spread-eagled naked and almost freezing to death.

After Florence Nightingale had finished her business, another nurse came in, this one dressed in light green surgical garb. I told her I was freezing. She covered me with a clean white sheet, skillfully inserted an intravenous needle into the vein on the top of my left hand, then taped it to a brace of some sort, to keep the IV secure. Another nurse came in, attached a plasma bottle to an overhead hanger of some kind, plugged me into the drip, and injected something into the IV tube. She told me it would help me to relax.

"You might feel a little sleepy, too," she added.

I drifted off almost immediately.

Sometime later, the anesthesiologist reappeared. "Roll over on your side," he said.

I complied obediently.

"Now bring your knees up to your chin."

I felt him rubbing something cool on my skin about halfway down my spine.

"You'll feel a little bee sting now," he said. He was right, but that was all there was to it.

"You can roll over on your back again now," he said. I did. "This will start to work in a few minutes. It'll numb you from your chest down. You've got to keep your head back, though, or you'll get a headache. Okay?"

"Okay," I said, settling back comfortably again and falling back to sleep.

When I woke up, I was lying facedown, and they were working on me. I wasn't fully awake, but I could hear the doctors talking, and feel them shoving and rolling me around. I could feel some pressure on my leg, too, but that was all.

I have no idea how long I lay on the operating table, but I remember the doctor telling me what he was doing, that he was debriding the wound, cleaning out all the stuff that had gotten into it, all the dirt and grit and mud. Then I could sense the tone of the doctors' voices changing somewhat. They couldn't find the bullet. No matter what they did, they couldn't find it. That was strange, because I'd seen it clearly on the X rays, right next to my femur, but there they were, digging around inside my leg, and they couldn't find it at all. Finally, I heard a voice asking me what I'd been doing when I was hit, and I told them I had been squatting and that the bullet had ricocheted up into my leg.

Oh, they said, that changes everything. Then I felt them lifting me up, sort of, and later, when I felt all squished up on my face, and twisted like a pretzel, I heard someone say, "There it is!"

Later, I heard the doctor telling me they were going to leave the bullet where it was, that they'd do more damage taking it out than leaving it in.

"You're the doc," I said, and fell asleep again.

I woke up being wheeled through a corridor. I could feel the gurney jiggling underneath me and see the curbed metal ribs of a Quonset hut corridor floating by me overhead. An IV tube was swaying in rhythm to a clear plasma bottle dangling over my chest. Someone was holding the bottle. She was a blonde, a beautiful blonde in army fatigues. Her hair was short, her complexion flawless, her eyes kind and gentle. She was absolutely gorgeous.

"Looks like he's going to smile," she said.

How could I not? I'd just fallen in love.

The gurney took a sharp left turn, stopped momentarily, then turned into a dimly lit room with curved sloping walls. To the calm, quiet commands of my new blond compadre, I felt myself maneuvered to the left again, lifted off the gurney, and placed in a bed—a real hospital bed, with stainless steel sidebars and clean white sheets. The Quonset hut's curved ceiling sloped down behind my head, and the wall on my right was painted light green. I'd been placed in the bed nearest the door. As the orderlies departed, I tried to lift my head to look around.

"Uh, uh, uh," said the blonde. She was a nurse, a second lieutenant. Her name tag read Allen. "You've got to lie flat on your back until the saddle block wears off. Otherwise you'll get a terrible headache."

Then I remembered. I couldn't feel my legs! I was paralyzed! Totally numb from the chest down! A sudden terror seized me, then passed. Would the feeling come back? Yes it would.

My new blond friend was attaching my IV to a hanger in back of my bed. While she worked, I admired the soft curves of her figure as she leaned over me. She was beautiful! She turned back, looked down, checked the IV in my hand, and asked, quietly, "Is there anything I can get for you?"

"When will the feeling come back to my legs?"

"It usually takes a few hours," she said. "You may want some painkillers then. Just ask. Anything else?"

"I'd love a cigarette," I said.

"Sorry. There's no smoking in the ICU (intensive care unit)," she answered, shaking her head.

"Oh, no!" I joked. "How am I gonna survive?"

"You'll be fine," she said. "You'll only be here twenty-four hours. Just be sure to keep your head flat on the bed. And get some sleep. I'm going to leave you now, okay? Remember, if you need something for the pain, just ask. See you later."

"Yeah. Thanks," I said.

She turned and walked away, every man's dream.

I turned my head to the left. I could see a bed next to mine.

Somebody in it. I could sense beds beyond it, too, all the way down to the far end of the Quonset hut. There were beds across the aisle, too. Lots of them. All full. I turned my head back. Lieutenant Allen was conferring with a nurse by a small table near the doorway. There were other nurses in fatigues and orderlies in white, quietly ministering to the wounded. I was safe. It was wonderful.

Then I shut my eyes and faded back into oblivion.

Sometime later, I woke up to the sounds of someone moaning. It was the man in the bed next to me. A doctor was working on his leg.

"Oh, oh, ooooooh, ah, ahhrrrrgg," the patient moaned.

"I'm sorry," the doctor said. "But we have to get as much as we can." He had a pair of long tweezers in his hand, using them to pick something out of the wounded man's leg. But the leg wasn't there. It was gone, traumatically amputated above the knee. The doctor was picking shrapnel out of the poor guy's stump!

"Oh, oh, oh, oh!" the guy groaned again, his body tense, his right hand gripping the steel sidebar of his bed. I could see his face now. It was pale. He was in agony, a young man with short blond hair, hurting terribly.

Jesus fucking Christ, Doc! Leave the poor guy alone!

The doctor kept probing.

The poor guy kept moaning.

I couldn't believe what was going on, what the doc was doing to the poor guy, but there was nothing I could do, so I turned away.

After what seemed like hours, I heard the doctor say, "That's enough for now. Get some sleep. You'll be out of here tomorrow."

The young man didn't respond.

I watched the doc get up and leave. Then I turned back to the poor guy and tried to say something, but couldn't. I tried to go back to sleep, too, but couldn't. I wanted to say something to the guy, something to alleviate his pain, something to make him feel better, something to help. But what can you say? Sorry about that, man. Hey, buddy, what happened to your leg? Hey, man, you're gonna be okay. Hey, man, they do great things with prostheses these days.

Nothing I could say would help the guy's sense of loss, or ease his pain, or give him his leg back, so I turned my head away and stared at the ceiling and tried not to think about what had happened, or the last few days, or how badly we'd been chopped up that time, or how many men we'd lost, or who they were. Then I realized I was out of it for a while, out of the fighting, and I felt a calming sense of relief, and safety, and peace, and, despite the unimaginable anguish of the poor guy lying next to me with his leg blown off, I knew he would be okay, would be going home, and was actually pretty lucky, compared to some. Then I drifted back to sleep.

Sometime later, I woke up to the gap-toothed smiling face of our balding Rasputin of a first sergeant, Frank Miller. He'd dropped by to pick up my gear, and visit. Good old Dockery was standing right behind him, too, looking a bit sheepish. Boy, was I delighted to see them. The first sergeant asked if there was anything he could get for me, but I couldn't think of a thing. Then they were gone. Though their visit was fleeting, it was one of the nicest things that happened to me in that hospital.

Much later, I think, because I had the distinct impression it was nighttime, I woke up again, this time to some commotion across the aisle. A team of doctors and nurses had wheeled a new patient into the ward, on the other side, three beds down from the nurse's station by the door.

I looked left. The traumatic amputee was asleep. But across the aisle, all kinds of activity was going on.

"Now, try coughing again," one of the doctors was saying. The patient just lay there, too out of it to understand. "Cough, Jonesy! You've got to cough!"

The guy was a mess. He had just come out of surgery, I learned later, where he'd had a sucking chest wound sealed and a broken jaw wired shut.

One of the doctors was inserting a rubber tube into the guy's chest, through the rib cage on his right side. Right there

across the aisle! At least that's what I think he was doing. He
worked on him for a while longer, fitting the tube into the
guy's lung so the fluid would drain from it. The tube ran down
the side of his bed and into a big glass bottle underneath it.
When the man coughed, small spurts of blood squirted into
the bottle. It was a quarter full. The man's arm and shoulder, I
think, were in a cast, too. As I said, he was a mess. But the
doctors wouldn't let up on him.

"You gotta cough, Jonesy. Try it one more time. You gotta
get the blood out of your lung, and coughing's the only way to
do it."

I heard Jonesy cough, just a little one, a single, dry hack,
and a spurt of blood splashed into the bottle.

"That's good. But you gotta give me more," the doctor said.

There was a nurse on the other side of Jonesy's bed, tow-
eling off his face, encouraging him in a softer, gentler voice.

"You can do it," I heard her say.

"Come on, Jonesy, cough! You can do better than that."

Jonesy moaned, and mumbled, and tried to cough again.
Another spurt splashed into the bottle.

I really didn't understand what was happening, but I knew
the guy was a mess. Later, having asked the orderlies, I
learned that he'd been boarding a chopper and was bent over
at the waist when a bullet hit him in the buttocks, breaking his
pelvis, continued up through his lung, coming out his chest
through the collar bone, then up into his jaw. He had a frac-
tured pelvis, a punctured lung, a shattered clavicle, and a
broken jaw—all from a single round! But they were working
on just his lung that night, and they worked on it for what
seemed like hours.

I drifted back and forth from consciousness to sleep, and
whenever I'd wake up, I would hear first one doctor, then another, urging Jonesy to cough. Finally, I drifted off again.
When I woke up the next morning, both the guy named
Jonesy and the traumatic amputation case were gone—
evacuated to Tokyo, I understand, where the medical facili-
ties were slightly more sophisticated.

With the new day came sensation in my legs, a sense of

blessed relief, and lots of pain, for which they gave me Darvon. Around midday, I was lifted onto another gurney and wheeled out of the ICU to another ward—a bright, full, happy place, where the friendly banter of wounded GIs made me feel right at home. They wheeled me and my IV rig almost all the way down to the end of the ward and put me in a clean, fresh bed on the left side of the aisle again. I felt great. I was back with the troops, part of a team again, just one of the boys. Who cared about the pain? (They gave me more Darvon for it, but it didn't help much.) Everyone in that ward was nice, I recall, and they made me feel welcome, even though I was an officer—the only one in the ward, I think. (Being wounded is a great equalizer.)

My recollections of that ward are hazy, but nice. After a day or so, the doctor who'd done my surgery came by to examine his handiwork. He showed it to me, too—an open six-inch gash in the back of my left thigh where he had debrided the wound. It looked awful! They'd cut away all the damaged flesh and left the wound open so it could drain, which it had been doing, into the bandage he peeled off. They'd stitched up only the inside part of the wound with self-dissolving sutures, he told me. After it drained some more and healed from the inside out, they'd stitch up the outside part. After I saw that ugly gash, I didn't look at it again. Pleased with his work and my progress, the good doctor asked a nurse to rebandage my leg, and left. I never saw him again.

The wound healed a little every day, and as it did, the pain lessened, and my spirits improved.

As the wound healed and the shock of that battle wore off, I found myself thinking more and more about what had happened, how George Polli had refused to come forward to help us out, how he'd disobeyed both the captain's and my orders to bring his platoon forward into the action. The more I thought about it, the angrier I got, and at some point during that first week in the MASH, as soon as I felt up to it, I wrote Captain Davison a letter and told him that if he didn't press charges against Lieutenant Polli for cowardice under fire, I would. After mailing the letter, I felt better. I'd said my piece.

I spent about a week in that ward, I think. I remember first the agony, then the relief, of using a bedpan (for the first and last time). At some point they came and took the IV out of my hand, which was wonderful because it was getting really sore. I also remember waking up at night and hearing the moans of the men around me, talking in their sleep. War dreams. They were awful. The man across the aisle was back for his third visit, he said, to get some shrapnel out of his back. He'd picked it up in the Ia Drang Valley in November. The shrapnel was simply working its way to the surface of his skin, and the doctors would cut it out when it got troublesome. He suffered terrible nightmares and woke me up several times with his screaming, but awake, he was one of the most laid-back guys I'd ever met.

I also remember one night when a team of orderlies worked on a man who was having a malaria attack. His fever had spiked dangerously high. They set up several fans by his bed and kept him cooled off by bathing him every minute or so, and letting the fans play over his body. I think they put mosquito netting up around him, too, but I'm not sure about that.

And I distinctly remember the day Nancy Kelly came into the ward. She was one of the three or four female Red Cross workers who had volunteered to join the Cav in early April. I'd met her during her brief visit to the 2d of the 7th's officers club soon after she and the other "donut dollies" had arrived. Our captains—Myron Diduryk and Skip Fesmire—had invited them to our O-club, and they'd caused quite a stir by their visit. The lieutenants had stood around shyly in the background and gawked as the ladies had oooh'd and aaah'd at what the captains said, but then Nancy Kelly came over to us and said hello.

"I didn't think you'd be interested in meeting us lowly young lieutenants," I'd said to her, jokingly. But she *had* been interested, and she'd made an indelible impression on us.

Suddenly, there she was again! She had come into the ward and was walking down the aisle, passing out little bags of goodies—toothpaste, soap, and toiletries from the Red

Cross. She looked fresh and clean and wonderful in her Red Cross outfit, coming down the aisle, smiling and talking to the guys. When she reached my bed and said, "Hi," I reminded her of her visit to our O-club. She said she remembered me, which I'm sure she didn't, and she smiled as if she cared, which I'm sure she did, about us all, and then she went on her kind and gentle way, dispensing hope. I made a mental note to see her again as soon as I could walk.

And now a word about my dear fiancee Nicole, whom I'd left at the Oakland Army Terminal back in July. We'd been writing to each other. She every day. I, when I could. Her letters had been my lifeline to the States, and I relied on them and looked forward to them every day. They helped keep my morale up. But geography plays a role in relationships, too, and not having seen her or talked to a round-eyed woman in more than nine months, I couldn't help myself when a Lieutenant Allen or a Nancy Kelly appeared on the scene. Just the sight of them was a thrill. But looking back on it now, I realize that my memories of the traumatic events of that year are clearly more distinct than those of my correspondence with Nickie, and that's why I haven't mentioned her since Chapter 1. But I did feel strongly about her and tried to be faithful. It's just that the circumstances of that year had their impact on the way I felt about things, and what I did. And though I still thought I loved her, I couldn't help but think that girls like Lieutenant Allen and Nancy Kelly were goddesses.

By the way, it turned out that Second Lieutenant Allen was married to one of the surgeons working at that MASH, and though I'd fallen "in love" with her when I first saw her, my ardor faded when I learned that. All I can remember about her after that was the envy I felt whenever I looked over at her living quarters, a tent in back of the MASH, and saw her bra and panties hanging from the clothesline by her tent.

After a week in that second ward, I may have undergone a minor surgical procedure involving the stitching up of the outside part of my wound, but I can't remember anything about it. Whatever, I could almost walk by then. At least I could hobble painfully from the ward to the mess hall or the latrine and back.

Our uniform, by the way, was light blue cotton pajamas. All the patients wore them, and we stood out from the staff of that hospital like a bunch of gaunt, vacant-eyed prisoners in a concentration camp. We probably looked like them, too. But we were happy. I'd venture that most of us felt lucky to be there, lucky to be alive—I certainly did—and the morale around the MASH was very high.

I especially enjoyed my trips to the mess hall. First, the food was generally excellent, usually fresh, a considerable improvement over C rations. Second, it was always good to get out and get some fresh air and smoke a cigarette. And third, I would keep my eyes peeled for Nancy Kelly, and on one occasion at least, I had the unexpected pleasure of running into her and talking to her for a few blissful minutes.

After about a week in that second ward, they moved me to a third, where the staff hardly ever showed up. The wounded in that ward were simply healing. Time, rest, and sleep were all we needed. I remember that ward, though, because that's where I was when Captain Davison visited. And he brought George Polli with him.

There wasn't much I could do about it. I remember waking up from a sound sleep and looking up and seeing Captain Davison, in a clean set of fatigues, standing over my bed. I was glad to see him, and shook his hand, but I realized almost immediately he wasn't alone. He said something, then turned toward the door (which was only three or four beds down on the left in this ward), and there was George Polli standing sheepishly by the door.

"I got your letter," the captain said. "But I've decided not to do what you suggest. I want you to make peace with George, instead. I want you to shake hands with him."

Bullshit! No way! No way was I going to shake hands with that fat-assed cowardly son of a bitch.

The captain turned and beckoned George to join us. And

he came. I watched him moving hesitantly toward my bed and wondered why the captain had brought him. He'd read my letter. He knew how I felt. And there he was, bringing that cowardly son of a bitch into the ward where I was lying helpless with a bullet in my leg, along with a bunch of other guys who'd been wounded fighting, not sitting back in some safe graveyard somewhere, staying out of the battle. And now he was right next to me, standing there with a shit-eating grin on his face, trying to be jovial, saying something like "How the hell are you?" with his hand thrust out, and I just lay there, simmering in disbelief, wondering what the captain had in mind.

I don't honestly remember whether I shook George's hand or not. I may have, but if I did, I don't remember it. And if I did, I don't know why. I know I was tired and still in pain and not completely healed. And I know I was angry as hell. But lots of things go through your mind when you're lying in a hospital bed, and having been through the crucible, and having seen so much in such a short time, and having had some time to reflect on it, I'd wondered why certain people had done certain things, like why Dick Hogarth had taken his platoon out into that open rice paddy, and why Marty Hammer had fought all afternoon with his three wounds and kept things together for his people, and how Jim Kelly, bless his soul, had had to stay there and continue fighting the next day. And so with the captain standing there in the background, and me lying flat on my back, feeling tired and confused and angry and hurt, I may have shaken George's hand, but I don't think I did.

He'd come to visit, though, and that wasn't lost on me, and the captain, by bringing him there, had let me know that he was handling things differently than I wanted him to handle them, and that was his option, his choice, his decision. I had let him know how I'd felt, and that was all that mattered to me at the time. Whatever, the captain and George visited me there, and for that I'm grateful, but I still don't know what really happened to the mortar platoon at Thanh Son 2, the village we assaulted that afternoon of May 6, 1966, and how

George had really behaved, and that remains a mystery to me to this day. Just as much of a mystery as my accepting the captain's decision and letting the matter drop. Captain Davison was certainly a more generous and forgiving man than I was. Then again, maybe he knew of some mitigating circumstance behind George's refusal to come forward into that fight. I don't know. All I know is what I saw and heard that day, and not having learned the truth of what had really happened, and not being able to learn about it while I was hors de combat, I simply relied on the captain's judgment and let it go. And that's them apples.

It was during the captain's visit that I learned what had happened after Marty Hammer and I had been medevac'd. Early the next morning, with Jim Kelly's platoon leading the way, Alpha Company had attacked across that rice paddy where Dick Hogarth's body lay. They'd overrun the remnants of what had been a battalion of hard-core PAVN troops (the North Vietnamese Army's Qyet Tam Regiment, to be exact). It had been quite a victory, the captain said.

I learned later that we killed 335 PAVN troops and captured 22 more during that battle. We even captured their colors! Most of the hard fighting had taken place on May 6, too, the day I was wounded. The seventh had been a mopping-up operation, and we'd suffered no further casualties.

Jim Kelly was put in for a Silver Star for his heroism that day, and he deserved it. Marty Hammer was awarded the Distinguished Service Cross for his extraordinary grit during that fight, as well. I never saw Marty again, but we corresponded after I returned to the States. He became a general's aide after he'd recovered from his wounds.

The battalion had done itself proud in that fight. At the time, of course, all I remember thinking was how many men we'd lost—almost a third of our company that day. I couldn't accept, or really appreciate, what a good job we'd done.

Whatever the case, Captain Davison and George Polli left, eventually, and I continued to heal up from my wound. But I never trusted Polli after that fight.

* * *

Two more events come to mind during my stay in that MASH. I got a letter from Nickie telling me that Burt McCord, my friend from the MATA course, Gene Cargile's West Point friend who'd been married and had two children, had been killed in action in the Iron Triangle. The news brought tears to my eyes, especially for poor Eddie McCord and her children. Why was it always the married guys who got killed?

The second event was slightly different. It was a visit from Maj. Gen. John Norton, our new division commander. The general came striding into our ward and pinned Purple Hearts on several of the men there. For some reason, I wasn't on his list. Perhaps it was too soon after the engagement. Whatever, I remember General Norton coming through the ward with his entourage behind him, pinning medals on the guys, and cheering everyone up with his no-nonsense, get-the-job-done approach. I was heartened by his arrival as our new division commander, but his visit to the ward was a joke.

I would be shaking his hand again about two weeks later, in the middle of the night, not more than a mile from where I was lying in that MASH. But that's another story.

I'd been recuperating for about three weeks when I got a note from George Johnson, the battalion adjutant—something to the effect that Captain Davison had just come down with typhus. He was going to be evacuated to Manila the next morning. Could I get released from the hospital and take command of Alpha Company? If I couldn't, George Polli would take over because he was the ranking officer.

Polli take command of Alpha Company? Over my dead body!

I scrounged a pair of fatigues and bummed a ride to battalion. I remember meeting with Captain Davison and First Sergeant Miller in the battalion aid station's quarantine tent that evening. The captain was really sick, just lying there behind his mosquito netting and really hurting. He wanted to know if I could handle the job. Of course, I said. He briefed me on the company's mission. We were manning a huge chunk of the division's perimeter, but I'd have access to a jeep to make my rounds. That sounded fine with me. I said good-bye and good luck to the captain, limped back to the jeep with Sergeant Miller, and told him I'd see him in the morning.

No matter what the doctors said, I'd be there.

Chapter 27

Command Time

If a man has any greatness in him, it comes to light, not in one flamboyant hour, but in the ledger of his daily work.

—BERYL MARKHAM,
West with the Night

I reported for work the next morning, checking in with Captain Johnson and Lieutenant Colonel Litle at battalion headquarters. They cordially welcomed me back, and the colonel briefed me on our mission. Then, I proceeded to the company area and found George Polli napping in his tent. He jumped up and almost saluted when he saw me. I let him know what I expected of him in his new capacity as my XO, rattling off almost the same spiel that Joel Sugdinis had given me back in October, but leaving out the manifesting and medevac procedures. I tried to emphasize how important it was to me that the men get everything they needed whenever they needed it—food, water, ammo, equipment, whatever. That had become his job. George nodded his head. Then I told him I was going to "walk the line," i.e., familiarize myself with the company's positions, and that while we were manning the Green Line, he could stay in the rear, i.e., the company area, with First Sergeant Miller. (That way, I could steer clear of George, and the first sergeant could keep an eye on him.) That's the way we left it until the captain returned.

Then I hopped into "my" jeep and toured the company front. Our positions ran from the western slope of Hong Kong Mountain, which was by then inside the division perimeter, all the way around, north and east, to a spot behind the 1st

Battalion's base camp—a distance of well over a thousand meters and impossible to defend if it weren't for the night riders, the hundreds of extra troops who came down every night from the division's support units to bolster our line. And by that time, with all the improvements that had been completed, the Green Line was a relatively safe place to be, with wooden watchtowers every hundred meters or so, and spotlights mounted on tall concrete poles interspersed among them. Between our well-dug, heavily sandbagged positions and the distant tree line there was a clear field of fire about 150 meters wide, crisscrossed with barbed wire, concertina, foot traps, trip flares, mines, and claymores. So all we really needed to man the line during the day were a couple of guys with machine guns as lookouts in each of the watchtowers. The rest of the company could spend the day lollygagging in the sun (yeah, sure), catching up on their sleep, cleaning their gear and weapons, playing cards, reading a bit, or writing letters home. We stayed awake at night. That was our job—manning the Green Line and staying alert. But with the hundreds of night riders who came down to fill in the gaps in our line, it wasn't that difficult to keep abreast of things. Or so I thought.

I didn't think much about "the burden of command." I was much too busy, though doing what, I'm not sure. (Looking back on it, I have no clear recollection of how I spent my time.) All I really cared about was taking care of my people and getting the job done. I spent lots of time driving around in the jeep visiting the platoon CPs, checking on this or that, and generally staying out of trouble. At least trying to. It found us, nonetheless.

Jim Kelly's 1st Platoon, which had done so well in our most recent fight, manned the left flank. They had good, easily defensible positions high up on the mountainside's rocky slope, and I didn't have to worry about them. The 3d Platoon, which had been pretty much decimated on May 5 and 6, was being refitted. Under the command of their platoon sergeant, S.Sgt. Rother A. Temple, they held the middle of our line. Sergeant Temple had been with us since the very beginning and was one of the best NCOs in the company. He knew what he was doing and was solid as a rock, and I was glad he was there. On our right flank, then, was the 2d Platoon, led now by S.Sgt. Walter Caple, another Ia Drang veteran. He'd taken over the platoon when Marty Hammer was medevac'd. Like Sergeant Temple, Sergeant Caple was an outstanding NCO, clearly the best man for the job, and I liked him tremendously.

The Mortar Platoon, with Sergeant First Class McGrath in charge while Polli was the XO, had placed two of their three tubes and their fire direction center on a knoll behind the 3d Platoon. The third tube was set up in back of battalion, no more than fifty yards behind the company street, to support our right flank. Sgt. (E-5) Jim Hibbitts was the man in charge of that tube, and he, too, was a solid veteran of the Ia Drang fight.

The company command post overlooked the 3d Platoon's positions in the center of our line, and was within shouting distance of Sergeant McGrath's mortar pits. The CP consisted of a small but well-dug, heavily sandbagged, single-entrance bunker, and I gather it had been the CP for not only Captain Davison, but also most of the other line companies that had manned that part of the perimeter. Why reinvent the wheel? I slept on the ground in back of the bunker, but it was there if we needed it.

One last observation. When I took over the company, we had three NCOs acting as platoon leaders, an indication that either we'd been badly chopped up at Thanh Son 2 or the division's line battalions were badly undermanned. Perhaps both. Luckily, we were only defending the Green Line, which had always been considered easy duty. If we'd been in the field, we'd have been hurting. And though my stitches had been removed, and the wound had fully closed, the scar tissue was still tender, and I could barely walk. Running was out of the question. Still, I felt fine about taking charge, though I can see now how the pressures of command can take their toll.

* * *

During my first week on the Green Line, we got rocketed. It was dusk, I recall. I was talking with Sergeant McGrath and some of the mortar guys about something, when all of a sudden rockets started whooshing in and exploding around us. I wasn't exactly sure what was happening until I saw a big gray dust ball materialize about fifty yards east of us. I saw another puff of dust farther down the line, heard someone yell "Incoming!", and finally figured it out. In they came, *boom! boom! boom!*, kicking up dust and debris as they landed. By that time, we'd all gotten off our duffs and were racing for cover. Racing is perhaps the wrong word in my case, but I legged it as fast as I could to our command bunker and ducked inside. There I was greeted by a wide-eyed Spec Four Gosey, who'd been on radio watch just outside the bunker when the rockets started coming in. He was fine, but I was puffing and giddy with relief that I'd made it to the bunker. I glanced at him, shook my head, and we both started giggling—I kid you not—while the rockets continued to smack into the ground around us—maybe a dozen or so—most of them falling into the 2d Brigade's base camp behind us.

I called battalion.

"Big Horse Base, this is Silent Slasher Six. Over."

The TOC RTO responded immediately.

"This is Slasher Six," I said, trying to sound as calm as I could. "We're receiving rocket fire—about fifteen or so rounds. They're falling into our Charlie Papa area and the Black Horse area behind us. Over."

The TOC RTO rogered that and told me to wait, and the rockets stopped falling.

While I was waiting, Sergeant McGrath appeared at the entrance to our bunker and told me they'd spotted the flashes from the rocket launchers. He had the coordinates, too.

"Great! Give 'em to me," I said. "Good job!"

He asked for permission to return fire.

"Of course," I said.

Then Lieutenant Colonel Litle's voice came over the radio. "This is Big Horse Six. Say again your sitrep. Over."

"This is Slasher Six. We just took about a dozen rockets in and around our position, over."

"This is Big Horse Six. Where are they falling? Over."

"This is Slasher Six. They've stopped now, but they were falling around our Charlie Papa and in back of us, in the Black Horse area, over."

"This is Big Horse Six. Say again where they're falling, over."

"I say again, into our Charlie Papa and the Black Horse unit, over."

Certainly he knew I meant the 2d Brigade. They were the Black Horse Brigade!

I could now hear the FDC guys shouting out gun settings and powder charges and was waiting for our first round to fire.

"This is Big Horse Six. Say again where they fell, over."

Jesus Christ Almighty! Was he drunk? And who gave a shit where they fell?! What mattered was where they were coming from.

"This is Slasher Six. We've spotted where they came from. I have the coordinates, over."

"This is Big Horse Six. Let's have them, over."

Now that's more like it!

While reading the coordinates to him over the radio, I heard the *whonk!* of our first round heading toward the target.

"We're returning fire at this time," I said, proudly.

"Say again those coordinates, over," the colonel said.

I repeated them as clearly as I could.

"Roger that," he said. "Wait. Out."

I could hear the FDC guys calling out adjustments for their second round, when the colonel came back on the horn and told us to cease fire.

Cease fire! Cease fire? We had the bastards in our sights and were about to drop a salvo of mortar rounds on their heads, and he was telling me to cease fire?

"Roger that. Over," I said. "Cease fire!" I yelled out the bunker doorway, as disappointed by that command as I've been about any I've given, and I'm sure the mortar guys were even more disappointed in hearing it.

The colonel came back on the line and asked again where the rockets had landed. I couldn't believe it. What was his goddamn problem? Who gave a fuck where they landed, as long as they didn't hurt anyone?

I repeated my message as best I could, adding that we'd suffered no casualties.

"Roger," he said. "Stand by. Out."

Thirty years later, I realized that my use of the term "Black Horse" didn't mean anything to the colonel that night. If I'd used the term "Black Knight" instead, he'd have understood immediately. Black Knights was the 2d Brigade's moniker, not Black Horse. Who said I wasn't excited by those incoming rockets? Who said adrenaline doesn't affect you? Who said I knew what I was doing?

Oh well, nobody got hurt, thank God, and for that, I was thankful. I was proud of our mortar guys, too. They'd spotted the enemy and returned fire quickly. That's what the game was all about. I congratulated them on doing a good job, but I knew they were disappointed. So was I.

Then a remarkable thing happened. Within a minute or so of our reporting the location of the rocket launcher flashes, we heard a low rumble growing from the vicinity of the Golf Course. A few minutes later, an entire rifle company, the quick-reaction force from the Black Knights of the 2d of the 5th, lifted off from the division helipad, flew over us in one long, spread-out formation, and air assaulted into that location. It was quite a show.

I was suddenly very glad I wasn't one of those Victor Charlies who'd had the temerity to set up that rocket and fire it at us. We'd brought the wrath of the 1st Air Cav down on their heads, and it was awesome.

After the ships returned to the Golf Course, the show was over. It was quiet the rest of the night.

The next morning, shortly after dawn, I noticed the colonel and some other field-grade officers I didn't recognize, probably from the 2d Brigade or division headquarters, walking around and surveying the damage. There wasn't any, really. None that I could see. Just a few holes in the ground where the rockets had exploded around us. But they were there, and I was glad they were in case the colonel thought we'd been hallucinating, or making the whole story up. The colonel and his compatriots didn't bother us, or come over and say hello, or anything like that. They just poked around the shell holes and went away. I should have reported to him, I guess, but it's hard to do that when you can barely walk, and he was a long way away.

Later that day, around noon, the men from the 2d of the 5th who'd flown out there the previous night came back into the perimeter through our positions. They told us they'd found the launch site, but no VC.

At least we'd given them the right coordinates. That was something to be proud of.

About a week later, we were probed. In two places.

It had been dark for some time. The night riders had come in and taken their positions, and I was settled in behind our CP. Suddenly, Sergeant Caple called with a report of activity to his front, way down in back of the 1st Battalion's base camp, by the shower point on our far right flank. One of his guys had seen a definite presence on the far side of the wire. A probe.

"I'll be right there," I said. Perhaps "right there" wasn't the right thing to say, because the jeep was parked about a hundred yards in back of our CP, and it took a while to make the walk, and to drive the drive took another ten minutes. Spec Four Gosey was my RTO, and Dockery the driver, I think. I'm not sure. But we did have radio contact with both our guys on the line and with battalion, where the artillery liaison officer hung out. (Normally, the artillery FO is with the CO—in his back pocket, so to speak—but on the Green Line, battalion controlled the artillery.)

We drove to the 2d Platoon positions, using the division interior road, parked in back of battalion, near Sergeant Hibbitts's mortar position, and arrived in decent time to check things out. Sergeant Caple was on the line, of course, and briefed me on what they had seen. His people were positive they'd seen someone in the wire. There didn't seem to be that much of a threat, though, so I suggested they keep an eye on things, and be sure to call me if they needed anything like artillery or illumination. Though there were spotlights around the Green Line, they wouldn't be turned on unless there was a full-scale attack. With only one or two men spotted in the wire, I didn't think an attack was imminent.

While I was conferring with Sergeant Caple, Sergeant Temple came on the line. His people had just reported movement—several men, he said, sneaking around the white stucco house about two hundred yards out on the other side of the wire. He wanted artillery illumination and ARA. Because the artillery guy was in the battalion TOC, I told Sergeant Temple to call him there and ask for it, then adjust it from his position. I was too far away. Shortly after speaking to Sergeant Temple and telling him I was on my way back to his position, someone from battalion called with considerable urgency in his voice and advised me that Pegasus was heading toward my Charlie Papa. Pegasus was the call sign for General Norton, the division commander. I rogered that and advised battalion that our Three-six had seen some bad guys across the wire from their positions, near the abandoned stucco building about two hundred meters out, and that he would be calling for artillery. The artillery guy called me then and asked if I was aware of what was going on. I said yes. He said my Three-six wanted support. I said I knew that, and if he wanted it, give it to him. He asked me to confirm things with my Three-six. I called Sergeant Temple again for a sitrep. He could see two or three men lurking around the building, he told me. He could see them clearly against the backdrop of the white stucco building. Okay, I said. Do what you think is right. I'll be there as soon as I can.

Sergeant Temple then called for an ARA strike on the white stucco building.

I was en route back to my jeep when it occurred. We could hear it, but couldn't see it. We were too far away.

And that stirred up a hornet's nest. Not in the VC camp, but in ours. Right after the strike, I got another urgent call from battalion, informing me that Pegasus was on his way down to check out what was going on.

Now that wasn't such a big deal to me. I thought it was just great that Maj. Gen. John Norton, formerly the commanding general of the 82d Airborne Division and our division commander, was going to come down and say hello to us, make sure we got what we wanted, and learn a thing or two. That was his prerogative. But for the brigade S-3 and the battalion S-3 and the other men who cared about their careers, General Norton's visit was a very big deal. You could hear it in their voices over the radio as I hobbled back to my jeep.

"Pegasus is coming!" I heard. And a few minutes later, "Pegasus is at your Charlie Papa! Where are you?" And a few minutes after that, "What's the delay? What's your position? Why aren't you there?"

I explained that I was in back of our far right flank, was proceeding to my Charlie Papa as expeditiously as I could, and would be there as soon as possible. I didn't say I couldn't move any faster, but I couldn't. We hustled, hustle being a relative term, back to our CP, which took about ten or fifteen minutes, I think, and during that time, I received at least two more transmissions from battalion telling me exactly where Pegasus was, and asking me why I wasn't there waiting for him. Enough.

Sergeant McGrath was there. He was the ranking man in charge, and he knew what to do, so I wasn't that excited. And Sergeant Temple was perfectly capable of handling things, too. No big deal.

When I finally made it back to our CP, Sergeant McGrath advised me that the general was down by the watchtower in back of 3d Platoon. Actually, I think he simply pointed down the hill and said, "They're all down there somewhere, sir."

So that's where we headed, down the slope, and into the dark silent night, Gosey and Dockery with their radios on their backs, and me with my slowly healing leg wound, all traipsing down to the 3d Platoon's CP looking for the general in the tower. It was my job, as acting CO, to report to the general, and I was going to do it, no matter what, but limping down the line, in the black pitch of that dark night, I was wondering what all the hoopla was about.

When we finally reached the watchtower, I could tell there were several men in it. Someone, I can't remember who, told me the general was up there, and I nodded. That was not the best place for the commanding general to be because if any place was targeted by a rocket launcher or a recoilless rifle (or a heavy machine gun, for that matter), the sandbagged parapet atop that tower would have been it. Saying a silent prayer that the VC didn't have anything aimed at us, I climbed up the ladder to report.

When I got up there and looked inside, I saw that the parapet was absolutely jammed with people, several of them whispering. I pulled myself up, clambered inside, found General Norton among the shadowy figures, and reported.

"First Lieutenant Gwin, Acting CO of Alpha Company, 2d of the 7th, reporting, sir!"

The general shook my hand. Captain Nadal, our S-3, was there, and Sergeant Temple standing ramrod straight and looking very serious. I think I said "hi" to him, and the others I could recognize, and then stood by to illuminate the general on our current situation. I may have apologized to him for having taken so long to get there, but I don't think so. Sometimes it's best to keep your mouth shut. The general seemed satisfied with what he'd seen and indicated that he'd be returning to his headquarters. Then he turned and started down the ladder, followed by our S-3, the brigade S-3, yours truly, Sergeant Temple, and everyone else who'd been up there, except, of course, the two or three stunned troopers who'd been there in the first place.

The general graciously shook my hand again and strode off into the night with his entourage following closely behind him. Our S-3 turned to me and said that the general had been satisfied, perhaps even pleased, by the way we were doing things, and with that, he, too, turned and strode off into the darkness. I turned to Sergeant Temple, told him what I'd just been told, and complimented him on the way he'd handled things.

"Spread the word, Sergeant," I said. "The men did good tonight."

And that was it. No big deal. But I learned that night that if you're a company commander, you have to be prepared to answer not only to your own people, the men who rely on you for leadership and support, but also to the brass above, at battalion, brigade, even division level—especially if you're calling for an ARA strike right outside the wire of the Green Line.

My reason for calling it was simple. One of my platoon leaders had asked for it. It was also clear to me that Sergeant Temple had been very sure about what his men had seen. And what the hell? If you see VC moving outside the wire, you should blast 'em, right? There was a war going on, wasn't there?

One last story before Captain Davison returned. It came to pass, during my cameo appearance as Alpha Company's commander, that two mortar rounds landed one night in the vicinity of the division G-1's tent. SFC Jim Gooden, who had been our battalion assistant operations sergeant at LZ Albany, confirmed this to me thirty years later. Wounded at Albany, he'd been reassigned after his recovery to assist Lt. Col. John D. White (Ole John D., our former battalion commander) in the division G-1's office. Sergeant Gooden told me that there were two mortar rounds, and that they had landed right next to the G-1's Conex container in the middle of the night, about the same time as our right flank mortar tube's scheduled H & I rounds were fired. (H & I stands for harassment and interdiction, sporadic nighttime fire designed to strike fear into the hearts of the enemy.) When the two rounds fell, they scared the bejesus out of Lieutenant Colonel White, and he, being the astute and gracious officer that he was, decided that since they had landed almost simultaneously with the firing of Alpha Company's right flank mortar tube, they must have come from it. Accordingly, he screamed for someone's head, and it happened to be mine.

An Article 32 Investigation was commenced the next morning.

Now an Article 32 Investigation is a prerequisite for a general court-martial, and an officer has to conduct it. That honor fell on none other than Capt. John "Skip" Fesmire, CO of Charlie Company, one of the best captains in our battalion.

I'll not forget the bright sunny morning back in our base camp when Captain Fesmire walked up to me, told me what he was doing, and proceeded to read me my rights. You know the rights. You've heard them on the cops and robbers shows on TV—that anything I say may be held against me— something like that. Captain Fesmire read me my rights and informed me of the charges against me, as the commanding officer of the company on line, made by our former battalion commander.

"He thinks the rounds that fell near his tent came from your tube," the captain said.

I remember getting angry about that. Sergeant Hibbitts was in command of that tube, a man who'd been a mortar squad leader through Xray, Albany, LZ 4, Thanh Son 2, and numerous other scraps, one of the best NCOs in our unit, bar none. And Old John D., who'd been shit-canned for incompetence back in October, thought we'd been dumb enough to turn our mortar tube around and fire a couple of rounds into our own perimeter!? Jesus fucking Christ! But I stifled my rage and answered the captain's questions, confident that our guys knew what they were doing.

I couldn't help asking, though. Why didn't they think they might have been VC mortar rounds?

The look on the captain's face told me everything.

After I was read my rights and asked a number of questions, and after I shared with Captain Fesmire my deepest and most personal thoughts on the merits of his investigation, I escorted him across the dry rice paddy that separated the headquarters from the troops, and up the hill to where Sergeant Hibbitts was tending his gun. I went over to him, told him what the captain was doing, told him to answer his questions without getting too pissed off, brought him back to Captain Fesmire, and introduced them. With that, I saluted, said "Garry Owen!" and left.

So that's what you get for doing the best job you can?! An Article 32 investigation and accusations of dropping mortar rounds on the G-1's tent! And only because of the timing! I hated H & I fires. Harassment and interdiction, my ass. All they did was harass our mortar platoon and interdict their night's rest. And now that senile old bastard, John D., was fucking with the troops once again. Goddamn it. Goddamn it to hell! What a bloody shame it had come down to this. Being accused of something so stupid. I was, to put it mildly, slightly pissed.

Long story short—and luckily for us—Captain Fesmire completed his investigation that very same afternoon and arrived at the not-too-implausible conclusion that it was more than likely that the mortar rounds that had exploded near Lieutenant Colonel White's Conex had been fired from outside the wire. And that was how it was left.

But I'll never forget the anger I felt, and the humiliation of the charge, and the rage at Lieutenant Colonel White for coming back so spitefully to haunt us.

And then, suddenly, it was over—my brief tour as acting company commander of Alpha 2/7.

Captain Davison returned just before the last week of June, and boy, was I happy to see him!

He'd recovered fully, he said, and felt good. I was glad. Then he told me that he'd heard I'd done a good job as CO, and that made me feel even better. And then he said something I'll never forget.

"Now that I'm back, you can relax. You and Jim Kelly. You've both got less than two weeks until your DEROS (date of expected return from overseas), so as far as I'm concerned, you don't have to go out into the field anymore."

That's what he said, more or less.

It took me a while to grasp it. I'd completely lost track of the time. I'd forgotten how close my DEROS was, and Kelly's. And then it began to sink in. I didn't have to go out into the field anymore. I'd had my last operation. No more air assaults. No more hot LZs. No more getting shot at. No more traipsing through the jungle looking for bad guys. No more gut-wrenching fear. No more death and dying.

My God, I was going to make it! I was going to make it through my tour! Unfucking believable!

"Are you sure?" I asked.

"Yes, I'm sure," the captain said.

And with that, I turned and walked out of his tent with my head spinning, my heart light and free, my head in the clouds, my mind in total disbelief. I was going to make it home!

I went immediately to the O-club to find Jim Kelly and celebrate. We were both going home. We were both going to make it. That was worth a beer.

I was going to make it home, I thought, heading to the club. I was going to make it home. I was going to make it home . . .

It was over!

Chapter 28

One Last Picnic

*The warrior knew [that] life and
death, and courage in the face of
death, were all that really mattered. Everything else, save for
love, was nonsense.*

—PHILIP CAPUTO,
Means of Escape

Two days later, Captain Davison reneged. The 101st Airborne, he said, had run into trouble south of Tuy Hoa, and the
3d Brigade was going down there the following morning to
help them out. The 2d Battalion was going to be airlifted by
C-130 to Tuy Hoa, and he was asking me to make the trip
with them.

My heart froze. Oh no, not again . . .

"Jim, too?" I asked, meaning Kelly.

"Yes," he said.

"You said we didn't have to go out into the field anymore."

"I know," the captain said, "but we're short of officers, and
we've got a new first sergeant, and your replacement needs
some time. So, I'm asking you to come with us."

God knows I couldn't refuse, but I thought about it.

Jim Kelly agreed to go as well, of course—not that we had
any choice in the matter—and we started gearing up for the
operation. The captain was right about needing us. We had an
almost brand-spanking-new second lieutenant, whose name,
I think, was McCarty, and though he turned out, ultimately, to
be my replacement, I can't remember what he looked like.
We also had a new first sergeant by the name of Sherman

Flanders. Frank Miller, after more than ten months of steadfast service with a line company, was going home. His replacement was fresh from the States, clearly untried, and,
from my perspective, slightly soft. (Perhaps because he wore
glasses.) But I was happy for First Sergeant Miller. He'd certainly earned a rest.

But what about us?! We'd earned a rest, too. Too bad we
couldn't take one. Bellyaching about it wouldn't do any good,
though, so Jim Kelly and I basically bit the bullet and carried
on. But it was very very hard. When you're "short," as they
say about those guys who have only a few weeks left in
country, you're thinking more about going home than getting
the job done, more about staying alive than taking care of
your people, so the 1st Cav's unspoken rule was that when
people had less than two weeks in country, they were usually
relieved of further field duty, and allowed to stay back at base
camp as if they were scheduled for R & R. And that made
sense, I thought. Too bad it didn't apply to us.

On the morning of June 22, 1966, then, we found ourselves
boarding a C-130 for a flight to Tuy Hoa. I tried not to think
about the C-123 that had crashed into the mountains five
months before, but I couldn't help it. Luckily, our thirty-
minute flight was uneventful. From Tuy Hoa, we were ferried
by CH-47 Chinook to the airstrip at Dong Tre. That's what
my flight record indicates, but I can't find Dong Tre on a map.

The Dong Tre airstrip was in the middle of nowhere, surrounded by mountains. When we landed, we simply walked
off the back of the Chinook, turned right, continued a hundred meters off the strip into tall, lush grass, and plopped
down in it until we got the word to move. I think the whole
battalion was there, lounging in the grass under the broiling
midday sun, just waiting for 1st Cav Hueys to pick us up and
take us into the fight. And that was the hard part. We'd been
told there was a fight going on, and we were being committed
to it immediately. Ode to Joy!

Captain Davison was called to battalion. We just lay in the
grass and waited. When he returned, he told us that we'd be

picked up in an hour or so and airlifted to an LZ named Mike, a couple thousand meters to the east. PAVN had been spotted near there, he said, so the LZ would be prep'd with artillery and ARA before we landed. Just another air assault.

An hour later, a formation of eighteen or so Hueys came in to pick us up, and we hopped on board and headed east. The flight took less than twenty minutes, but I remember it because the whole time we seemed to be descending due east into a long, narrow valley. The whole valley seemed to slope gently to the sea, and the closer we got to the LZ, the lower we seemed to be. The terrain was completely unfamiliar, too— hilly and uneven. Then, out the right door, the LZ came into view. It was a large open field set in a bowl surrounded by high ground—an unforgiving place if the bad guys were up in the hills. Then I heard Jim Kelly on the radio reporting that he could see mortar pits on the far slope of the hill mass to our left. Mortar pits! They had mortar pits within range of our LZ! I looked out the left door, and sure enough, there they were, three well-dug mortar pits that I could see, but no PAVN. Oh, shit, here we go again, I thought.

Our assault was flawless, if such a thing is possible. We veered to the south, leaving the hill with the mortar pits behind us, and roared into the LZ. I was with my usual team, two RTOs, our new first sergeant, and a couple of guys from the mortar platoon. I jumped out the right door onto a flat, dry-stubble field, no grass at all, no cover or concealment of any kind, and sprinted all the way off the LZ to the edge of the field, my team right behind me. We jumped into a shallow ravine that ran along the LZ's southwestern edge. I was expecting incoming fire, but there wasn't any. As the choppers lifted off, I could see the platoons deploying to their respective sections of the LZ. The captain and his team were heading east across the LZ to a dike or stone wall of some kind. It ran along the base of a large grass-covered hill that loomed over us like a giant green skull.

And there we waited while the platoons settled in.

Within just a few minutes of our assault, I was lying there

on the side of our little ravine, glancing back toward the northern edge of the LZ, where I'd seen the mortar pits, when suddenly four or five PAVN in gray uniforms came hot-footing it down the side of the hill. They were armed and coming right at us!

"There they are!" I screamed, raising my M-16 to my shoulder, and letting fly with a couple bursts of three or four rounds each. I saw my tracers falling away behind the sprint-ing PAVN as they dodged to the right and disappeared behind the grass-covered hill. Other guys were shouting and firing at them, too, but they got away. Furious at myself for missing them, I glanced angrily at First Sergeant Flanders. Where the hell had he been? He looked back at me, all eyes. Welcome to the war, First Sergeant.

Instead of sending someone to follow the PAVN, the cap-tain, bless his soul, called for artillery to blast the area they had been heading for. The map showed it to be a low swampy area on the other side of the grass-covered hill mass, and when two or three salvos of 105mm rounds came *whooshing* into the place, I felt very much reassured. One, that we had artillery on call if we needed it. Two, that it was already being registered. And three, that the captain had chosen to use it in-stead of sending a platoon of our people out there to see what they might find.

After the artillery had pounded the far side of that hill mass and the swampy area behind it, the captain advised everyone to dig in for the night. We'd move south the following morning. That was fine with me. I moved my team to the cap-tain's side of the LZ, and we dug three or four decent foxholes in case we needed them.

That evening, as the sun set, we lay low and oriented our-selves to the terrain features around us. The bowl we were in was dominated by several high peaks—the green giant's skull to our east, the one with the mortar pits to our north, and a more ominous ridgeline, covered with thick vegetation, to our south. It, too, loomed over us like a dark brooding giant, and that was where we were headed the following morning. The only thing that separated us from that brooding mass of jungle was the small ravine we'd jumped into during the air assault, but our people had dug in along the edge of the LZ by then, so I felt pretty good about our positions that night.

After we'd dug in, there wasn't much to do except stay alert. Knowing that the 101st was in trouble, knowing that we'd already seen PAVN troops and well-dug-in mortar pits, and knowing that we'd already called in artillery on a suspected enemy position nearby, combined to keep us in a state of high alert as we settled in. I was doing okay, I thought, but I felt like I was sinking slowly into a morass. It's hard to go back out into the field after you've been wounded, but I didn't quite appreciate that yet.

Around ten P.M., I think it was, the eerie stillness of the night was shattered by the sounds of a fierce firefight breaking out near the top of that ominous brooding ridgeline to the south, and we could hear, over the radio, our battalion recon platoon leader advising battalion of his situation. We were the closest friendly unit so I prayed they would be okay. If they weren't, we'd have to help them out. After that brief but vicious firefight, the recon guys managed to break contact, and the platoon leader reported that they were "going to ground," which meant they were going to sink into the earth, to hide so well that the enemy wouldn't be able to find them, even if they were looking. He'd suffered no casualties, thank God, but he was taking his people into the thick brush to wait out the night.

Boy, was I glad I wasn't with them. I could picture his people, scared shitless, hiding in the thick underbrush while PAVN searched for them.

In the morning, when dawn came, they reported that a large unit had passed right by them that night. Maybe a battalion, they thought. Oh, my.

Alpha Company was ordered to trek up that high ground and relieve the recon platoon, but first we sent a reinforced squad to spec out that swamp where we'd fired artillery the day before—just to check out the damage, if any, and see what might be there. A squad from the 2d Platoon filled that bill, and when they came back, they brought several bent, broken, and twisted AK-47s with them, reporting that the artillery had indeed had some effect, that they'd seen definite presence of enemy there—lots of blood trails and gore.

So, we'd inflicted some damage on the bad guys—that was clear—and the captain seemed pleased about that. I was, too, because it hadn't cost us anyone. But I was also angry at myself for having missed those fleeing PAVN in the first place, and I was worried about what lay ahead, up that mountain to our south.

I went over to listen to the squad leader's report, and when I looked at the weapons he'd brought back with him, three smashed and broken AK-47s, I noticed some gray goo on the bent and twisted barrel of one of them—up near the sight.

"Them's splattered brains, sir," I heard him say, proudly.

I almost retched. I gagged and staggered backward, away from those AK-47s and the putrid gray obscenity that marked them. I had seen a lot of things during my ten months with the Cav, but I'd never seen brains splattered before. It was awful. It looked like gray curd, or globs of gray custard, and my stomach simply revolted at the sight. I staggered backward and looked away, trying not to let my reaction show, trying to regain my composure, but I'll never forget seeing that gray brain curd on the barrel of that weapon and almost puking. I was slowly coming unglued.

Shortly after the patrol came back, we headed out, platoons in column, crossing the ravine to our south and heading up that ridgeline to relieve the recon platoon. We hadn't gone more than three hundred meters when our lead platoon called to report that they'd captured a PAVN soldier guarding an arms cache in a hootch. The company halted, and the captain called me forward. When I got there, he was standing next to a tall skinny PAVN soldier dressed in gray. He was already bound and gagged and looking grim. Defiant might be the better word. The arms cache he'd been guarding consisted of a couple satchel charges, some packs filled with ammo and grenades, and two antitank mines.

The captain told me battalion was sending a chopper to pick up the prisoner. I was to put him and his stuff on that chopper. The LZ was just ahead—a small open field, partially cultivated, and surrounded by tall trees and lots of heavy underbrush. The company would continue up the mountain, and we were to rejoin it when we could.

No sweat. We gathered everything up, pushed the PAVN along with us (the satchel charges draped around his neck), and found a spot near the small field to wait for the chopper. The company continued past us into the dense undergrowth and started up the mountain.

While waiting for the chopper to come in to pick up the prisoner, I started to get anxious. It must have been early, the day having just begun, but it was hot already, I know that. The LZ picked for the extraction was just half the size of a football field—just barely enough room for one ship—and surrounded by tall trees and heavy undergrowth. We had no idea what was on the other side of that field, either. Perhaps PAVN, just waiting for the ship to fly in. The longer we waited, the more agitated I got.

The tail end of the company had just disappeared up the mountain when the Huey hove into view. I had it on my radio, threw smoke for it, and waited for it to land. Actually, we didn't wait for it to land. Both Gosey, carrying the PAVN's weapon, packs, and mines, and I with the PAVN, headed out into the open field to meet the chopper as it landed. We had fifty yards to go. I had the prisoner's bony left elbow in the grasp of my right hand. The two satchel charges were still draped around his neck. Gosey sprinted ahead of us toward the chopper. We were hustling as fast as we could in case there were PAVN on the other side of the LZ just waiting for the ship to land before they opened up.

But the prisoner wasn't moving fast enough. He didn't want to go at all. He was fighting me, holding back as defiantly as he could. So I kicked him in the ass and started yelling at him. I was yelling at him and shoving him forward as we went. But he still wasn't moving fast enough. So, I kicked him again, and he fell to his knees. "Get up, you fuck!" I screamed at him. He shook his head no. I kicked him again, but he refused to get up. So, I literally dragged him off the ground, stood him up, shoved him forward and kicked him again. This time he started moving, and I pushed him and herded him as fast as I could to the waiting ship, its crew chief beckoning to us to move faster. Finally, I shoved that poor recalcitrant PAVN prisoner into the waiting arms of the crew chief, and together we managed to get the son of a bitch into the Huey.

As soon as he was in, I turned tail and sprinted back to the cover of the tree line, plopping down to the ground as soon as I got there, and turning to see the ship lifting off safely above the treetops. When I turned back and looked at the first sergeant, he was staring at me. He was shocked. He'd been shocked at what he'd just seen, and rightly so, and I realized with an acute sense of shame that I had definitely crossed the line. I'd lost it.

Then I got angry and stared back at him. I just stared. He'd learn. He'd learn soon enough. He'd learn how it felt to be scared. He'd learn to hate, too. I was sure of that. He'd find out what it was all about eventually, but the look on his face was something I've not forgotten all these years, and it told me a lot. I was close to the edge, but I didn't know it.

After the chopper left, we picked ourselves up and continued up the mountain, catching up easily with the rest of the company and, an hour or so later, reaching the top. And there we rested.

The recon guys were still there, I remember, and very glad to see us. They reported that a large enemy unit had passed right by them in the night, heading south. Battalion ordered us to follow them, and that's what we did. But first we had some time to take a break.

I remember there was a small LZ near the top of that mountain. A chopper flew in and disgorged some reporters, who, as usual, took off in all directions looking for a story. I remember one of them thrusting a sound mike into my face, and my brushing it away, angry at his intrusion. Reporters were like pariahs as far as I was concerned—bloodsuckers looking for a story—and they pissed me off. When another asked if I could answer some questions, I brushed past him and said I didn't want to talk to him. But First Sergeant Flanders had no such compunctions, and I noticed with some amusement that he was standing there under a tall tree and happily answering questions like a pro.

He'd learn, I thought.

And what the hell did he think he was doing? One day out in the field and he was answering questions like he'd been doing it for ten months? Oh well, at least he'd taken the heat off of us. All I wanted to do was find some shade, eat some Cs, and get some rest.

Later, after lunch, we picked ourselves up and continued the search for that large PAVN unit that had walked past the recon platoon. We started humping hills again. All that hot afternoon, we followed that enemy unit up and down the mountains. It was a miserable day, hot as Hades, and the terrain changed from the steep, heavily vegetated mountains to a hot, dry valley of parched red earth, almost barren, with unfettered vistas of the terrain still to cross. We kept going, humping under the hot sun all afternoon. I recall looking up and seeing a butte, or a high plateau of some kind, and being struck by its color. The earth was red, like the dust of Plei Me, and I could see the striations of sedimentary rock as I looked up the side of the butte. The plateaus south and west of Tuy Hoa were unlike any terrain I'd seen that year.

We were ordered to turn west and climb that plateau. Approaching it, I could see funnels of erosion down its red clay slope. Without stopping, we began to climb, using a dry streambed as a trail. It was late afternoon when we reached its scrub-covered peak.

Orders came to dig in and wait. The ground around us was flat now, arid and perfect for digging foxholes. Interspersed around our perimeter were clumps of thick, impenetrable, small-leafed bushes, not quite tea plants, about six feet wide and eight feet tall. They reminded me of the mountain laurel in the mountains of north Georgia, a bane to infantry on the move, but excellent for concealment or an ambush. Because the earth was soft and easy to dig, however, we were able to set up our night defensive perimeter quickly, even though most of us were exhausted from the long day's trek in the relentless heat.

We were up early and on our way the next morning and had covered three klicks before the sun reached its zenith. We'd found nothing, not a hint, not a single trace of PAVN's presence. We swept through a recently deserted village and saw no one. Silence hung over us like a pall. At noon we came upon a farm—rows of abandoned crops eloquently attesting to the war and its devastation. I saw a bomb crater, the biggest I'd seen, twenty yards wide and six feet deep to its water line. It was half filled with muck. Beyond it stood an abandoned hootch and a dusty furrowed field that yielded a crop of small green pineapples, round as grapefruit. I ate one greedily, and the meat and juice were delicious after the long morning's march, but ten minutes later, I regretted it. The unripe fruit ran through me like prune juice. Everyone who ate them suffered severe stomach cramps and a bad case of the green-apple quickstep, but we kept on going.

Emerging from a forest, we began a steady climb up a gently rising slope that seemed to have no end. My map told me we had another thousand meters to go before we reached the peak of that particular ridgeline. Beyond it, we would continue west, descending into a valley that ended with another series of hills. The ground turned red-brown again, like North Carolina tobacco land, and the "mountain laurel" reappeared along our route.

After eight hours of mindless plodding through deserted countryside, we were bushed. Heads were lolling, eyes closing, everyone simply putting one foot in front of the other, trying to keep pace without falling asleep. Captain Davison was up with our 1st Platoon, which had the point. I was walking with the 2d Platoon, which was next in the column. We were followed by the Mortar Platoon, and in the rear, our 3d Platoon with its new lieutenant, McCarty.

Suddenly, the men ahead of us stopped and raised their hand, signaling a halt. The sign was passed down the line. I heard the low hum of a chopper passing far to our south, behind us. A breeze whispered through the laurel bushes, and a puff of red dust blew past the toe of my boot.

Then a burst of three rounds broke the air overhead, and we dove to the ground. They'd come from a heavy weapon of some kind, up ahead of us, but I didn't recognize the sound. It was big, though. Maybe a .50-caliber. I reached over and took the handset of Gosey's radio. M-16 fire and grenade explosions shattered the stillness to our front. They, in turn, were answered by a staccato of incoming AK-47 rounds that snapped over our heads, then more deep thumps from the PAVN's heavy weapon. When our M-60s started rattling out fire, I knew we'd run into something big.

"Bunkers ahead," Jim Kelly's voice came over the radio. "They've got a .50-caliber or something up there. Our point's spotted at least two Victor Charlies with AKs in the trench line."

"Roger that," the captain said. "We're coming forward. Two-six, this is Six. Move up on the right. Out."

I heard Sergeant Caple barking commands, and watched his people rise and move forward and to the right, his squad leaders shouting encouragement, the troops reacting without hesitation, sprinting forward in short rushes toward the sound of contact, keeping sight of the men to their front, dodging ten yards at a clip, up, run, down on one knee, up again, and running, the muffled clinking and banging of gear, the pounding of boots on the hard ground, the grunts and groans and barked commands stirring something in me that I'd felt before but never understood. I watched with a mixture of pride, admiration, and fear as the 2d Platoon maneuvered into battle.

Our new lieutenant came up the hill with his platoon strung out behind him, keeping visual contact with the men in front of them. As the 3d Platoon closed up, the firing picked up ahead. I pushed myself up off the ground and moved forward, too, but kept my head low. When I saw Captain Davison and his team crouched safely behind an embankment of some kind, I stopped about thirty yards behind them and simply lay down in the red dust to wait and see what happened. George Polli appeared behind me, too. This time, he was striding forward. The captain looked back, saw us, and pushed his flat hand out and down, signaling us to stay put. The firing up ahead suddenly stopped, and it got quiet.

I could see very little of the terrain to our front, even when I stuck my head up, but I guessed we were close to the top of that ridgeline, maybe a hundred meters or so to go. Beyond the captain I could see other mounds of red-brown earth, maybe a trench line with bunkers, recently dug. The laurel bushes along the trail we'd been following were about chest high, but they stopped near the captain's position, marking the end of the trail.

Where I was lying, though, the trail was about thirty yards wide and open enough for a small landing zone just behind us to the left. From the way the rounds were popping overhead, I could tell we were in defilade, protected by the captain's embankment from any firing from our front. The 1st Platoon was near the top of the ridgeline, but we were protected by the slope of the hill. I felt safe enough to light a cigarette.

The firefight resumed quickly enough. Several short bursts of M-16 fire were answered by a blast from PAVN's heavy weapon. Then a fierce exchange exploded on our right front, where the 2d Platoon had gone. Sergeant Caple had run into something.

Oh Jesus, not again . . . I felt exhausted, suddenly heavy-limbed, as the firefight swelled ahead.

Sergeant Caple's voice broke into the net. "We ran into it good," he said. "Couple of bunkers here, too, and a long trench line dead ahead. I've lost two people. Over."

"Don't force it," the captain advised. "Pull back and we'll get some help."

Captain Davison had both handsets up to his ears, talking with his platoons on one, and with battalion on the other. The firefight ahead had subsided, but sporadic exchanges on our right front kept it alive. The deadly game of sniping had begun.

"We've got three wounded—two serious—and a KIA," Caple said in the clear. "Can we get 'em out?"

"This is Five," I said. "I'm back here on the trail near a Lima Zulu. If you can get 'em back here, I'll get 'em out."

He rogered that. I suddenly felt exhausted, almost too tired to move. I could feel the fear closing in. I had to get moving or I'd freeze up.

"Look at that, sir!" the first sergeant said, pointing into the sky.

I looked up where he was pointing and saw the silver glint of an air force L-19, a single-engine Bird Dog, circling a thousand feet up. I watched it make three rotations, dipping its wing each time it reached a certain spot. He was pointing out the enemy's positions.

"Will you look at that!" the first sergeant said, again, in awe.

As the little thin-skinned Bird Dog continued to circle, it lost altitude, down to eight hundred feet, then seven hundred feet. Then I saw tracer rounds wafting from the enemy's trenches up into the sky, heading for the Bird Dog, and the plane seemed to stagger in midair. Its nose dipped, and it dove to the right, trying desperately to shake the PAVN gunner's aim, then disappeared behind the ridgeline, its engine straining, and for a breathless moment, we sat there and waited for the sounds of a crash, but the silver glint appeared again, in a climb this time. A scattering of cheers broke from some of the grunts around me as the silver-winged FAC climbed steadily into the cloudless blue sky, away from danger, then returned to its original circling pattern at a higher altitude.

"Man's got guts," someone said.

"Man's crazy as shit," Gosey said.

"A little of both, I'd say," the first sergeant observed.

Then we saw a team of Caple's troopers, four of them dragging a poncho out of the trench line and struggling through the laurel toward our position. Sergeant Wittlesey was in charge. I could see a man in the poncho but couldn't recognize him. He was unconscious, lying on his side, his head wrapped in a dirty field bandage, his shoulder dark with blood.

"It's Gordon, sir," Wittlesey said, gasping for air. "He got hit in the eye. Couple more wounded on the way."

They laid Gordon's body in the shade of the laurel bushes and stood tottering over it for a minute trying to catch their breath. Doc Ambrose, who'd sprinted to our position from the captain's embankment, began working on Gordon, and I called for medevac.

"Okay, let's get back there," Sergeant Wittlesey shouted to his men, and with hardly a pause, they began dodging and weaving their way back through the trench line. As they did, they passed another four-man team coming toward us, dragging another poncho.

The Dustoff dispatcher told me medevac was on the way.

Beyond the second stretcher team, another appeared, four more men straining with another heavy load. I watched them struggling toward us. Behind the two stretcher-bearer teams I could see two more men, bandaged and filthy, weaving slowly toward us, too. I turned to see how Doc was doing. He was checking Gordon's bandage, opening his shirt, searching for other wounds. Poor Gordon lay on his side, twisted unnaturally in the poncho, his boots turned inward, his limbs limp and still. His face had turned gray. Or was it dust? He was going into shock, that was clear.

Suddenly George Polli was behind me, encouraging the stretcher bearers heading our way. "Easy, easy," he said.

They stumbled by him and dropped their heavy load on the ground. Sergeant Kimura was in charge of this team. "He's gone, sir," he said to me, shaking his head. His men were just standing there, too exhausted to move.

Polli stepped over to the inert poncho. "Are you sure this man is dead?" he asked.

I saw him lift the corner of the poncho, then jerk his head up and stagger away from the corpse. Sergeant Kimura and his men simply stood there, motionless, and watched. Polli lurched to the right and turned away. He'd gone deathly pale. "Yes, I guess he is," was all he said.

I looked down. The body in the poncho was lying chest-down, headless. The man's harness and web gear were still on, but his head had been sheared off at the neck, flush with the shoulders, and gray brain curd was splattered all over his back.

I felt the retch coming, helpless to do anything about it. My stomach simply revolted at the sight, and I almost puked. Somehow, I held on.

"It's Williams, sir," I heard Kimura say. His voice came through a haze. "He took a .50-caliber in the face."

All I could do was shake my head. Then Sergeant Kimura turned and yelled, "Okay! Let's go!" and his four-man team made a quick dash back through the laurel and disappeared back into the trench line from where they'd come.

By then, the third litter team had managed to clamber over the trench line and was lugging its precious cargo toward us, too.

"Hold on, man! Here we are. You gonna make it," one of them was saying. It was Chandler, from the 82d Airborne. I'd greeted him back in January when he was young. Now his gaunt and haggard face was looking to me for guidance. "Where do we put him, sir?"

Summoning the last vestige of my strength, I pointed to a spot next to Gordon, and looked at the man in the poncho.

It was Johnson, Sp4. Davey Johnson. He'd been with us as far back as Albany, and he was a good man, a really good man! But now he was lying sprawled on his face, his eyes shut, three tissue-tinged bullet holes ran diagonally across his back, from his shoulder to his hip. He'd been hit with a burst of automatic-weapons fire, and he was just barely holding on.

They laid him gently down on the ground next to Gordon.

"Help this man, Doc!" I said. "You've done what you can for Gordon."

Ambrose looked up, nodded, and scrambled around to start working on Johnson.

"Hang on, Davey," Chandler said. "Hang on!" The wounded man's eyes flickered open and his lips started to move. I leaned forward to hear what he said.

"Fuckin' A, man. Fuckin' A," he said. Bloody spittle

dribbled from his mouth. "Got some water? Gimme some water." Then he moaned again and shut his eyes.

Doc kneeled at his side and began ripping bandages apart frantically. "Help me with this!" he said to the first sergeant, and the two worked feverishly to get the bandages ready. They had to plug the holes before Johnson's lungs filled with blood. "Wet his lips," Doc said to Chandler. Doc was coaching him. Chandler reached around, grabbed his canteen, unscrewed the top, and gently splashed some water onto Johnson's parched lips. What he couldn't sip formed a puddle by his face. The doc kept working. "Yeah, that's it," he said. "That's the way. You gonna make it, Davey Boy. You gonna be out of here in a flash, man. Million-dollar wound, baby. You gonna be okay. Just hang in there, man."

I could hear Polli's voice behind me. "Move away. Give him some room. Give the man some air."

I whipped around, angry that he was interfering, but then I saw his eyes, and knew he was trying to help. Maybe George would be okay after all.

"Take a break," I said to Chandler. "Sit over there and help us when the medevac comes." He put his hand on Johnson's shoulder, said something I couldn't hear, then struggled to his feet. He turned and joined his team of exhausted stretcher bearers, and they backed away and dropped to the ground.

Doc was still working furiously on Johnson, and it looked to me like he might have a chance. I kneeled down and spoke into his ear. "It's Lieutenant Gwin, Johnson. You're gonna make it. Just hang on! Medevac's on the way, Johnson. It's almost here. So hang on, buddy. Hang in there!"

His eyes flickered open, and he licked at the water by his lips, but I have no idea if he heard me.

Then I heard the Dustoff approaching and began the simple routine of guiding it in.

I'd done it too many times, I guess. Calling for medevac, throwing smoke, guiding the ship into the best place for it to land, and watching as the men carried their wounded comrades toward the waiting, red-crossed Huey, the medics or crew chiefs aboard, helping, encouraging, and pulling the wounded onto the ship, or sliding the inert bodies of corpses onto the chopper's floor, and all the time the Huey's rotors kicking up the dust, and the roaring of the turbine, and the general confusion and shouting above the chopper's noise, and the urgency, don't forget the urgency, as we did what we could to help them into the ship and then stepped back and watched it lift away, slowly rising through the swirling dust, and flying off to safety. And then, after it had gone, the inevitable quiet, or the apparent quiet, until the firing began again, or the battle started up once more. But this time was different, and when the ship lifted off and flew away, something left me, too. I just staggered back to the laurel bushes, lay down in the dirt, buried my head in my arms, and didn't move.

Sometime later, I don't know how long it was, we got the word to pull back fifty meters and dig in. Pull back from the top of the ridgeline and dig in. We'd call in artillery, pound the shit out of that bunker complex, and attack it the next morning. I heard that on the radio, I think. I knew we were supposed to pick up and fall back fifty meters, and that sounded smart to me. But I couldn't seem to move. I just wanted to lie there in that red dust and sleep.

At some point, I was able to push myself up and rejoin the headquarters group, following them back down the trail for a hundred meters or so, until we came to a copse of trees, well below the crest of the ridge, and that's where the captain chose to set up his command post. And that's where I crashed.

I don't remember much about that night, or much of anything else that happened out there the next two days, but I do have vague recollections, and this is what I can make of them.

First, as soon as we reached that copse of trees, I sat down with my back against one of them and just stayed there. I had no will to move. No will to fight anymore. No energy. No spirit. I didn't care about anything. I'd run out of gas. I didn't bother digging a foxhole that night, either. We always dug foxholes. Everyone had one, or shared one. But that night, all I remember doing was sitting with my back against that tree, and waiting for the morning to come. That was when I was going to die. I knew it. So why bother digging a foxhole?

And that morning, after sleeping as soundly as I'd slept all year, I remember seeing Colonel Moore, the brigade commander. He was coming with us, on the ground. He was going to participate in the attack. At dawn, we picked up from our positions, the company headquarters moving from the copse of trees to a place on the line of departure for the attack, and we all found positions along that line. I picked a spot behind some boulders, I remember, along with my RTOs and Doc Ambrose, and lay down and waited for the artillery barrage to begin. I could look down the line and see men finding positions, Captain Davison, Colonel Moore, Jim Kelly, and all of our people, finding whatever cover they could against the possibility of a short round. And there we waited. After the barrage, we were simply going to stand up and charge across the open field to our front, charge the bunkers and the trench line in the woods across the way, charge across a hundred meters of open ground. That's when I'd get it, I knew. Charging across the open ground. I was too tired to fight it. Too tired to care. Too bloody sick of the bloody fucking war to worry about it. I just didn't care.

I remember the artillery barrage. It went on for five or ten minutes, the rounds coming directly over our heads from the batteries behind us. If you've never been waiting on the line of departure for an attack, with salvo after salvo of 105mm and 155mm heavy explosive rounds roaring over your head like locomotives, and crashing a hundred meters in front of you, into a dark forest, with the *crack!* of each round and the *whack!* of the heavy explosives whamming into the ground, dozens at a time, and the ground shaking with the impact of each one, and the smell of cordite and the unbelievable noise of the fire growing and growing as the rounds come closer and closer to your position, you have no idea of how terrifying it is, how awesome the power and destruction of it all, and there we lay, hugging the ground as closely as we could, trusting that the artillery would fall where it was supposed to, and simply letting it do its job, yet knowing that, when it lifted, we'd hear the command to move out, to move forward, and we'd have to pick ourselves up off that ground and start across that open field, firing from the hip, walking steadily forward and attacking that enemy bunker complex with its heavy machine guns, and its brave, little, determined defenders, and hope and pray that we'd make it across that open field before the bastards could set up their guns. And then suddenly the last salvo came in, blasting the shit out of the forest on the far side of that field, and I could hear a whistle blow, and see men rising to my left and my right, and I pushed myself up off the ground, and stepped over the boulders, and started walking doggedly across that open field, listening to the men shouting and yelling as they charged across that open ground, some firing from their hips, others taking aimed shots, and the dust and smoke of the barrage not yet settled, and we walked into the tree line, anxiously scanning the treetops and the ground ahead of us, and still waiting for the enemy to open up.

But they didn't, because they'd gone. They'd picked up and fled, and the forest we'd just blasted was empty.

My flight log tells me we made another air assault into an LZ named Yankee that afternoon, but I don't remember it. All I can remember after that artillery barrage and the attack across that open field was the captain calling Jim Kelly and me to his foxhole the next morning and telling us to catch the incoming resupply chopper out of there, to go back to the base camp, and to clean up for our trip home.

Chapter 29

Going Home

Hear me my chiefs. I am tired; my heart is sick and sad. From where the sun now sets, I will fight no more forever.

—CHIEF JOSEPH

Jim Kelly and I spent the next few days in our boxer shorts and shower togs, lollygagging around the O-club, drinking beer, bagging rays, catching zzzs, and packing for the long trip home. I shoved some of my favorite gear—my MACV jungle pack, camouflage poncho liner, jungle boots, and spare uniforms—into a duffel bag and shipped it home. I wrote Nickie and my folks and told them I'd be back in about a week. (I asked Nickie if she could meet me at my parents' house in Boston when I arrived.) And last but not least, I cleaned up Voluptua and donated her to the 2/7th's O-club, in perpetuity, tacking her cardboard-backed, full-page, spread-eagled, more-than-bounteous beauty to a prominent spot near the bar. No one in the club seemed to mind.

It was all a drunken haze, really, trying to reorient ourselves to the once-implausible concept that we were going to survive our tour. It was really hard to grasp. What else was there to do to celebrate that unbelievable news, that newly discovered knowledge, that dawning realization, that we were indeed going home in one piece?

Raid the Red Cross compound, that's what.

One of our last nights in country, Jim and I commandeered a jeep and drove to the MASH I'd spent some time at. It happened to be right next to the Red Cross workers' quarters. I remember finding Nancy Kelly somehow, and asking her if she'd like to come back to our O-club and have a drink with us. And she accepted. Just like that!

What a bittersweet night that was, one of my last in country. She was so lovely, so gentle, so nice and kind to us, and so happy for us that we were going home, that the hours melted away while she was with us. And Jim and I were so love-struck, so shy, and so traumatized by what we'd been through, that we just sat around and sipped our beers and talked of whatever it was we talked about, and then, at much too reasonable an hour of the evening (the Red Cross girls had a curfew), I drove Nancy back to her quarters and said good-bye. There was a moment, though, a star-lit moment, when we were sitting in the jeep together, under the moonlight, all alone, when I thought fleetingly of kissing her. Just kissing her. But I didn't. She was too sweet, too precious, and I was too scared to try. I'd soon be with Nickie, too, so I let the moment pass. (Years later, thinking about that moment on more than one occasion, I have kicked myself in the ass several times.) But I was also too shell-shocked by what had happened to us that year, and I realize that I couldn't have made a pass at her, even if I'd wanted to. (For months after coming home—more months than I care to admit—I was totally sexually dysfunctional.) I do remember shaking Nancy's hand, though, and saying good-bye, and watching her disappear behind the tent flap of her quarters. And driving back to base camp, I had the sad but clear realization that I would never see her again. (I was wrong.)

The battalion returned to base camp the next day. They'd had no further contact since Jim and I had left it, and Alpha Company had suffered no more casualties. Thank God.

My last day at An Khe is a blur. I remember the colonel calling me and Jim Kelly down to his tent and presenting us with the apparently customary Bronze Stars for meritorious service (which meant nothing to me, frankly). That done, the colonel invited us to attend a farewell party in our honor at the O-club that night—ours and Mr. King's, who was also flying home the next morning. And that night, at the party, I remember feeling very sad, confused, and emotional about leaving (guilty, now that I know better), and when the colonel presented us with our 7th Cav brush hooks, the unit's standard farewell memento, and asked us to say a few words, I just stood there, too filled with emotion to speak, and when my turn came, I said, simply, that there was nothing I could say. And with that, we all got drunk.

The next morning, I did manage to say farewell to the men of Alpha Company at their early work-call formation. I said something to the effect that I was going home that day, and that if I could make it home, they could make it home, and that I had never in my life worked with a finer group of men, and that I had never been so proud as I had been serving with the troops of Alpha Company, 2d of the 7th. With that, I wished them Godspeed, saluted, and walked off without looking back.

Jim had been scheduled to leave at a different time than I had, and I don't remember saying good-bye to him, but it didn't matter. We'd had five days of drinking beer and lying around in the sun to say our farewells. Without further adieu, then, I signed out of the battalion, hopped a jeep to the airstrip, and caught a Caribou to Da Nang, where my flight would leave for the States the following morning.

The officers' DEROS shack at Da Nang was nothing more than a general-purpose tent with a double row of cots and a makeshift wooden bar near the entrance. With the tent flaps up, you could look out and see the huge Marine base at Da Nang—another sprawling perimeter manned by Marines guarding the airstrip. Glowering over the airbase were more dark, foreboding, jungle-covered mountains, but inside the DEROS tent, we didn't care a hoot about that. All we had to do was make it through the night, catch our freedom bird out of there the next morning, and fly ten thousand miles home.

I tied in with some Cav guys, and we started drinking. Later that evening, I was flabbergasted to look up and see Myron Diduryk, George Johnson, and Tony Nadal—three captains from the 2/7th—come bursting through the front entrance of our tent. They were coming right at me, and they looked very grim. Wondering what the hell they were doing there, I stood dumbfounded and stared as they walked up to me.

"You're out of uniform, Lieutenant!" said Myron Diduryk, his face close to mine, looking me straight in the eye, without so much as a smile. He looked as tough as he had at Albany, the day he'd flown in to save us.

I had no idea what he was talking about, or why they were there, so I glanced at George Johnson, behind him, and the adjutant had a grin on his face, so I gathered it wasn't that serious, and relaxed.

"You're out of uniform, *Captain*," Myron said, emphasizing captain, then reaching up to pull my lieutenant's bar off my collar.

So that was it. Well I'll be damned.

He turned and took the captain's bars that George Johnson handed him and pinned them carefully where they were supposed to be on my collar.

"That's better," he said, with a smile.

"Your name's on the list," George said. "It came down this afternoon. Congratulations."

Well I'll be damned, I thought, grinning. I'd made captain, and those three guys had been good enough to fly up to Da Nang, deliver the news, and pin captain's bars on me before I went home. What a nice thing to do, I thought, grinning from ear to ear. They were grinning now, too. After that brief informal ceremony, and congratulations all around, they turned briskly toward the door and strode happily out of the DEROS shack, on their way, I assume, to the nurses' quarters at the hospital in Da Nang.

And that was how I made captain.

(It turned out they were a few days premature. They knew my name was on the list, though, and they guessed my orders would come through by the time I got home, and they wanted to surprise me, too. I appreciated that, because it made a difference, somehow, coming home a captain. My dad had been a captain once, and my grandfather, and my grandfather's father. It meant a lot.)

Sometime later that night, I can't remember when, exactly, the entire perimeter opened up, all at once it seemed, small-arms fire and mortars and tracers lighting up the night, and I, along with all the other combat vets in that tent, dove to the ground and started hugging the earth. There was no doubt about it—the goddamned perimeter was getting hit from three sides—and I was struck with the sudden realization that I was going to die on my last night in Vietnam.

And I had no weapon! We'd had to turn in our M-16s back at An Khe, and I'd given my Colt .45 to my replacement because we weren't supposed to carry weapons back to the States. So, there I was, lying facedown in the dirt on the floor of the DEROS tent in the middle of a huge firefight going on all around us, thinking oh, shit, this is it, when over the noise and confusion, I heard someone laughing. It was the sergeant who'd been our bartender all night. He was looking over the makeshift bar at us and laughing.

"It's okay, gentlemen," he said. "It's just the Fourth of July, and the Gyrenes are shooting off their fireworks."

And he was right.

Sheepishly, we got up, dusted ourselves off, and went back to our drinking.

The next morning, wearing my brand-new captain's bars on the collar of my short-sleeve khaki shirt, my Combat Infantryman's Badge and jump wings over my left breast pocket, a pair of khaki trousers that actually had a crease in them, and my newly spit-shined Corcoran paratrooper boots (which I hadn't worn since the day I'd arrived in country), I joined a hundred or so other homeward-bound GIs and followed an NCO guide down the hill to our freedom bird, an air force C-141, a huge jet transport that I'd never flown in before. We filed on board, found a seat (the interior was set up like a civilian passenger plane), and settled in. Eventually, after what seemed like hours while the huge plane's engines warmed up, we felt the aircraft jerk a bit as it started down the runway. As we taxied to the end of the runway for takeoff, the captain's voice came over the speaker.

"For those of you who've never flown in this bird," he said, "let me warn you. It's like nothing you've ever flown in before. When we cut in the afterburners, you'll feel like you've been shot into the sky in a rocket. But don't let our climbing angle scare you. That's just the way this baby flies.

"Think of it like this," he continued. "There are more than fifty thousand horses pulling this baby up into the sky. So sit back, folks, relax, and have a pleasant trip."

And with that, he released the brakes and started down the runway in earnest.

I felt the plane pick up speed, faster and faster as it bumped and rumbled and bounced along the tarmac. Then the nose lifted slightly, and the bumping stopped, and I knew we'd lifted off. A ragged spattering of cheers broke out among the passengers as we lifted off the runway, and I remember a ground swell of relief. Then the captain "turned on the afterburners," and we were thrust back into our seats. The huge plane roared into the cloudless blue sky, banked gently to the east, and headed for home.

We were out of range, at last.

Appendix

Unit Roster

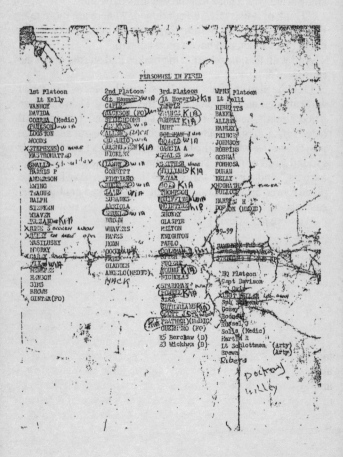

PERSONNEL IN FIELD

1st Platoon	2nd Platoon	3rd Platoon	WPNS Platoon
Lt Kelly	Lt Harmon WIA	Lt Hogarth KIA	Lt Folli
VANNOY	CAPIE	TEMPLE	HIBBITTS
DAVIDA	JACKSON (FO)	CARCE KIA	BAKER
CORRA (Medic)	STITHCOMB	BRUBAT KIA	ALLRED
PAULSON WIA	NEWTON WIA	HUNT	HANLEY
LOGSTON	ALLEN 12A CH	SOLFAN Jim	PRINCE
WOODS	CID ARIO WIA	GOULD WIA	JOHNSON
STEPHENS O WIA	RASMUSSEN KIA	GARCIA A	ROBBINS
MASTROMATTeO	DICKLEY	SEALES WIA	OGGHA
SMALL Shoulder	TOMY WIA	STATLER WIA	FORMOSA
HARRIS P	CORNITT	WILLIAMS KIA	DURAH
ANDERSON	PINILABO	R. YAN	KELLY
EWING	LAB WIA	MOE KIA	McGRATH finger
TEAGUE	SIMANEK	THOMPSON	BULLOCK
RALPH	AKNOLA	CHIPPEUBI WIA	HARRIS H LT
STEFKEN	CRUMB WIA	REINTHAL hip	DOBSON (MEDIC)
WEAVER	BROM	STOKEY	
BRILAND WIA KM	WRAVER	GLASPIE	
RICE broken elbow	HAYES	MILTON	
KELY cut ankle olive	HIXON	KNIGHTON	
WASILUSKY	GOODMAN	PABLO	
McGRAY	WALSH	COLEMAN	
CARY	GLADDEN	SMITH	RAMBERT FEB D
AK WIA	ANGELO (MEDIC)	FUGATE	STANNIES II WIA
NENTEE	NACK	YOUNG KIA	
HANSON		NICHOLAS	HQ Platoon
SIMS			Capt Davison
BROM		SPAUGH	Gale
GINTER (FO)		FOSTER KIA	KNOT SINGH Lt.
		SISK	Spl. Sergent
		SUTHERLAND KIA	Cosby
		GOTT LSR	Boone
		PRATHER (MEDIC)	Kussel J
		GUERRERO (FO)	Solis (Medic)
			Martin R
		25 Bereslaw (D)	Lt Schlottman (Arty)
		23 Wickham (D)	Brown (Arty)
			Ribera

Doctor?
Willey

About the Author

Larry Gwin was commissioned as an infantry lieutenant out of Yale University in 1963. After two years with the 82d Airborne Division, he served as an adviser to a South Vietnamese Army battalion in the Mekong Delta before joining the 1st Cavalry Division (Airmobile) in September 1965. Assigned to Alpha Company, 2d Battalion, 7th Cavalry Regiment (A 2/7), he served as their executive officer for almost nine months. During that time, A 2/7 made more than forty-five combat assaults, fought in five major engagements, usually against North Vietnamese regulars, and suffered in excess of 70 percent casualties.

Gwin returned from Vietnam as a captain and taught history as an ROTC instructor at Northeastern University before leaving the army and heading to Boston University Law School in 1968. Graduating in 1971, he practiced law in Boston until 1982, when he "dropped out" to write and teach. Since then he has written more than ninety published pieces, taught at prep school and college levels, and commenced an arbitration practice. He has two grown sons, Sam and Rob, and resides north of Boston where he continues to write and arbitrate securities cases. In 1996, he was awarded a Silver Star for his extraordinary heroism in the Ia Drang Valley. *Baptism* is his first book.

THE ONLY WAR WE HAD
A Platoon Leader's Journal of Vietnam

by Michael Lee Lanning

During his tour in Vietnam with the 199th Light Infantry Brigade, Lt. Michael Lee Lanning and his men slogged through booby-trapped rice paddies and hacked their way through triple-canopy forest in pursuit of elusive Viet Cong and North Vietnamese Army regulars. Lanning's entire year in Vietnam was spent in the field, and he saw a lot of combat, as an infantry platoon leader, as a reconnaissance platoon leader, and as a first-lieutenant company commander.

In this book, based on the journal he kept in Nam, Lanning writes of his experiences—and of the terror, boredom, rage, and excitement he shared with countless other American soldiers.

Published by The Ballantine Publishing Group.
Available in bookstores everywhere.